THE COMPLETE BOOK OF FURNITURE REPAIR AND REFINISHING

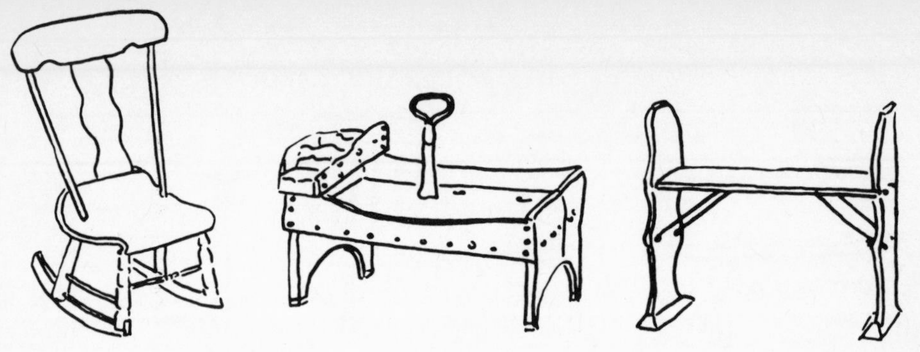

THE COMPLETE BOOK OF *Furniture Repair*

Easy to Follow Guide

CHARLES SCRIBNER'S SONS, LTD., LONDON

and Refinishing

with Step-by-Step Methods

by

RALPH PARSONS KINNEY

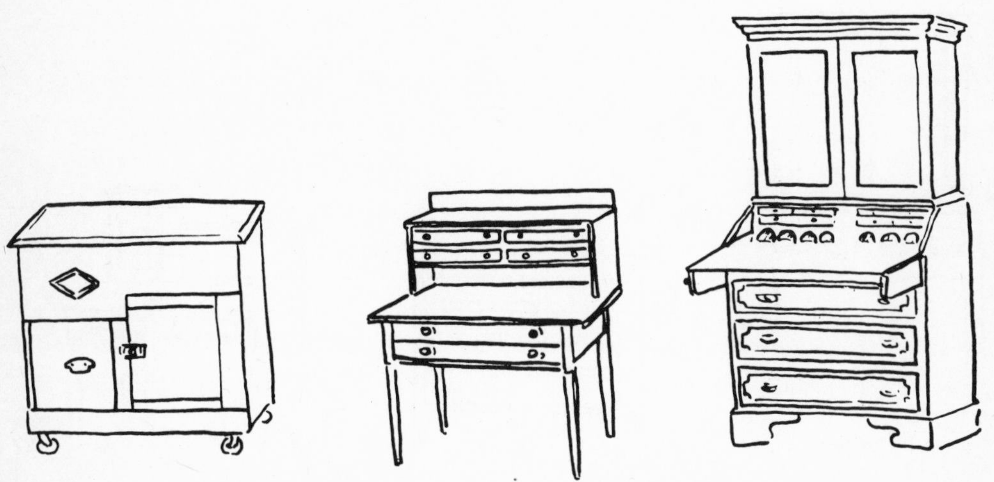

CHARLES SCRIBNER'S SONS, NEW YORK

Printed in the United States of America

O-2.64[MH]

PREFACE

Purpose of the Book

1—The primary aim is to furnish workers with information and practical suggestions, regarding the repair and refinishing of Antique and all other types of furniture. It is written in a form which is easy to read and understand, and it is intended to be used as a manual during the work.

2—The book is also intended for persons who hesitate to attempt restoration because they lack knowledge regarding equipment and tools, but who, if properly enlightened, might adopt it as a hobby.

How the Book Is Written

1—Subjects are divided into carefully defined chapters containing no long, involved descriptions.

2—Subjects are further divided into *titled* step-by-step methods. Notes are often added.

3—The worker is told not only *how* to do each operation but *why* it is done that way.

4—Cross references are often used and all of the material is indexed.

Added Features

1—The book is in two parts. Part I refers to the selection and buying of Antique furniture, the four steps of restoration, the work and materials used, etc. Part II describes the tools used, the shop, shop practice and hints, etc.

2—Many of the illustrations show an "untouched" piece of furniture and the same piece after repair and refinish. Others show tools, hardware used, my shop, and other pertinent information.

Working from the Book

1—The work of repair and refinishing, with the materials and tools to be used, is made easy to follow, due to the manner in which the subject is subdivided, titled, and cross-indexed.

2—Some of the materials, methods, and suggestions are new; some are old. All should prove beneficial and instructive, whether the worker be a beginner or an expert.

3—The work is neither difficult nor involved. A conscientious worker may follow instructions to success. This calls for repeated practice, cultivation of patience, sincere effort, and friendly encouragement. Anyone can turn out creditable work if he or she will but sincerely try.

RALPH PARSONS KINNEY

Laguna Beach
California

CONTENTS

ILLUSTRATIONS

Antiques shown in all illustrations have been finished by the Author. Interior views are of the Author's home.

THE COMPLETE BOOK OF FURNITURE REPAIR AND REFINISHING

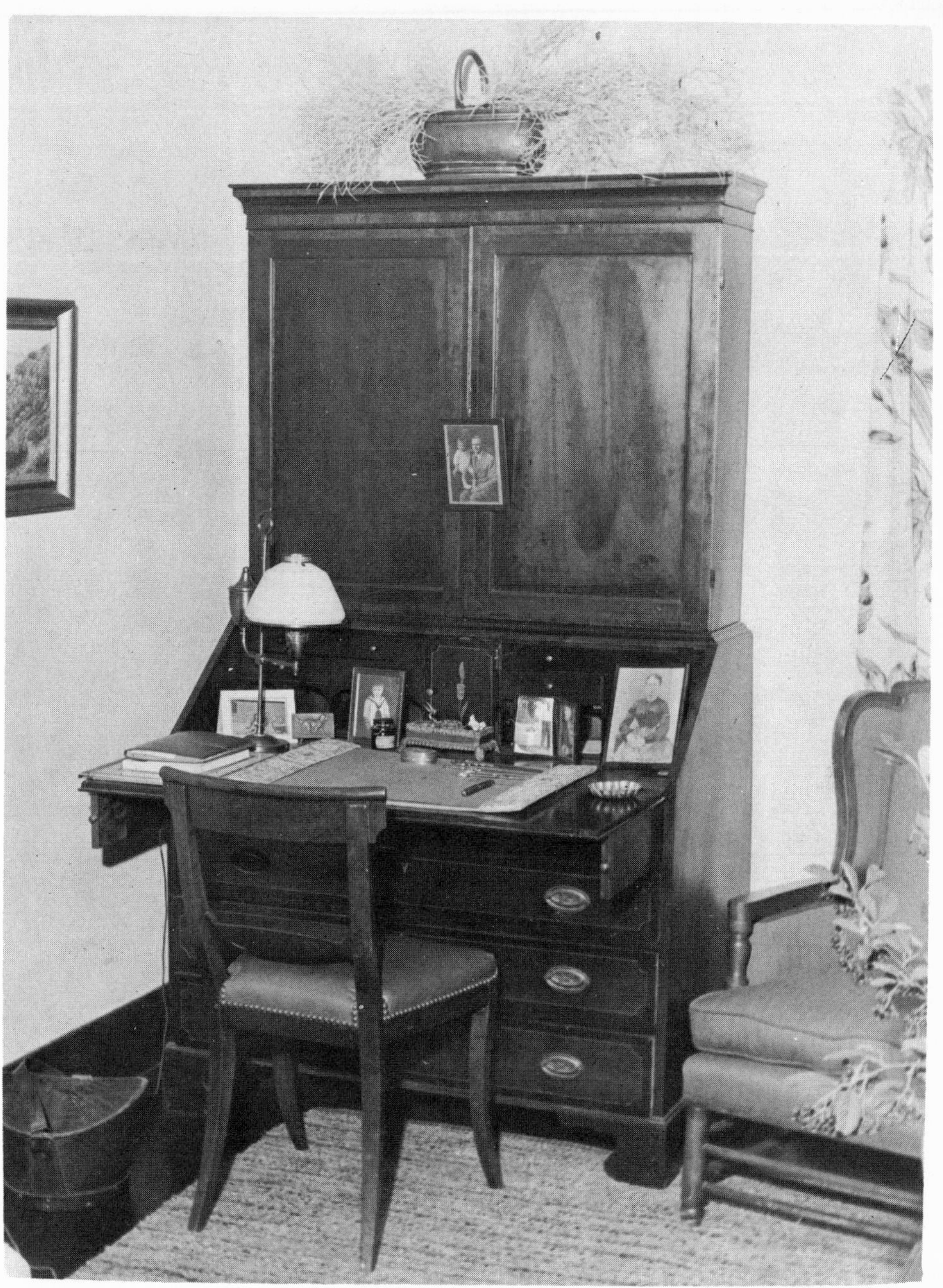

MAHOGANY COUNTRY CHIPPENDALE TYPE DESK

PLATE 1. Grey paint and an undercoat of shellac was easily removed with a commercial remover. Disclosed top cupboard has no inlay; was therefore earlier or later in construction than the body of the piece. No repair was necessary. "Varnish and oil" finish was applied and waxed.

Chair of cherry. Merely sanded and finished same; green leather seat cover added.

INTRODUCTION

The restoration of Antique and other types of furniture holds a strong allure and fascination for those with a natural aptitude in the use of tools, be they beginners or expert craftsmen. Every undertaking presents a new problem and there is no satisfaction equaling that of its successful solution. A well done job will require all the skill and craftsmanship to which the individual can attain.

Over-restoration has ruined many a fine piece of furniture. A beginner, through lack of knowledge and an excess of enthusiasm, will often attempt to remove every scar and blemish. This robs the piece of all that evidence which attests to its age and long usage, and as a result you have a piece which looks like a reproduction.

The question of just how far restoration should be carried is a difficult one, particularly when the piece is an Antique. True lovers of Antiques cherish the evidence of age in an old piece. This is lost when restoration is so extensive that it becomes an actual rebuilding of the piece. Where the original finish is still intact and in good condition, no attempt should be made to remove it. A great part of the beauty lies in this old finish. A thorough cleaning and polishing will often be sufficient. Don't carry restoration too far!

There is always something new to be learned about restoration of furniture. This knowledge is acquired by the "trial and error" method. The desired result can be reached by various procedures but those selected should be the ones which have been tested and proven.

It is not the intent to convey the impression that the methods and procedure set forth herein are the only ones that will accomplish your purpose. The experienced amateur, or the professional, may prefer something different. Therefore, not everyone will agree with all that is suggested in this book.

Most of the work outlined herein requires only a limited supply of hand tools and the work can be done by one who has merely a sketchy knowledge of how to use them. In working with old furniture, we gain great respect for that excellence of construction and craftsmanship which was accomplished with only a few crude hand tools.

Among those who read this book will be some whose interest lies in learning about restoration, even though they never intend doing the work themselves. This knowledge will enable them to direct others in their work and to recognize when a piece has undergone too much restoration.

Those who plan to undertake the work themselves should read the book in its entirety before undertaking a job of restoration. Step follows step and each should be thoroughly understood, for circumstances and conditions may offer a choice of procedure, or of the sequence in which the steps should be done.

Many people feel they have no natural talent for mechanical work and are loath to undertake anything of this kind. If such people would handle an object carefully and study it with their eyes, instead of deciding at once that it is beyond their ability, they would soon find that most of the problems which they had felt were impossible for them to undertake, could be readily solved.

From this it is clear that any adult person can at least attempt the work of furniture restoration if he will only try. They may not, at first, be perfect but improvement will come quickly with repeated practice. Even though you feel that repair work is beyond you, the work of refinishing can be done if you will follow the directions given in this book.

If you feel your talents are not yet developed to a point where you will no longer run the risk of ruining a piece, engage a professional to do the job. The knowledge you have gained from this book will enable you to recognize that point beyond which even the professional should not go in his efforts at restoration.

The quality of the work you do yourself is in direct proportion to the painstaking effort you put into it, rather than to your natural ability as a cabinetmaker or refinisher. Careful work throughout is the only way to achieve results comparable to that of a conscientious professional.

Check operations in each step with care, using the book on your workbench for reference. Do not depend on memory if you are a beginner. It is natural to forget and not do all that is told, and such omission might cause damage or result in a poor finish. All procedures may be found in the index.

Selecting Antique Furniture

When choosing a piece of Antique furniture, for your own use, the following factors should be considered carefully:

1—Utility.

2—Wood and condition.

3—Beauty of design.

4—Rarity or value.

Age alone does not make Antique furniture worthy of a place in your home. Condition, workmanship, materials, and design are also important. Be cautious about buying a piece in particularly bad condition. The cost of restoring may not warrant the purchase price.

Items that are at least one hundred years old are classified by the U. S. Customs Department as Antiques and are permitted entry into the country, duty free. Collectors do not consider a piece valuable if its replaced parts amount to more than ten percent of the entire piece, or if its original shape or design has been altered.

Most buyers more often choose a piece for its decorative value, the wood of which it is made, and its usefulness, than for its age or rarity only. These latter factors are much more interesting to the collector.

Testing Before Buying

At first it may be difficult for a beginner to recognize the value in an "untouched" piece of furniture because of its condition or its surroundings. A piece may be covered with dirt or a heavy layer of dust, the finish may be badly checked and cracked, it may have many coats of old paint, and its surface may be rough and scarred. It may be in need of considerable repair and there may be one or more of the parts missing. Often it is stored in a place where the light is poor and where it is crowded in with other pieces, some perhaps refinished. All of this confuses the untrained buyer.

When, through experience, in restoring pieces found under these conditions, and when you have trained yourself to recognize the good and the bad, you will know which pieces to choose and which to let alone. You will have learned what can be done with a piece that, at first glance, seemed utterly hopeless. You will have developed sense of imagination in regard to furniture that will enable you to recognize more readily those "untouched" pieces of good value. You will also have become an ardent enthusiast for the work of restoration.

If the construction or condition of a piece is doubtful and you are not certain what woods were used when it was made, there are several ways of testing and examining the piece in order to arrive at a decision regarding its value.

If the piece is tucked away in a dark corner where the light is bad, move it out into the open, if possible, or use a strong flashlight. Wipe off as much of the dust and grime as you can and proceed as follows:

1—Look for missing parts.

2—Check for necessary repairs.

3—Examine the part where the drawer sides meet the front and note the construction of these joints. If these are well fitted "dove-tail" or of another good type of joint, you may usually presume that the rest of the piece is well constructed and of equal quality of workmanship. (See Plate 10, page 49, "Types of Glue Joints," and Plate 11, page 51, "Joints and Fastenings.")

4—Check the piece for loose joints by wobbling it.

5—Test the wood for hardness with your fingernail or with the point of a knife blade, unless its species is obvious. It must be remembered that several kinds of wood may have been used in the construction.

6—If the piece is covered with old paint, you will often be granted permission to scrape off a small place on a surface with a knife blade, so you may examine the bare wood, to learn its color or species. In doing this, you can also determine how many coats of paint are on the piece, as these coats may be seen at the feathered edge of the spot scraped off. If the piece is very old and the undercoat is red, black, or green, this will be difficult to remove. These are called "Refractory Paints."

7—The ability of wood to take a fine color, when refinished, may be tested by wetting a spot, free from paint or finish, with water or saliva on a finger tip. Old wood will usually show a rich color while a newer wood will not. (See "Wet Test for Color," page 105.)

Collecting Antique Furniture

In recent years, the price and scarcity of good Antique furniture has risen because the demand for it has steadily increased while the supply has decreased. This is particularly true of the better grades and rarer items. However, if you will search patiently and diligently, many choice items may still be found.

There are many places to look for Antique furniture. If you know even a little about Antiques, you will get much enjoyment in hunting for them in the out-of-the-way places, if for no other reason than for the satisfaction of boasting to your friends about the bargains you have thus found. When your "find" has been repaired and refinished and you have done the work yourself, your pleasure will be increased.

Buying direct from the home has become increasingly difficult, particularly in the Eastern states where this field has been combed by the amateur enthusiasts and those who are scouting for the dealers. Much Antique furniture and other items of Antique value, now come onto the market when decedents' estates are sold. These are usually disposed of by means of private or auction sales.

The difference between the two methods is that, at an auction the items are sold to the highest bidder, while at private sales the prices are marked on the pieces before the sale. Bargains can still be picked up at either type of sale.

In cities, a visit to second hand, Good Will or Salvation Army store may often reward you by the discovery of a choice piece at a bargain price. However, even there, the storekeeper is becoming more and more aware of true values.

The safest place for the uninitiated to buy Antiques is from an Antique dealer, particularly a dealer who has earned a reputation for fair prices and fair practice. They will gladly show you their stock of "untouched" pieces and you can generally rely on their integrity.

If, after you have picked up a piece of Antique furniture, in an out-of-the-way place at a bargain price, and you later see a similar piece for sale in an Antique store, at a far higher price, you should recognize the reason for this increase. Consider the facts. Shop owners can not afford the time to hunt for and buy very much of their merchandise direct. This is particularly true if they are situated at any great distance from the source of supply. They must buy from wholesalers or dealers who attend the auctions and other sales, or who buy from "Scouts" who comb the countryside for them. Antiques, like other kinds of merchandise (food, luxuries, autos, etc.), move from the original source to the wholesaler, and through him to the retailer. Each takes his profit and to this profit he is entitled. Antiques are not gov-

OLD ODD SHAPED TABLE

PLATE 2A. Enameled yellow, with undercoats of white, black, and red "refractory" paint. Top of pine with knots; legs of poplar (white); stretcher of maple.

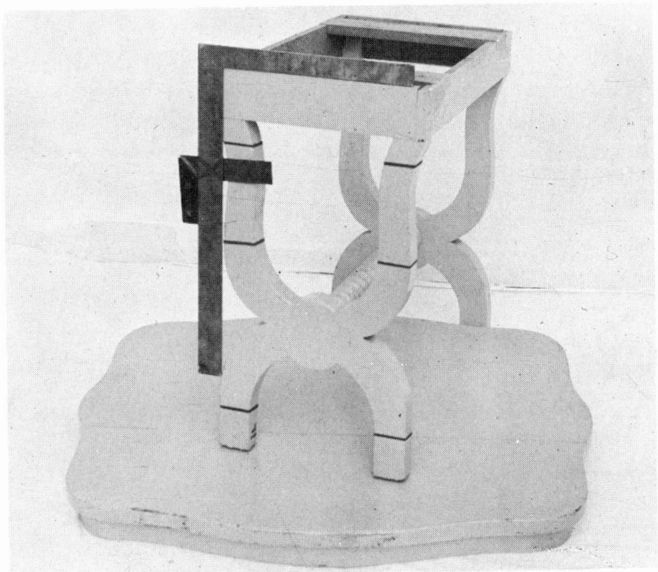

PLATE 2B. The problem—cut down table to 19″ high. Framing square placed on frame top, body touching at 2 marks; try square against framing square showed true right angle; when marked, sections were cut out and joints met squarely; contacting surfaces were doweled, glued, and clamped; later sanded. Bottom of legs sawed off.

erned by established market prices to any great extent. Reputable dealers are content with a reasonable profit.

It is well for the beginner to hunt around in his own home to find some piece of old furniture on which to start work. Furniture which has been stored away and forgotten may often be refinished and restored to a useful piece. For example, a table can be cut down in height for use in front of a couch. (See Plate 2-A, B, C, pages 5 and 6.) An "ugly duckling" can often be transformed into a thing of beauty, particularly when the removal of an old finish reveals the beauty of the natural wood.

You will be surprised at what may be unearthed in the "Dump Yard" of a small city or town. You may find in there whole pieces of good furniture or pieces of old wood for repair. Such pieces can often be purchased at a nominal sum and, when repaired and refinished, they make attractive items for your home or as gifts.

Note If you wish to increase your store of knowledge about Antique furniture, the Public Libraries contain many excellent books on this subject. (See Chapter 16, "Reference Books.")

PLATE 2C. Outer paint removed with 'commercial remover'; red undercoat with 'tri-sodium phosphate'; some spots scraped. Legs stained to match pine. Top replaced; piece finished with 'varnish and oil' and waxed. Now lovely piece of good proportions.

CHAPTER 1

RESTORATION

Divisions of Restoration

The actual work of restoration can be divided into but four categories. These are fully covered in separate chapters as follows:

Chapter 2—"Repairs."
Chapter 3—"Removing Old Finish."
Chapter 4—"Preparing for New Finish."
Chapter 5—"Refinishing."

All other chapters are supplementary to these four and contain information on materials, tools, the shop, and suggestions of general value.

You were told in the preface that this book was written not only to furnish information and suggestions regarding the restoration of furniture, but also that the material is in a form which will permit the book to be used as a manual while working.

When the book is used for this purpose, it would be a good plan to place index tabs on the edge of the sheets at the beginning of those chapters pertaining to the actual work involved, if not on all the chapters. Such tabs may be purchased in small packages at stationery stores at a reasonable price and may often be found with numbers printed on them from "one" upwards.

Planning Work

When repairing or refinishing a piece of furniture, each step should be planned carefully and in advance. The work and the selection of materials and tools should follow this plan closely, except in those cases where unforeseen conditions arise, during the course of the work, which make a deviation from the plan necessary.

In commercial plants, the materials to be used and the sequence of the work is planned in advance and the plan set forth on written orders. The work is routed through the various departments, each of which specializes in a particular phase of the work. Restoration work must be done in separate steps and these in their proper order. With good advance planning, many errors can be avoided.

Prepare your work plan as follows:

1—Examine the piece and determine what repairs are necessary.

2—Examine the finish or paint covering the piece and decide whether it must be removed and, if so, the best method for its removal.

3—Choose the type of final finish you wish to use. This should be done from the standpoint of the effect and utility of the piece.

4—Plan in advance, when possible, to prepare the surface for the type of finish selected. This is difficult when paint must be removed. At other times, it is obvious.

Note The condition of the piece or its utility will often govern the nature and extent of the repairs necessary, the method of removal of an old finish, the steps required to prepare it for a new finish, and the type of new finish that should be applied.

Using Imagination

Imagination plays an important part in restoration work. By this is meant the ability to visualize what the finished piece will ultimately look like while it is still in its rough and untouched state. Imagination will aid in the selection of materials to be used, the work to be done, the color, and the approximate final finish.

Without imagination, you will find it almost impossible to plan your work in advance, to alter a piece, or to adapt it for changed utility. (Example: a spinet adapted for use as a desk.) You should be able to see the finished piece in your mind's eye, to visualize what the finish will look like, and to know that an altered or modified piece will not destroy its beauty or proportions.

In childhood, most of us had strong imaginative ability. As we grow older this sometimes wanes, but it can be developed and strengthened for restoration work by planning and thinking ahead so that we can see the results we are striving to attain.

For examples of the use of imagination, see Plates 3, 4, and 5, pages 2, 3 and 4.

Keeping Time and Cost Records

Additional pleasure and interest in restoration work may be derived by keeping a record of time spent and materials used, as well as costs for each job.

Such records are easy to keep. Their purpose is for a basis of comparison between doing the work yourself or having it done by a professional—and as a prop to your ego. You will find that what you have accomplished, and the pleasure you have had, while not completely reducible to dollars and cents, is your "excess profit."

If you are interested in keeping such records, this may be done in a simple manner, as follows:

1—Keep data in a small notebook as a permanent record. Allot a separate page for each job and give it a job number. Set down the date the work is started, a brief description of the piece, and work to be done.

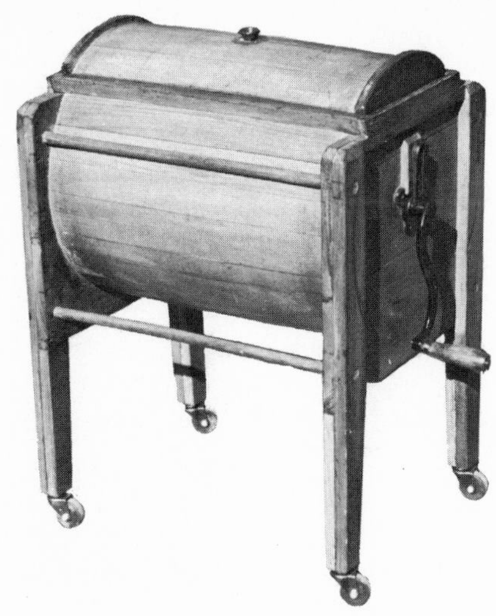

PLATE 2D. BARREL TYPE CHURN

The problem—convert churn to mobile bar with attached level tray. Blue top paint and undercoat of white removed with lye (would not respond to commercial remover). Legs shortened; made double thickness; tea-cart rubber wheels added. No repair.

2—A line or two below, write the word "Hours." Enter here the number of hours worked on the job at different periods. (Example: 3–½–1–2, etc.)

3—Farther down the page write "Materials." Enter those used, together with their approximate or estimated cost.

4—Enter lower down the words "Total Cost." Decide upon the hourly rate you think your ability warrants, compared to local professional rates. Multiply the total hours spent by this rate to get your labor cost. Add to this the approximate cost of materials. The total of the two will be the cost of the job.

Note Many workers, when proficient, may augment their income by doing work for others. Past records are then of great value in making estimates.

Patina

Patina, as used in connection with Antique furniture, is that mellowness and texture of surface color or condition attained by age, as a result of long usage and repeated polishings. It appeals both to the sense of touch and sight. Age alone can produce it, and once destroyed, it is impossible to replace.

The patina of old furniture should be guarded carefully. If there is any question of your ability to refinish a piece without destroying the patina, let it alone and call in an expert who understands its value.

Those who have been engaged in refinishing old furniture for any con-

EARLY PINE KITCHEN CUPBOARD

PLATE 3A. A homely piece, untouched. Had 11 coats of paint, cracked and scaled; top coat light green; under coat red 'refractory' paint. Upper coats removed with 'commercial remover'; under coat responded to 'alcohol.'

PLATE 3B. The problem—change upper doors for better proportions. Whole front removed; spacing of shelves changed and grooved in back for standing plates; truly a problem—all were secured with cut nails. Pine boards over 125 years old used for doors, with narrow strips around them. Hardware exchanged for wooden knobs; slight repair. Piece sanded; colored with linseed oil; finished with 'shellac and wax,' orange shellac added to white. Now a stunning piece.

PLATE 3C. BARREL TYPE CHURN

Curved inside top leveled with hardwood plyboard; trimmed with mitred ¼-round moulding (for tray sides); attached with bent "T" hinges. Inside bottom leveled for bottles, side racks made for glasses, end compartment for equipment—of plyboard and old maple. Surfaces stained to match old pine; finished with "satin rubbed" varnish and waxed. Untouched churn bought in Maine for $2.00.

siderable time, have gained an admiration and respect for old surface finish. If this evidence of age and usage is removed, much of the charm of the piece is lost. No one, however, wants to let deposits of grime and dirt remain on a furniture surface and these, as well as deposits of paint, can be removed without damaging the patina.

The patina is best protected by removing old finishes and paint with liquid solvents, rather than removing them by sanding or scraping. Commercial "paint and varnish removers" are harmless to patina but "lye" should never be used without a full understanding of its nature and the proper method for its application. On some woods lye should never be used.

Sanding, Scraping, Planing

Some beginners employ an abrasive paper, a scraper or plane, without having sufficient knowledge of the damage they may cause through improper use. As a result the patina is destroyed and all evidence of age removed, so important to the collector and those who know and admire Antiques. These harsh methods also leave the surface in such condition that no new finish will hide the scars left by such treatment.

A professional or an experienced amateur knows how to handle abrasive paper, scrapers, or planes. They have learned to love and respect a

HANDMADE EARLY PINE COMMODE
(Sometimes called a 'Bonnet Chest')

PLATE 4A. Painted brown, scraped spots (see upper right front surface and edge of top) revealed white, with 'refractory' undercoat of red. Outer coats removed with 'commercial remover'; undercoat with 'sal soda.' Repairs made.

PLATE 4B. (*below*) The problem—deep compartment over drawer suggested conversion to a mobile bar. Thick rough back (not shown) sanded and finished around edges with quarter-round moulding, mitred at corners. Sliding tray in drawer added to hold accessories. Tea-cart rubber wheels installed. Diamond of moulding placed on front for ornamentation. Finished with "varnish and oil" and waxed. Untouched commode bought in Maine back country for $1.75

PLANTATION DESK

PLATE 5A. Disassembled for regluing; some repairs. Removal of brown paint and stained varnish disclosed maple with mahogany trim. Bought in Maine for $1.50, falling apart. Back was low, broken, out of proportion. Old mahogany table leaves (see in back—25¢ each at junk yard) used for new back, end and shelf.

PLANTATION DESK

PLATE 5B. Desk completed with new green felt glued to slant top; 'varnish and oil' finish, waxed.

fine finish and can smooth and restore a surface without injury to the patina.

Abrasive papers must be used in many phases of restoration work and no harm will result, if the right grades are chosen and correctly used. Full instructions for use and information as to types and grades are given hereafter.

A piece of broken glass should never be used as a scraper, under any circumstances or conditions. An examination under a magnifying glass will show the edges are not smooth but jagged. If used, it will mangle a surface and do serious damage.

A plane should never be used on a fine old surface. Its use should be restricted to those occasions when it is necessary to remove a surface completely and build up a new one.

If you will examine the flat surface of an old piece of furniture, you may find shallow and slightly rounded tracks. These are marks of the old type planes which were made with a slight curve to the cutting edge. This proof of age is lost and destroyed forever, when such surfaces are taken down with a scraper or plane.

No scraper, plane, or abrasive paper should be used on the turnings of old furniture. These parts were made on hand lathes which revolved at low speeds. The turnings were often left a little rough and with slightly spiraled grooves on the surface, as a result of the slow speed at which the old lathe revolved and the curved chisel which was used.

Steel wool of correct grades may be used for such work without fear of surface injury and should be the only material employed.

Original Brasses

In refinishing rare old furniture, do not remove the original brasses to get at the surface more easily. These brasses include handles, handle plates, keyhole plates, and escutcheons. Old brasses should never be removed when they are held in place, on the inside, with cotter pins or iron wire bent and driven into the surface of the wood. Their removal may break the fasteners or leave holes and marks in the wood.

Work around the brasses and leave a little of the old finish near their edges. Their removal will reduce its value to a collector who might suspect that the brasses had been recently added and were not originals.

Real old pieces will seldom be found with all the original hardware in place and in good condition. Some of the hardware may be broken or missing entirely. In the latter case the missing pieces should be replaced with similar old hardware or exact reproductions, which may be obtained from manufacturers who advertise in magazines and trade journals published for the Antique trade.

Inflammables

Many materials used in refinishing are inflammable and great care must be taken in their storage and use. Some are volatile and, because of this, are a constant fire or explosion hazard unless used and stored properly. Some materials, among them linseed oil, are also subject to spontaneous combustion when conditions for this are favorable. Others, like alcohol, lacquer-thinner, gasoline, benzine, etc., will evaporate rapidly and the vapors from them, when mixed in the proper proportion with air, form a dangerous explosive gas.

Neither turpentine, which evaporates rapidly, nor kerosene, which evaporates more slowly, are volatile but both burn freely, as do paints, enamels, varnishes, shellacs, lacquers, paint and varnish removers, stains, etc., when exposed to fire.

In spite of the dangers from these materials, they can all be used with safety, if the necessary precautions are taken. They should be used only in a well-ventilated room, even though they might never be exposed to a spark or flame, as the fumes of some have a toxic (poisonous) effect on the user. One should not light a match in a room when volatile materials have recently been used, even though the room is well ventilated. It might be safe to do so or to smoke in such a room, but the "no smoking" rule is a good one to follow where volatile materials are used.

The storage of more than a small amount of these materials in your house is usually forbidden in your fire insurance policy and a violation of this prohibition may render your insurance void in case of fire. If you have a shop in your house, it is best to arrange a storage place for these materials somewhere outside so that the danger from keeping them will be reduced to a minimum. A very small quantity of dangerous materials are kept in my basement shop. These are stored in tight containers, carefully labelled. The balance of the supply is stored in a cabinet in the yard about fifty feet from the house. (See Plate 6, below.)

OUTSIDE STORAGE CABINET

FOR PAINT AND FINISHING MATERIAL

PLATE 6. Stock of burnable and volatile materials stored outside, greatly reducing fire hazard in workshop. Door lifts up and locks; shelves correctly spaced for convenient storage; ventilation through narrow spaces at top and bottom of cabinet.

CHAPTER
2

REPAIRS

Repair is the most difficult phase in restoration. If you lack the necessary tools or doubt your ability to accomplish fine work, you will do well to take the job to a professional who has the necessary skill and equipment. However, do not avoid repair work entirely. An honest trial may perhaps surprise you by uncovering a skill and aptitude which you had no idea you possessed.

Comprehensive directions for furniture repair will be found in the detailed procedures of this chapter. The steps are easy to follow. Even those unaccustomed to the use of tools will not find their use too difficult, as a fair trial will prove.

It is the purpose in this chapter to describe the various methods and use of materials, for making *general* repairs on *all* kinds of furniture, rather than to dwell on *special* repairs or replacement of parts for particular types of furniture.

Inspecting Furniture

Suggestions are offered to enable you to plan your work and aid you in its execution, as follows:

1—Examine the piece thoroughly. To do this—

a—Search all surfaces for cracks, bruises, small holes, or dents and for evidence of dry rot which may have to be cut out and patched.

b—Check veneer for loose edges, blisters, waves, cracks, dents or bruises, and for missing pieces.

c—Look for missing parts that must be replaced and for parts damaged or broken which may need repair or replacement, depending on their condition.

d—Place the piece on a level surface and see that it is in balance. If not in balance, one or more legs may be of unequal length and this must be corrected. Long usage may have shortened all the legs so much that you may wish to lengthen them to restore the piece to its correct height.

e—Check drawers and doors for loose fit or bind.

f—Make sure the hardware, such as handles, escutcheons, bolts and nuts, hinges, etc., are in place. If missing, they should be replaced.

g—Check surfaces for board warps. If found, decide whether they are bad enough to warrant repair.

2—Rock frame to locate any loose joints. Remove drawers, doors, and top of piece, when feasible or necessary.

3—Examine drawers and doors for loose joints in their construction and for repair or replacements which may be necessary. Keep all the hardware and fastenings, if removed, in a separate container.

4—Plan your work from the repair to the final finish.

5—Select the procedures necessary for your repair work and read and understand them thoroughly. Each and every step is important, for a step in one procedure may often be worked in with that in another. There are often optional procedures for achieving the same result. Do not deviate from the method you have selected unless unforeseen conditions arise.

6—Make your repairs before you start to refinish so that the repair will not injure that which follows. The usefulness of a piece depends upon its soundness. The parts and surfaces must be intact and the alignment correct.

7—Recheck all measurements before cutting lumber. Material cut too short is unusable, and if it is slightly too long it cannot be resawed. Make allowances when rip-sawing for smoothing with a plane.

8—Before putting any strain upon a recently glued joint, be sure you have allowed sufficient time for the glue to harden.

9—If you are not familiar with various types of furniture joints, see Plate 10, "Types of Glue Joints," page 49; and Plate 11, "Joints and Fastenings," page 51.

10—All tools mentioned in the various procedures of this chapter may be found in Chapter 9, titled "Tools for the Beginner," and in Chapter 10, titled "More Hand Tools." Also see Plate 24, page 186, titled "Woodworking Tools Commonly Used," Plate 25, page 187, showing a group of hand tools recommended for use; and Plate 7, page 25, illustrating clamps and a screw jack.

11—Have confidence in yourself. However, do not undertake work far beyond your ability. Any beginner can do simple repairs in a satisfactory manner. The rest will come with experience but do not underestimate yourself.

12—Don't carry repair work too far. The work must be done thoroughly but it is important that you understand that point beyond which you should not proceed. Many fine old pieces have lost their charm, beauty, and much of their value, because repairs have been carried too far. This is a failing found not only among beginners but also among professionals.

Note See Chapter 16, "Reference Books," for books regarding tools and methods of advance work and for special types of repairs.

. . . .

GLUES

In the early days of furniture construction, there is little evidence that glue was used except for veneers. Most furniture joints were fastened with nails, screws, dowels, pegs, or wedges.

The glue used in those days was made from hides, horns, and hoofs of animals, boiled down to a jelly and then allowed to harden. This dried mass was broken into flakes or ground into coarse powder. When used, it was mixed with water and gently heated in an iron glue-pot. This glue was hard, brittle, brown in color, was not waterproof, and often left a stain on wood.

In recent years, several new types of glue have come on the market which are far superior in holding power and lasting quality than the glues of former days. Of these there are two types especially recommended for amateur use in the repair of furniture and other objects.

These are the "Synthetic Resin" type of glue which is best for woods and the "Plastic" type which is fine for "spot" gluing with wood, leather, or glazed surfaces. Both are completely waterproof, hold and last well, and will not stain anything to which they are applied. In addition, the "old fashioned" liquid glue may still be used at times to advantage.

Information is given regarding each of these glues and their specialized uses, following "General Rules for Gluing."

In factories or shops, where glue is constantly used, you usually find it heated in glue-pots because of its continuous use, but this glue is generally a modern or recently developed type. It is best for the amateur worker to use only the types of glues recommended because of their convenience.

GENERAL RULES FOR GLUING

For satisfactory results in gluing, follow these rules:

1—Scrape, or otherwise remove from surfaces to be glued, all old glue, paint, dust, oil, wax, grease, old finish, etc. Materials to be glued must be thoroughly clean and dry.

2—Many old glues may be softened with hot vinegar. Where possible, scrub with old tooth brush.

3—Sponge "lacquer thinner" on oily woods for better holding power before using the above mentioned old type glue.

4—Uneven surfaces must be planed, sanded, or scraped to make perfect, well fitted contact surfaces. Glue alone will not hold.

5—When possible, slightly roughen or slash surfaces to be glued to increase holding power of the glue. This forms a "tooth" for holding power.

6—Glue is used to hold contacting surfaces together. These may be outside surfaces that touch one another or at a joint, where the end of one piece fits into another. In either case, the surfaces to be glued should fit correctly against each other or the glue will not hold. A thin layer of glue, correctly applied, will hold better than a thick layer, poorly applied.

7—Apply glue to both surfaces of joints and assemble the parts. Place piece to be glued on old newspapers to catch any glue which might drop.

8—Apply pressure with clamps or tourniquet, placing under jaws of clamps or contact points of the tourniquet, thin pieces of wood or folded pads of newspaper, so as not to injure surfaces. Use "wax paper" under the wood pieces or pads, when it is likely that glue will run out under them from the pressure applied, as this type of paper will not stick to the glue. Wipe off with a damp cloth any glue squeezed out. (An illustration of the uses of various types of clamps and tourniquets may be seen in Plates No. 7 and 8, pages 25 and 26.)

9—Test on a flat surface all pieces that have many glued joints (chairs, tables, etc.) for perfect alignment. Should this not be done and the piece be out of alignment, it would be impossible to rectify the trouble after the glue has dried.

10—Allow to dry for at least 24 hours in a warm room before releasing clamps or tourniquet and 48 hours before working on further or using a piece thus glued.

11—When the clamps or tourniquets have been released, clean off all glue that was squeezed out from joints which was not reached previously. Often the glue may not be crystal hard. Remove carefully with a knife blade, taking care not to injure the surface. Any glue remaining on a surface will cause spots to show through a clear finish.

Important No type of glue will function properly if it or the piece to be glued is too cold. Gluing and drying of glue should be done in room temperatures of 70 to 75 degrees for best results. Forcing a glue to dry too rapidly will also bring bad results.

SYNTHETIC RESIN WATERPROOF GLUE

This powdered glue is one of the newer types which have been developed for use as wood glue. If all the directions herein are followed and the recommended type is used, the glued joints will be stronger than the wood itself. The wood will break before the joint will give way, should it be necessary to take it apart later.

These glues come in cans in sizes from ¼ pint to 1 gallon and may be purchased in paint, hardware stores, and lumber yards carrying building supplies. It is best to buy the smaller size cans as required, because if not tightly sealed the glue will harden through absorption of moisture from the air and thus be rendered worthless.

Important *Always* use this type of glue for gluing woods where the factor of holding power is primary.

Directions for Mixing

1—Place in a clean receptacle the amount of the powdered glue you expect to use. Add little by little a very small quantity of water (70 to 75 degree temperature), stirring constantly until the mixture reaches the desired consistency. It is surprising how very little water it takes to prepare the glue. A thicker mixture is more easily applied, stays in place better, and shrinks less.

2—Some makes of this type of glue may be used immediately after mixing while others must stand about twenty minutes. See directions on the can.

3—Synthetic resin glues cannot be "retempered." That is, when mixed and allowed to stand, they cannot be thinned by adding more water. However, during the mixing, if the consistency is too thin, more glue may then be added.

Directions for Use

See "General Rules for Gluing."

Note 1—At times, this type of glue becomes hard enough in but a few hours to proceed with the work on a piece, if used correctly and temperatures of glue and room where used are favorable. However, it is better to wait 24 hours before releasing clamps and 48 hours before subjecting the piece to strain or use.

2—A paper cup is the best receptacle in which to mix this glue. Use that type which is rather shallow, made of heavy, waxed material, and available at any grocery store. The thin, unwaxed type is useless. A small, shallow tin can of the kind in which baby foods come, is also good. Throw the receptacle away when through gluing.

3—A "patching tool" is excellent for taking the powdered glue from the can, mixing, and applying it. The blades are thin (one is pointed) and glue may be forced deep into cracks with it. After using, set the tool aside uncleaned. The dried glue may later be removed easily with a knife. (See Tool No. 7 on Plate No. 25, page 187. For mention of tool, see pages 188 and 189, in Chapter 9 on "Tools for the Beginner.")

PLASTIC-TYPE GLUE

Practically anything can be glued with plastic-type glue, including china, leather, and wood. It dries rapidly when in a place where air can reach it. The glue is transparent, holds well, comes ready-mixed in tubes, and is easily applied. It may be purchased almost anywhere, including drug, department, and ten-cent stores.

This type of glue is recommended for "spot-gluing" on wood, in cases of loosened veneer, replacing a broken chip or sliver, or even for tightening a joint, if such joint is where there will be little strain. It works perfectly for such purposes and is more convenient than mixing powdered glue with water.

Directions for Use

Plastic-type glue is used differently than other glues. Directions on tubes are substantially as follows:

1—On *non-porous* surfaces, such as glass, apply a thin coat to both surfaces, place them together at once, clamp or hold firmly in place, and leave until thoroughly dry.

2—On *porous* surfaces, such as wood, apply a thin coat to both surfaces, and allow to dry. Then apply a second coat to one surface only, put them together at once, and clamp as above.

Note 1—In both of the above cases, wipe off all excess glue squeezed out by pressure. If this does not come off easily, wipe with denatured alcohol on a cloth. If it is in a spot difficult to reach when clamped, the excess should be scraped off carefully after the glue has dried.

2—Follow other directions in "General Rules for Gluing."

WHITE RESIN PLASTIC TYPE LIQUID GLUE

A new type of glue for woods (also paper, fabrics and plastics) has recently come on the market. It looks like white cream but dries transparent. It comes ready for use and has great holding power.

A great advantage of this glue is that for most woodwork it usually dries hard enough in from 30 to 40 minutes for pieces glued to be worked. However, hardwoods and those containing acids may take an hour or longer. It requires 24 hours of drying time for the glue to have full strength.

A disadvantage of the glue is that metals cause it to stain. Consequently, this glue comes in and should only be used from glass containers. It must be protected from freezing, and like all other glues, it should be used at 70 degrees or warmer.

For the past few years this type of glue was sold in bulk only to woodworking mills and factories, where it was used with great satisfaction. It is now available in many sized containers in hardware, paint, and builder's supply stores.

Directions for Use

1—Apply an even coat to both surfaces, place together at once, and clamp or bind firmly.

2—Immediately after using, wipe threads of top and jar and secure top firmly, so that the drying glue will not make it difficult or impossible to again remove the cover.

Note See notes for "Plastic Type Glue," immediately preceding.

OLD FASHIONED LIQUID GLUE

The "old fashioned" liquid glue which can be readily purchased in tubes, bottles, or cans, may often be used to good advantage. It has its place as do the other types of recommended glues but, in most cases, these latter are preferred.

Do not use this glue as a substitute for the "synthetic resin" type of glue which has no equal for gluing woods. However, it is recommended for use on parts or surfaces where there is little strain or need for great strength, particularly because of its convenience, as it comes ready mixed.

This type of glue may be used for "spot-gluing" on wood, in those same places where "plastic-type" glue was recommended, and is preferred to that glue on larger areas. However, this glue dries slowly and is not waterproof.

This liquid glue is also fine for gluing fabrics to wood surfaces, such as felt to desk tops, etc. (See "Gluing Felt to Wood," page 75.)

Directions for Use

The glue is applied and used in the same way as the mixed "synthetic resin" glues. Also see "General Rules for Gluing."

FLAKED GLUES

There is one other type of glue recommended for restoration work. This glue is similar to the old fashioned "liquid glue."

Flaked glue is dissolved in water to the proper consistency and then heated in a glue-pot. When applied hot, it dries faster and has better holding power than when used cold.

Do not use this glue as a substitute for the "synthetic resin" type which has no equal.

CLAMPS AND TOURNIQUETS

Clamps and tourniquets are used on freshly glued furniture and other articles to hold the glued joints firmly together and in alignment while glue is hardening.

Before clamps or tourniquets are tightened, the piece should be placed on a level surface to assure correct alignment. Joints to be glued should be checked to see that they are in proper position. Once glue has hardened, it is impossible to change the position without damage.

(See Plate 8, page 26, for illustration of use of "Wood Clamp," "C-Clamp," "Bar Clamp," and single or double "Tourniquets.")

Clamps

See Plate 7, page 25, for various types of clamps used in applying pressure to glue joints. They are as follows:

1—"Wood Clamp" (the technical name) is more commonly called a "Hand Screw Clamp." These clamps come in various sizes with jaws from about 5″ to 20″ long and with maximum openings from about 2″ to 15″. These clamps are important shop equipment.

The quickest and easiest way to open or close the jaws is to grip a handle in each hand and swing the clamp around. This keeps the jaws parallel as they move on the screw threads. Clamp the jaws evenly and firmly against pieces to be held together and then tighten the outer screw to give extra tension.

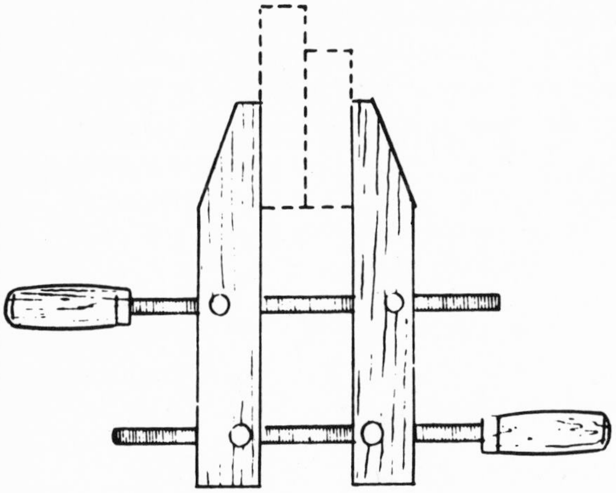

1. WOOD CLAMP

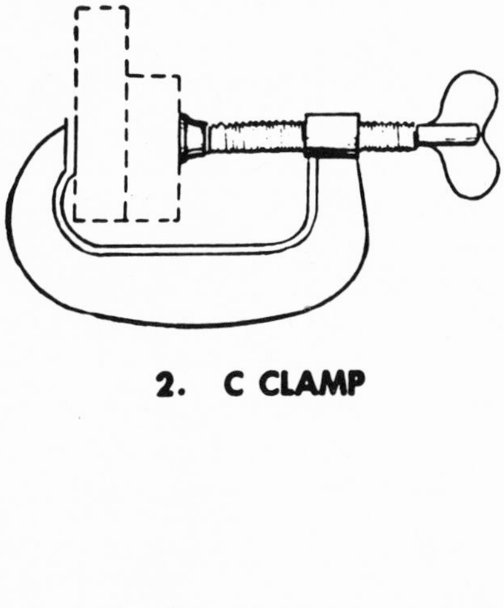

2. C CLAMP

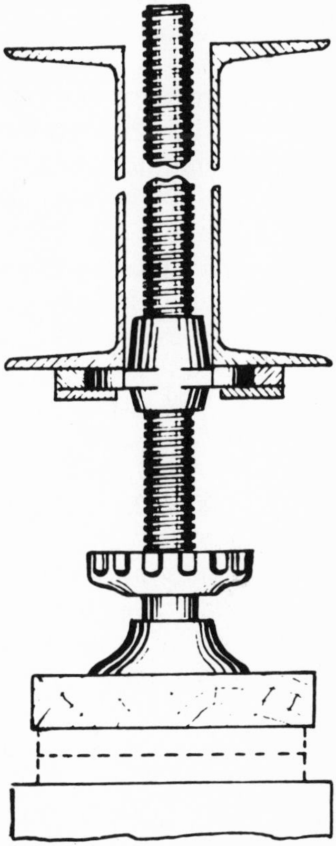

4. JACK SCREW

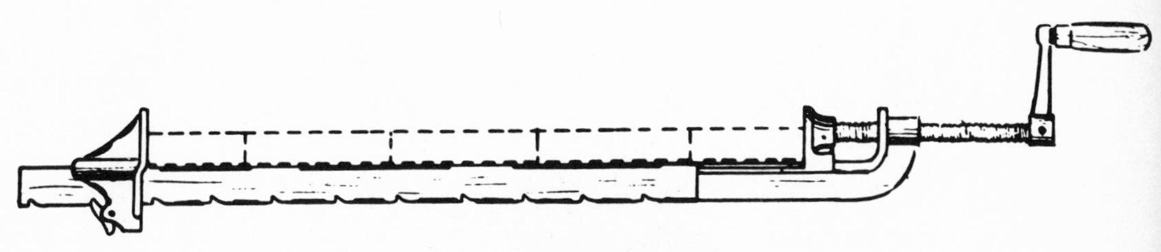

3. BAR CLAMP

Hand devices used in applying pressure to glue joints.

PLATE 7. Photographed from U.S. Government book.

The ordinary use of clamps is obvious. Here is an example of a more complicated use of a Hand Screw Clamp. Should you wish to clamp a table frame to the underside of the top, and hold it in place while glue on glue-blocks is drying (or to otherwise strengthen the joint), place a stiff piece of material (such as a 2″ x 4″) across and under the frame and clamp this to the top, providing, of course, the clamp jaws are not long enough to reach into the frame.

2—"C-Clamp." This type of clamp is for "spot clamping" only. Use a folded wad of paper or a small flat block of wood under each jaw to prevent injury to the wood surface. The sizes vary with jaw openings from about 2″ to 12″.

3—"Bar Clamp." This clamp is adjustable lengthwise, comes in various lengths and is used for horizontal clamping on wide widths. You will note in the illustration that there are pieces of wood under the jaws of the Bar Clamp holding the back-slats of the chair in place. The wood strips are placed there to distribute the pressure of the clamp and prevent the jaws from injuring the chair surface. A well equipped shop should include this type of clamp but is not essential, as a "tourniquet" may often be used as a substitute.

4—"Jack Screw." This is a fine tool to have but is not often found in an amateur shop. It is used for high pressure where large pieces are to be glued together.

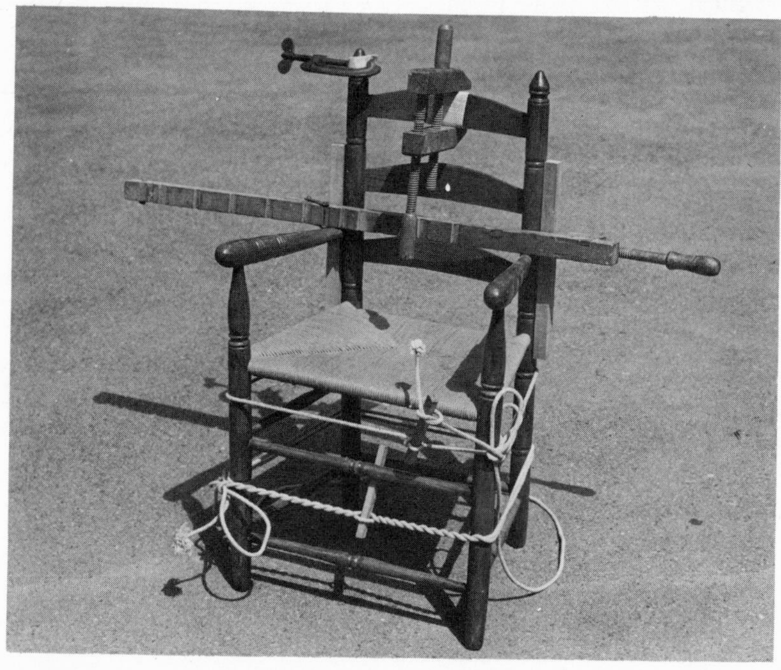

USE OF FURNITURE CLAMPS AND TOURNIQUETS

PLATE 8. See "Clamps and Tourniquets," page 24.

Tourniquets

The use of a tourniquet is often more satisfactory than a mechanical clamp when properly applied, as it distributes the pressure more evenly. (Examples of the use of a "Single Tourniquet" and a "Double Tourniquet" are shown in Plate 8, page 26, where the rungs of the chair are being held into the legs.)

A single tourniquet is made by placing the rope once around the article, while in the double tourniquet the rope is passed around twice. The ends of the rope are tied together (bow knot good) and a stick (short dowel or large spike good) is twisted in the rope until the desired tension is obtained.

Many people use the single tourniquet. However, the double type is better because, when a stick or spike is twisted between the two turns of the rope, it can be pushed back of some portion of the furniture to maintain the tension. In the single type the stick or spike must be tied in position. Moreover, the double type gives more even distribution of pressure.

The best rope to use is a heavy cotton clothesline. It is soft, strong, and closely woven. There is no need of cutting a rope to the size needed. When two tourniquets are needed on a single job, each end of the rope may be used.

HOMEMADE WEDGE CLAMP

A homemade wedge clamp is excellent for binding boards which are to be glued together, edge to edge. It is easy to make and use as shown in the drawing.

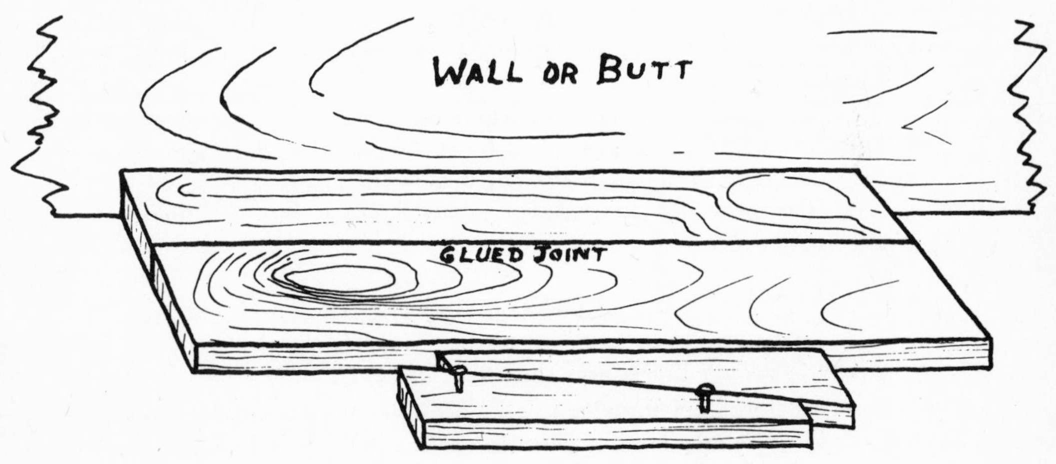

Look the drawing over carefully and get the picture of the procedure in your mind. It will clarify the method of making and using the clamp, as follows:

1—Construct this clamp from scrap lumber, ¾″ to 1″ in thickness, 6″ to 8″ wide and about one-half as long as the boards to be glued. On the wide side of the clamp material, mark at each end the mid-point from the sides. Now measure up and mark a point ½″ above the center on one end and on the other end ½″ below. Connect these two points by a diagonal line and saw through the material lengthwise along the line. This will give you two wedge-shaped pieces of the required angle, regardless of the length of the material.

2—Apply glue to both contact edges of the boards to be glued and place these edges in the correct permanent position, on a level wood surface, over wax paper, and against a backboard or butt.

3—Drive a nail, which is about one and one-half times longer than the thickness of the wedges, into, but not through, one of the wedges *only*, on the flat surface near each end, as shown in the drawing.

4—Put the wedges together as sawed, having on the outside and near the middle of the board, the one into which the nails were driven; the other one against the outside edge of the board to be clamped.

5—Then drive the nails partly through into the surface below, deeply enough to hold the outer wedge firmly in place, but leaving the nail heads above the surface in order that they may later be pulled out easily.

6—Pound the inner wedge tightly in place from the wider end, creating a strong tension against the glued boards. If the boards to be glued are thin, it will be necessary to place a weight on them to keep them from buckling.

7—Wipe off with a damp cloth any excess glue squeezed out on the upper surface and keep the boards clamped for 48 hours. The bottom side may be cleared later of any excess glue with a knife.

Note 1—This work must be done on a level, clean surface, such as a work bench with a back or wall to butt against. A section of a wood floor adjoining a wall is an excellent spot, provided you do not object to nail holes in the flooring.

2—If you have "bar clamps," the work can be done with them alone, if the boards to be glued are raised by sticks placed under them, in order to have the edges of the boards centered with the clamp screws.

3—The best glue for holding board edges is the "Synthetic Resin Waterproof" type.

GLUING FURNITURE

The following procedures should be followed:

Inspection Before applying glue to an assembled piece of furniture, examine it carefully to see whether any parts should be replaced or if, perhaps, screws, hidden nails, dowels, or braces might not be used to better advantage instead of relying on glued joints for strength. (See "Inspecting Furniture," page 18.)

Alignment Before gluing, place the piece on a level surface and see that it is in correct and natural alignment. Clamps or a tourniquet are used to hold freshly-glued joints firmly and properly together. They should not, however, be used to force an alignment.

Gluing without Dismantling 1—Shaky and rickety joints in furniture may be reglued, if clean, without taking a piece apart. When joints fit fairly closely, apply glue with a toothpick and work or rock the piece to and fro, to get the glue well into the joint. Whenever possible, turn the piece so as to have the joint-opening in a vertical position, so that the glue can flow downward into the joint.

2—When gluing, it is advisable to wedge toothpicks down into joints and to cut them off at or below the surface with a sharp knife. Such wedges will hold the joint in place better. Toothpicks are preferable to sharpened match-sticks as they are made of hard wood.

3—To prevent the glue from running out of a newly glued joint, when the piece is to be turned to a different position to glue another joint, wipe off the excess glue and wind a piece of string around the joint several times and knot it. A few hours later, and before the glue becomes hard, remove the string. Any excess glue remaining may be removed later with a knife (after the glue has become crystal hard) and without damage to the surface.

Dismantling to Glue 1—It is impossible to glue loose or rickety furniture properly, if the joints are filled with old glue and dirt. In such cases, if possible, dismantle the piece and clean all the joints thoroughly.

2—When dismantling, it is best to take out one piece at a time, clean and replace, unless it is obvious how to assemble and there are no similar parts. Otherwise, mark the ends of the parts as they come out and the inside of the joints from which they were removed, so you may reassemble properly. This is particularly important as, in many cases, a joint would not be loose unless there has been wear, and these worn parts must be returned to the place from which they were taken.

3—When marking dismantled pieces, it is well to make small grooves with a three-cornered file or a chisel (showing the number) on similar pieces such as chair rungs, back slats, etc., because pencil marks may be obliterated in removing dirt, old glue, or paint. However, it is usually sufficient to mark the side wall of the hole with a pencil as these marks are not apt to be lost in cleaning.

Note There are many pieces of very old furniture that should never be dismantled at all the joints. This is particularly true of some of the old chair rungs. The reason for this is that, in the days before glue was used, except for veneers, a chair rung may have been shaped or turned out of dry wood, with a bulb on the end. This was fitted closely into a hole of a green or unseasoned leg. As the wood in the leg dried it shrank and the joint became tight around the bulb. Such a joint may become loose with wear, but it cannot be taken apart without damage. Many fine old pieces were put together with wooden pins or wedges and cannot be taken apart without damage to the pin, wedge, or to the surrounding wood.

GLUING CRACKS

A large percentage of cracks in furniture and other articles of wood may be glued and clamped together, resulting in a permanent repair. In every case, the accumulated dirt, old glue, and paint must be removed or the new glue will not hold. Usually, this may be done with the point of a narrow bladed knife, a pin, or any other thin tool. If the crack is straight, it may often be well cleaned with an old hack-saw blade, by dragging it through the crack, with the teeth down and pointing towards the worker. The loose material can then be dumped or blown out.

The procedures for this work are as follows:

Crack Near an Edge Widen the crack with several small and thin soft-wood wedges, when possible or necessary. Gently drive in one wedge at a time until the crack is wide enough to insert glue. Remove the wedges, and apply clamps. Place over wax paper and put flat sticks under the jaws of the clamps, so as not to injure the wood surface. A "tourniquet" may often be used on wide surfaces, should you not own "bar-clamps." (See "Clamps and Tourniquets," page 24.)

Note "Brads" (thin, small headed nails) may be used, if preferred, to draw the crack together, after gluing. Drive into the board edge with care (with small hammer), sink the head below the surface with a "nail-set" and fill the hole left with stick shellac or wood dough of the same color as the finish. Smooth off carefully with a knife or fine abrasive paper.

Crack a Distance from an Edge After the crack has been thoroughly cleaned, test with a strong "bar-clamp" (with blocks of wood under the jaws so as not to injure the surface) to see if it is possible to draw the crack together. If this can be done, apply glue and clamp.

Where it is not possible to draw the crack together with the clamp, it will have to be filled. (See "Filling Cracks," page 77.)

Note 1—The proper glue for this work is "Synthetic Resin Waterproof Glue." Allow the glue to dry 24 hours or longer before removing clamps.

2—If the crack runs to the end of thick boards, in crude pieces, it is sometimes well to give added strength on the end by "toe-nailing" with finishing nails. (See "Repairing with Small Headed Nails," page 44.) The head of the nail may be driven below the wood surface and filled, as described in Note under "crack near an edge."

3—If the crack is wide and long, it may be well to reinforce it on the underside of the board with "mending plates," provided such a repair cannot be seen. (See "Hardware Frequently Used," page 46.)

4—Do not confuse a space between two boards, caused by shrinkage, with a crack. (See "Repairing Cracks Due to Shrinkage," page 38.)

USING WOOD SCREWS

When using screws to hold together two pieces of *hardwood*, drill holes of two sizes, the larger in the upper piece of wood, and the smaller in the lower. A screw driven in hardwood without proper sized holes is apt to crack or split the wood, the screw may refuse to enter it, or may break off.

The upper or "clearance" hole (also called a "pilot hole"), should be sufficiently large so that the screw can be inserted with the fingers, while the lower or "anchor" hole, drilled for the threaded part of the screw, must be small enough to give adequate holding power. In using a flat-head screw, countersink the mouth of the upper hole to accommodate the screw head, so it will be flush with or below the surface.

When working with *softwood*, holes of different sizes are not necessary unless near an edge. However, it will help to drill a small hole in both pieces of wood, smaller in size than the diameter of the screw thread, to serve as a guide for the screw.

The selection of a screw of correct length is very important, particularly for use in hardwood. The shank or smooth part of the screw should be the same length as the thickness of the upper board, to permit free passage of the screw, and leave the entire threaded part for holding power in the lower board.

Directions for Use

1—Before drilling a hole or using a screw, mark a small "x" with a pencil at the exact spot where the hole or screw is to be located, using for this purpose, if possible, a "try-square." At the intersection of the diagonals of the "x," make a small dent with a "center punch" hit lightly.

2—If the boards are not already fastened together, remove the upper one and place a flat piece of scrap wood under the board where you wish to drill, to prevent the lower side of the board from tearing or splintering, as the drill comes through. Drill the clearance hole, using the proper size "twist-drill."

3—Replace the upper board in the proper position over the lower, change the twist-drill to the size for the anchor hole and drill through the clearance hole, into the lower board, the full length of the screw.

4—Insert the screw and turn it down to its full length, taking care that the screw-driver does not slip from the slot and injure the wood.

Note 1—A small amount of soap or beeswax applied to the thread of the screw will make it go in more easily.

2—When there are a number of screws in a surface, leave the slots of the screws in a line with the grain of the wood for better appearance. If the screws are on a vertical surface, have the slots parallel with the floor.

3—The tip of a screw-driver should fit closely into the screw slot and be as wide as the screw head. This prevents slipping and tearing the slot. It is best to use an ordinary screw-driver for furniture, particularly on fine woods. An automatic screw-driver (such as a "Yankee") is apt to slip from the slot and mar the wood. Power hand drills are excellent for drilling screw holes in hardwoods, providing they are handled with care.

4—When using steel screws, a screw-driver bit in a brace is good for the final tightening of the screws. Use it for the full drive with large screws. Never use a bit with a brace for brass screws. This metal is weak and will break off easily, usually in the threaded section, causing much trouble.

5—For information regarding various types of screws, and size of "clearance" and "anchor" holes see "Wood Screws," page 179.

REMOVING WOOD SCREWS

A wood screw is often difficult to remove, particularly a steel one that has become rusted in wood, or a deeply buried flat-head screw with a damaged slot. Methods for removing stubborn screws follow:

General Rules

1—Use a screw-driver having a blade tip as wide as the screw head and which fits snugly into the slot. If too narrow, and the screw is stubborn, you are apt to tear and damage the slot, and make your work more difficult.

2—If unable to remove the screw with a hand screw-driver, try a "brace" with a screw-driver "bit." Press down firmly on the brace, so as not to injure the slot by slippage of the bit, and give a quick turn to the left (counter clock-wise), to unthread the screw. If the screw will not move, follow with a quick thrust to the right (tightening the screw) and quickly reverse the motion to the left again. This action will often start the screw.

3—Finally, try to jar the screw loose from its hole in the wood (particularly if the screw is rusted) by pounding it sharply on the head. To do this, place the tip of the screw-driver in the slot and strike a fairly heavy blow with a hammer. (For a flat-head screw, a round, short steel bar not larger than the screw head may be used, in place of the screw-driver.) Then, try to move the screw with a hand screw-driver. If not successful, use a brace with a screw-driver bit.

Round-Head Screw with Damaged Slot

The slot can often be widened or deepened with a hack saw as the screw head is above the surface. If necessary, remove the saw blade from the frame. Then follow the above general rules.

Flat-head Screw with Damaged Slot

A flat-head screw with a damaged slot is difficult to remove as the head is flush with, or buried below the wood surface. Use the following procedures *in the order given:*

1—Place the point of a nail-set in the extreme right hand end of the screw slot and at right angles to the slot. Slant it as nearly as possible toward the surface of the board (with the point still in the slot) and strike the nail-set with a hammer. If this will start the screw to unthread, repeat until the screw can be removed with a screw-driver, or until the head is raised enough to grip it in the jaws of "diagonal cutters." It may then be worked out with that tool.

2—When the above method fails, try this one. Drill a shallow hole (with a twist drill about one-half the diameter of the screw head) down through the center of the head, taking care not to let the drill go so deep that it will go through the head. Select a screw-driver with a point that is *slightly wider* than the width of the hole and pound it down into the hole, thus cutting slots on each side of the hole. Continue pounding to loosen the grip of the screw threads in the wood. Press down firmly on the screw-driver and apply a quick jerky motion to turn it toward the left (counter clock-wise). Should greater leverage be required, tighten a monkey-wrench over the lower flattened part of the screw-driver blade and push the wrench as you would a brace, while pressing down firmly on the screw-driver, so it will not be torn from the screw top.

3—If both of the above methods fail, drill the hole deeper until the head of the screw is cut off from its stem. The upper board may then be lifted off from the lower, the head of the screw picked out from the upper board (or driven out from the underside with a nail-set) and the protruding shaft of the screw may be unscrewed from the lower board with a pair of pliers.

Note A little kerosene put on the screw head and allowed to soak well into the wood will often help loosen a rusted screw. However, this may darken the wood, particularly softwood, in which case it should be avoided, unless the final finish is to be over a dark stain or painted.

REMOVING NAILS

Many old pieces of crude furniture were fastened with nails. It is often difficult to extract such nails, particularly the old iron "cut nails" if rusted.

Before attempting to remove a nail having a large head, especially if embedded, attempt to break its "bind" against the side of the hole. To do this, strike the head a sharp blow but take care that the force is not such that the nail will be driven deeper into the wood. For this, hold a spike, with the point sawed off, or a blunt tool of the proper size, against the head, and strike one sharp blow with a hammer.

Then use the following procedures *in the order given*. The first is less drastic than the second.

1—If the nail is situated where it can be raised by pounding from the underside of the board, as in the case of a nail holding a table top to the frame, place a block of wood (6″ to 8″ in length) under the top and as nearly as possible below the nail and strike against the block with a hammer and then pound the board back.

If this raises the nail sufficiently, draw it out a short way with a claw-hammer, having first placed a thin piece of metal (flat scraper good) under the hammer head, to prevent injury to the wood surface. Next, place a block of wood, about an inch thick, under the head of the hammer and continue to draw the nail upward. The block under the hammer head gives a more nearly perpendicular pull.

If it is possible to raise the nail only slightly by the blow, insert a hack-saw blade (removed from the frame) between the two pieces, nailed together, saw the nail through and punch it out from the underside of the top board with a nail-set.

2—As a last resort, remove the nail with "diagonal cutters" (see Tool No. 13 on Plate 25, page 187, and Note 5 in Chapter 9). The points of the jaws will leave a slightly larger hole in the wood surface but this can be filled with stick shellac, wood dough, or wood putty.

To remove a nail by this method, force the jaw points under the nail head, squeeze the handles firmly and push down. As the jaws are set at a slight angle from the handles, this downward push will exert a leverage which will lift the nail straight up. When the nail has been raised a little, release the grip, take a lower hold on the nail and repeat until the nail has been entirely withdrawn.

It is well to place a thin piece of metal under the jaws to prevent injury to the surface. Once you have mastered this method of extracting a stubborn nail you will marvel at the ease with which it is done.

Note 1—The "diagonal cutters" may be used in the first method in place of the hammer but must be used when the nail head cannot be raised. It can also be used for removing the remaining portion of the nail from the lower board when a nail has been sawed between the boards.

2—For information regarding various kinds of nails, see "Types of Nails," page 180.

WOOD DOUGH

"Wood dough" is often called "Plastic Wood." The name is incorrect, as that is a registered "Trade Mark" name of a popular brand of wood dough, just like "Duratite" is the registered trade name of another brand.

Wood dough dries quickly and may be sanded, planed, drilled, or carved. It will hold nails or screws and can be used to fill cracks, nail or knot holes, etc., and even for building up broken off wooden parts. It is one of the cheapest and quickest materials for repairing. If properly applied it will make a strong and permanent repair, but has one limitation. No matter how carefully it is smoothed, stained, and finished, it seldom will be entirely unnoticeable in a surface. The main reason for this is that, like "stick shellac," it has no grain, in contrast to the wood in which it has been used.

Wood dough has a definite use, and cannot be replaced by other materials. Use it preferably in inconspicuous places, or in those places where a part must be built up, then shaped or carved, stained and finished. Use it also in places where the repair required strength, ability to withstand moderate shock without chipping, or where nails or screws must be employed.

Wood dough cannot replace "stick shellac" (hard and brittle) for spot repairing, filling small holes, etc., and matching to an exact shade of color, to make a repair in a surface inconspicuous.

Wood dough is composed of finely ground wood, mixed with a binder and softened with quickly evaporating materials. Most of it comes in "natural" color (something like light oak), to be later stained, if desired, but is also available in colors to match various woods.

Wood dough comes in tubes and cans of various sizes. Immediately after using any, close the container tightly, as the solvent evaporates very rapidly, causing the contents to harden. Additional solvent may often be purchased for softening wood dough which has thickened beyond practical use, but that which has dried too far can never be again softened for use. A high grade "Lacquer Thinner" is recommended by many stores, as a substitute, when a prepared thinner is not available.

Directions for Use

1—See that the place where wood dough is to be applied is thoroughly dry and free from dust and dirt. However, it will stick to old paint if it has been roughed.

2—Apply to the spot to be filled or added to, taking extra precaution to keep it from the surrounding surface. Pack it deeply into holes. Wet the tip of your finger and press firmly in place. Allow to dry thoroughly.

3—Strip off surplus with a sharp knife or chisel and, if on a finished surface, sand smooth with 7/0 or 8/0 abrasive paper, taking care to sand only where applied.

Note 1—Wood dough shrinks slightly in drying. Should the place to be filled or added to be large, use several applications, one over the other, but only after the previous one has dried thoroughly. Finally, build up the surface to a height slightly higher than the desired final level. This coat to be cut and smoothed down.

2—Where it is necessary to build up a part and there is sufficient depth, drive screws partly into the surface to be repaired, leaving the heads exposed but beneath the surface of the repair, when cut down to the proper level or finished by carving. The wood dough should be packed tightly around the screws. This gives added hidden strength to the repair when finally completed.

3—When applying wood dough, if it should get on the surface surrounding the repair, it embeds deeply into the pores of the wood and is difficult to remove, especially from a wood with open pores or from a rough surface. It can be removed by sanding but it is better to use lacquer thinner. (Not to be used on a lacquer finish. The material should not be harmful to other finish.)

If wood dough must be stained it would be well to place a coat of wood dough on a piece of scrap wood. Allow it to dry, smooth and sand, and then apply a coat of stain. After the stain has dried, compare the color with that of the place in the piece where the repair is to be effected. Stain usually lightens somewhat in drying, and if too dark, cannot be removed. (A single coat of about 1/4th white shellac and 3/4ths denatured alcohol, applied carefully to the smoothed surface of the wood dough repair, will greatly lessen the absorption of stain.)

WOOD PUTTY

Many workers prefer "wood putty" to "wood dough." Each has its advantages and are of equal importance in a shop. Wood putty is a ready mixed powder to which water is added when used and is purchased at paint and hardware stores.

Its advantages over wood dough are that the best types harden more quickly and with less shrinkage, result in a smooth finish, are preferable for use under non-transparent finishes, and because it can be colored with "dry powder color" to match wood surfaces. (See "Homemade Dry Powder Stains," page 114.)

The disadvantages are that wood putty does dry to a flat surface and even though stained, does not look like wood and is, consequently, a poor material to use on a surface that will be conspicuous, such as in building up a broken off part. That can be done better with the wood dough. Furthermore, neither wood putty nor wood dough should be used for filling small holes in wood surfaces, where they will be conspicuous. "Stick shellac" (see following) is the perfect material for such work.

Directions for Use

1—Put as much as you believe you will use immediately in a waxed paper cup or small tin can, add only a very small amount of cold water at a time, and stir to a heavy dough. It cannot be "retempered," that is, used again by adding more water.

2—Dampen slightly the hole or crack to be filled and the immediate surrounding surface, apply the dough, pack it down with a dampened finger, to slightly above the desired level, to allow for possible shrinkage, and take care to keep it off the surface.

3—Wipe the surrounding surface with a dampened cloth over a finger and allow to dry. Then shave off any surplus with a knife.

Note 1—If the wood putty is to be stained with a "dry powder color," add the color to the dry putty powder, but make the mixture slightly darker than the wood as it lightens in drying.

2—If necessary to stain a patched spot or crack after the wood putty has dried, paint it first with white shellac, thinned with denatured alcohol (about 6 to 1) in order to prevent the stain soaking in and darkening too much. Test the color before applying to repair.

STICK SHELLAC

Stick shellac is used for filling cracks, small holes, dents, or gouges in either solid or veneered wood surfaces. It is more often used in hardwood furniture, such as maple and mahogany, where every small hole or depression should be filled smoothly, as such pieces require a fine finish.

It is extensively used by professionals in restoring fine Antiques and for repairing high grade and highly finished new furniture which may have received surface damage in shipment or from handling.

The end of a shellac stick is softened with heat and applied with a flexible spatula where needed. This is called "burning" it in.

When such a repair is properly finished, it is unnoticeable in surfaces having no grain, but stick shellac should not be used in surfaces with a distinct grain, except for a small area, as the repair would show distinctly.

This shellac is brittle, like sealing wax, resembles it in texture, and it too comes in sticks. It is produced in a great variety of colors and shades, from light buff through brown and into deep red, to match different woods and finishes. Some manufacturers produce these colored sticks in two types: transparent or opaque (non-transparent). Sealing wax may also be used for a repair, if it is the proper shade or color.

Stick shellac is sometimes difficult to find. It can usually be purchased in the larger paint stores. If not, an inquiry from a cabinetmaker or one of the better woodworking shops will disclose their source of supply. A set of about ten shades will be found sufficient for most work. However, if it is easily available, it is a good plan to purchase various shades as needed. One stick should last a long time. It is well to own a color chart. Many manufacturers furnish them and they are for sale by their dealers.

Directions for Use

1—Select a stick shellac of the correct color and shade to match the finish of the wood to which it is to be applied.

2—Melt the end of the stick with an electric soldering iron, holding the stick against the iron and directly over the place to be repaired and permit the molten shellac to fall upon that spot. Excessive heat will burn the shellac, destroy the color, and create bubbles.

3—Before the shellac hardens, flatten it out in the depression with a dampened finger or with the blade of a small spatula. The depression should be filled slightly higher than the surface. If necessary, melt and add more shellac. Finally, heat the blade of the spatula over an alcohol spirit lamp and smooth the surface. Allow it to stand until thoroughly hard.

4—Cut the raised shellac down flush with the wood surface with a sharp knife, razor blade, or, better still, with a sharp chisel, laid flat on the surface with the beveled edge of the blade up.

5—Finish the surface of the shellac with either a worn piece of "wet or dry" finishing abrasive paper, with "pumice stone," or "rottenstone" and oil.

Note 1—A place to be repaired with stick shellac should be cleaned thoroughly of dirt and old finish. Scratching or pricking holes in its bottom will give better holding power.

2—The point of a medium sized screw-driver or the large blade of a pocket knife may be used to heat and melt the stick shellac, if you do not have a soldering iron. Heat will destroy the temper of the metal, so the tool should be an old one.

3—A tool for smoothing the shellac can be made (as in step 3), from an old round end table knife, by heating and bending its blade at a 45 degree angle, about an inch from the end.

4—A spirit lamp which burns alcohol or "canned heat" (a jelly substance bought in cans), must be used for heating tools. An inexpensive one can be purchased or made from the base of a small oil can, with wadded string in the top as a wick. Gas or wood flame leaves a deposit of carbon (soot) on the metal and therefore should not be used as this will discolor the shellac.

5—If you wish to repair with stick shellac a surface that is to be stained later, the stain should be applied and allowed to dry thoroughly before the repair is made. Stains change color slightly as they dry, and it would be impossible to select the proper shellac color for the repair until the stain has dried.

6—The use of opaque stick shellac for deep cracks or depressions and the transparent type for those that are shallow, results in a more professional-like job.

REPAIRING CRACKS DUE TO SHRINKAGE

When two boards which are placed edge to edge in furniture shrink cross-grain, there will be a crack between them. This condition is often found in the tops of tables, dressers, cabinets, etc. The directions given for the repair of these cracks, when they run the full length of the boards, are intended to apply to such cases. They may also be used for cracks occurring in other parts and types of furniture.

The procedure is as follows:

Tops Which Cannot Be Removed 1—Remove from the crack any accumulation of dirt, old glue, or paint. Usually this may be accomplished with a thin knife blade, although it sometimes is easier to scrape out with the teeth of a worn hack-saw blade. Either must be handled with care.

2—Fill the crack with stick shellac of the right shade of color. In the case of a wide crack, this filling will be a slow and tedious job, but it is the only method to use on high grade furniture. If the work is done properly, the crack will not be visible, except that it will show no grain.

Note Wood dough may be used for the repair, but it is almost impossible to stain it to proper color and not have it conspicuous, no matter how carefully it is smoothed, stained, and finished.

Tops Which Can Be Removed 1—Remove the boards and clear dirt, old paint, or glue from the edges. Roughen or scratch the cleaned edges, for new glue to have a "tooth" to hold on to. Place the boards together again and test for close contact. If necessary, plane the edges at high spots.

2—If the boards were held in place with screws, fill the screw holes with wood dough, packed in firmly, as the boards, when replaced, will not assume their exact original position.

3—Apply waterproof glue to the edges of the boards, place them together, over wax paper, on a level surface, with their ends evenly in line, and draw them firmly together with two bar clamps or a wedge clamp. Wipe off surplus glue, squeezed out, with a damp cloth. Do not release the pressure for 24 hours, or handle roughly for 48 hours.

4—Replace the boards in their former position and refasten by the same means as originally used. Where convenient, use small angle irons and mending plates for additional strength and holding power. (See "Hardware Frequently Used," page 46.)

5—Strength may often be added to boards at the ends by "toe-nailing" in a manner which cannot be seen. (See "Repairs with Small Headed Nails," page 44.)

REMOVING DENTS AND BRUISES

Dents and depressions in furniture surfaces may usually be removed in softwoods, and most hardwoods, by the use of water or water and heat. However, it will seldom work satisfactorily with hard maple and this must be sanded to remove dents.

Various procedures are as follows:

1—**For Softwoods—without Heat** Water only to be used.

Apply water to depression with finger tip until water level is above the surrounding surface. Allow the water to absorb into the wood, adding more until the surface of the depression has lifted higher than that around it. The wood will shrink back a little as it dries.

2—**For Hardwoods—with Heat** With use of water and heat.

Fill depression with water as in Method 1. Heat the tip of a spike (a worthless screw-driver or blade of old pocket knife also good), and place it in the water until it steams, taking care not to burn the wood with the heated tool. Repeat until the wood fibres are raised to or above the surrounding surface.

3—**Using Marble or Thimble—with Heat** For depression near glued joint. With use of blotter and heated flatiron.

Fill the depression with water as in Method 1. Place a clean blotter carefully over the water. Press the blotter into the depression with a marble or the rounded end of a thimble. Hold moderately heated flatiron against the top of the marble or thimble, causing the water to steam and the wood fibres to swell.

4—**Using Woolen Cloth—with Heat** For large or obstinate depressions away from glued joints. With use of heated flatiron.

Lay a damp cloth on the depression and place over it a moderately heated flatiron. The warm moisture will cause the wood to swell and raise back to the normal level.

Note A—Water will soften the old type animal glue, causing joints to loosen or give way. Be careful when using any of the above methods near glued joints.

B—Prick a few minute holes in the surface of the depression with a very fine needle to hasten water absorption. Such holes will close and be invisible.

C—Water thus applied will turn non-waterproof final finishes white. (For reviving the color and finish, see "Removing White Spots," page 159.)

D—When an operation is applied to a wood surface without a finish, smooth it later with fine abrasive papers of grades from 6/0 to 8/0. (See "Sanding and Smoothing," page 97.)

WOODEN DOWELS

Dowels are cylindrical pieces of hardwood (usually birch), from which are cut short sections, called "dowel pins," which are used in fastening furniture. They hold two members of the furniture together, when glued into holes directly opposite each other. Dowel pins give a hidden strength in flush joints, as they pass through the joint into matching holes and are invisible from the outside. (For illustrations of dowel joints, see "F" on Plate 10, page 49, "Types of Glue Joints," and "P" on Plate 11, page 51, "Joints and Fastenings.")

Examples—In the construction of tables, the top is usually made of several boards, doweled and glued together, edge to edge, to appear as a single board. The upper frames and stretchers are usually doweled into the legs. The arms of chairs, if butted against the back, and seat members, are doweled. The spare leaves of extension dining tables are doweled to make them match and fit together, but here these pins are glued into the holes on one board only.

Dowels may be purchased from hardware stores and lumber yards. They ordinarily come in three foot lengths and are from 1/8″ to 1″ in diameter. The type of doweling having a spirally grooved surface is the best.

When making doweled joints, plan your work in advance. There are two factors to consider.

1—The thickness and length of dowel pins should be in direct proportion to the strain to which the joint is to be subjected. Thick, wide, heavy boards exert more strain on the joint and require heavier dowel pins. Dowel pins are seldom used more than 4″ long and, where possible, not less than 2″. (One half the length goes into each board.) The length is often limited by the thickness of one or both boards.

2—When it is possible to use two or more dowel pins at a joint, it will be better and stronger than if only one were used. Two small pins are stronger than one large one. The holding power with two pins is more widely distributed.

Note Bear in mind that a joint may often be reinforced from the underside or inside surface with angle irons or mending plates. (See "Hardware Frequently Used," page 46.)

MARKING FOR DOWEL HOLES

Marking for dowel holes may seem difficult to the beginner. The holes must be bored directly opposite each other, at an exact mark, so that when the dowel pins are placed in the holes, the surfaces of the boards thus doweled will come together properly, as had been planned. Marking for the holes is a relatively simple matter but must be carefully followed.

The two procedures, according to where the dowels are to be used, are as follows:

Edge Joints

Used when two boards of *equal thickness* are to be doweled together, edge to edge. Example—table tops.

1—With a pencil, mark the sides of the boards which are the under surface, unless it is obvious from the finish on one of the surfaces.

2—Clamp the boards together with the *ends flush* and the edge surfaces to be marked for the holes, *upwards* and *level* with each other. Have the under surfaces of the boards outward, as the finish side might be damaged by the clamps (or vise, if used).

3—Measure from the ends of the boards the spot where you wish to mark for dowel holes. Hold a "try-square" firmly against the side of one board, at those spots, and draw lines across the edge surface of both boards, with a knife blade, the point of an ice-pick, or awl. (A pencil line will be too coarse.)

4—With a rule (steel type best), locate the exact middle of each board edge. (Measure from the *outside* surface on each board.) Make a small hole on the line at those points, with the point of an ice-pick or awl. Enlarge the hole slightly with a center-punch. These holes indicate the exact center of the hole you are to bore for the dowel pins.

Note When there are more than two boards to be doweled together, as in a table top, the center boards will have to be marked and bored on both sides, to match the holes in the adjacent boards. Therefore, the boards should be marked (1, 2, 3, etc.) on the underside, to designate the order in which boards and edges go together. The adjoining boards must be treated as pairs.

Butt Joints

These are joints in furniture where the end of a board or other members butts against the side of another. In most cases, the dimensions of these boards or members differ at the joint, a smaller one butting against a larger. Here, the exact place where the smaller member butts against the larger must be determined, and both members marked for dowel holes, directly opposite each other.

Example—In table construction, the ends of the upper side members of the frame (thin boards) butt against the sides of the legs (wider, thicker, and usually square.)

The procedure for marking butt joints is as follows:

1—Make a template from heavy paper that is the exact size and shape of the end of the smaller board, by placing the end of this board on the paper and drawing around it with a sharp pencil. Cut the paper on this line and, if necessary, trim it so that it will be the exact size of the board end. Write "Top" on one side of the template.

2—Measure and locate the spot on the template where you wish the center of the dowel holes to come. (Wherever possible, use more than one dowel pin.)

3—Place the template back on the end of the piece from which it was drawn with the "Top" mark *outward*, and prick through the dots into the wood.

4—Place the template on the surface of the piece to be butted against, in the proper position with the "Top" mark *inward,* and prick through the holes in the template into the wood.

5—Enlarge these holes, in both pieces, with a centerpunch. These indicate the center of the holes to be bored for the dowel pins.

Note 1—The reason for the "Top" mark on the template being placed inward in step "4" is that, should you have the mark for the hole or holes *off* the center line in the template and it were placed on the second surface with the "Top" mark outward, the holes marked would be on the opposite side of the center line.

2—It must be remembered that the holes do not go all of the way through the board or member butted into, and the dowel pins are hidden in the joint. Therefore, it is impossible to locate the spot for the holes except on the faces into which they are to be bored. Follow the steps carefully.

3—The procedure for marking two boards of equal thickness and width, which are to butt against each other, is the same as that given above.

DRILLING HOLES FOR DOWELS

It is assumed that you have already planned on the thickness and the number of dowel pins to be used at each joint. Proceed as follows:

1—Use a drill or auger bit of the same diameter as that of the dowel pin selected. It is advisable to use "twist drills" for holes of small diameter. With only a limited tool equipment, you will have to use "auger bits" for larger holes. Either may be used in a bit brace.

2—Drill the holes, where marked, to a depth of about 1/4″ deeper than *one-half* the length of the dowel pin, if the hole is to be small in diameter. When the hole is of larger diameter (5/8″ to 1″), the added depth should be about 1/2″. The extra depth is to allow space for excess glue in the bottom of the hole. (One half the length of the dowel pin goes into each hole.)

Note 1—Holes may be drilled to an even depth by the use of a "bit depth gauge," easy to adjust and inexpensive. (See Tool No. 12, on Plate 25, page 187, mentioned in Chapter 10, page 191.)

A gauge may be made for twist drills by drilling a hole through a cork and leaving the cork on the bit at the depth desired. For auger bits, use a small block of wood in the same manner.

2—It is essential that the holes be drilled exactly perpendicular to the face of the board. A dowel pin will not slip freely into the holes in both members to be fastened if one hole is at an angle to the other.

3—To aid in drilling a perpendicular hole in the face of a board, place a "try-square" on it, with the steel rule part up, standing upright, next to the bit. If the hole is being drilled in the end of the board, tack small sticks of wood on two sides of the board, extending above it a few inches, to serve as a guide. By these means you can tell with considerable accuracy whether you are drilling in a truly perpendicular position.

PREPARING DOWEL PINS

It is important that dowel pins do not bind in the side of the holes, that their sides be grooved or roughened to give a "tooth" to which the glue will hold, and that the pins be of the proper length. Prepare them as follows:

1—If the dowel material is not of the kind that comes with a spiral groove, roughen its side surface with a wood rasp (shoemaker's file good. See Tool No. 5, Plate 25, page 187, and Note 6, Chapter 9, page 189.) This should be done on the dowel material before the pins are cut to length. The pins should not be a "sloppy" fit, but should slide into the holes with use of the fingers alone. A proper fit permits air to escape and the excess glue to be forced up the sides when the dowel is put into the hole. Since the holes were drilled with a diameter the same as that of the dowels, even the spirally grooved dowels may have to be eased a little, with abrasive paper or a file.

2—Saw the pins from the piece of doweling to a proper length to fit the hole depths. Take these depth measurements with a small piece of doweling or a nail. Make allowance for the extra depth in the hole to take care of excess glue.

3—Bevel the edges at the ends of the pins slightly, to permit easy entrance of the pin into the hole, and for the glue to pass up along the sides of the pin.

Note 1—When there are a number of pins to be cut and installed, mark the holes and pins with a corresponding number, in order that you may know where each pin is to go. (In doing hand work, it is impossible to drill holes to the same depth and cut pins all to the same length.)

2—When a dowel pin is to be used in a hole that has been drilled from the outside of a surface, where it will be later seen, cut it a little longer. After the glue has dried, trim it close and later sand it to the surface level.

GLUING DOWEL PINS

Before gluing dowel pins in place, first test to see if the pins will go into both holes, without binding. If they won't, the holes may not be directly opposite each other, or they may not have been drilled perpendicular. In either case, it is best to plug up the holes and redrill them, or start again and drill new holes, depending upon the circumstances and conditions found. Sometimes the hole may be slightly enlarged or the pin made a little smaller in diameter. However, don't do anything that will weaken the joint. Since the pins were made to slip into the holes with comparative ease, they should not be the cause of any binding.

When everything is in proper order, the pins and the contacting surfaces may be glued as follows:

1—Apply synthetic waterproof glue mixed fairly thick to the sides of the holes with a matchstick or nail. Apply glue to the contacting surfaces. Do not use too much glue, particularly in the holes.

2—Insert the pins in the holes of one member and put the other member in place. Wipe off any glue squeezed out with a damp cloth.

The two members should go together firmly with hand pressure only. If too much pressure is used (as when clamped) and the pieces forced together, the result will be disastrous cracks. The cause is often in having used too much glue. The bottom of the hole fills and the glue is unable to force itself up along the sides of the pin.

3—Bind the parts firmly together with clamps or a tourniquet, being sure the parts are properly aligned. Keep in a warm room to dry. The clamps may be removed in 24 hours but no strain should be put on the joint for 48 hours.

REPAIRS WITH SMALL HEADED NAILS

Repairing with thin, small headed nails has been common practice for years. You are here given a method for using "brads" (thin nails for light repairs) and "finishing nails" or "casing nails" (thicker nails for stronger repairs) that is not commonly known.

The new step in this method lies in drilling a hole for the nail to be used, with a *nail* of same size and from which the head has been cut off. The beheaded nail is held in the chuck of a hand-drill for drilling the hole. (Should the head not have been cut off, the jaws of the chuck would bind on the bulging head only, instead of on the side of the nail.)

When using nails in hardwood or before driving them into a narrow surface of softwood, holes should be drilled for the nails, for, otherwise, the nail may bend or split the wood.

The use of a beheaded nail as a drill, of the same thickness and length as the one to be used, results in fine holding power. The reason is that, when a hole is drilled with a nail and another one of the same thickness is driven into the hole, the final nail used binds on its *side* the full length of the hole.

Furthermore, the hole drilled is not as long as the nail to be finally used, as the nail for drilling has been beheaded and is held in the chuck. Consequently, the nail driven in the hole has holding power in the wood *beyond* the depth of the hole.

The hole can be more easily drilled with a "twist drill," especially in extremely hard woods. This would require the purchase of a variety of sizes (thickness) of drills, and it would be difficult to match the drills to the exact size of the nail, without the use of a mechanic's calipers. If the drill was smaller than the thickness of the nail, the latter might bend or split the wood when driven in. If the hole was larger than the nail, it would be a "sloppy" fit with no binding power.

The only difficulty you may have in drilling a hole with a beheaded nail is when using very thin "brads." They must be properly centered in the chuck, and care taken against bending the brad while drilling, as they are made of soft steel. (A small power hand drill is fine for this work.)

Examples in joints: A spindle, banister, slat, rung, stretcher, arm post, leg, etc., may often be given added strength by using this method of repair, after the parts have been glued and assembled and if the joint is near an edge.

This may be accomplished by drilling a hole in the side of the part with (or into) which the other part fits, at an angle and depth, so that the hole passes through the center of the part that fits into or with the other part. A full length small headed nail is then driven into the hole.

Should the nail head be in an exposed position, it may be driven under the surface with a nail set and the hole filled with stick shellac, of color to match the surface, or with wood dough or wood putty which may be stained.

Practically every joint shown on Plates 10 and 11, pages 49 and 51, may be strengthened with nails used in this way, if they can be driven in from an outside surface. Even splits near an edge of wood 1/8″ thick may be repaired by this method.

The procedure is as follows: 1—Choose a small headed nail of the thickness and length deemed best for the work. Cut the head off close, center in chuck of a hand-drill with a short "bite," and secure firmly.

2—Drill the hole without allowing the face of the chuck to touch the wood surface, thus marring it. When using thin nails, hold the drill steady and straight so there will be no undue strain on the nail. When drilling into the edge of a very thin board, be sure the hole is centered and parallel to the sides.

3—Drive a *whole* nail (of the same length and thickness as the one used for drilling) cautiously with a tack hammer, until the head is flush with the wood surface.

4—For information regarding various types of nails, see "Types of Nails," page 180.

Toe-nailing

Very often a joint may be strengthened by toe-nailing, which may be made a hidden repair, rather than using mending plates, corner angles, etc., which may be seen. (See "Hardware Frequently Used," below.)

Toe-nailing is a method of driving a nail at an angle, through one wooden member into another, to secure them tightly together. Examples: 1—A vertical upright being nailed into a horizontal member. 2—Two boards matched against one another in a flat position may be toe-nailed together at the ends. (See "Gluing Cracks," page 29, and "Repairing Cracks Due to Shrinkage," page 38.)

The work is done as outlined above, by drilling the hole for the small headed nail at an angle, while the boards are held or clamped together. The nail is then driven in place. Should the repair be located where it may be seen, the nail is driven below the surface with a nail-set and the hole filled. (Use as large a nail as possible for the greatest strength.)

HARDWARE FREQUENTLY USED

Many amateur workers do not know the technical names of various types of hardware frequently used around the house and for furniture repair. To enlighten such people and for their convenience, others than those commonly used in furniture repair are illustrated. All may be purchased in hardware stores. (See Plate No. 9, page 47. Information regarding nails and screws follows later.)

From the items illustrated, only those used most frequently in furniture repair are discussed, as follows:

Hinges

The type of hinges most commonly found on Antique or more recently made furniture is the "butt hinge" with "fast" pins (as opposed to "loose" pins which may be removed). Both kinds are termed "cabinet butts." The ornamental hinge is called a "butterfly hinge." (See illustration for both types.)

These come in many sizes and shapes, of brass or steel. The steel hinges may be had in a variety of finishes, including galvanized, dull or bright brass, bronze or copper, nickle plated, dead black, etc. The best for furniture repair are the solid brass or dead black.

Chest Lid Support or Desk Slide

A variety of kinds may be had and are sold by either of these names. This device should be used on lids of cabinets and chests which open upwards, so that the lid will stop just beyond the vertical position, and stand there by itself. The slide prevents the lid from falling back and breaking the hinge, or pulling out its screws. Use only one slide on the inside at one end. It is easily installed, the only problem being to have it in alignment and properly adjusted.

Corner Irons, Flat Corner Irons, Mending Plates, T-plates

These are the most important kinds of hardware to use in furniture repair. They give added strength at joints and, when used, should be

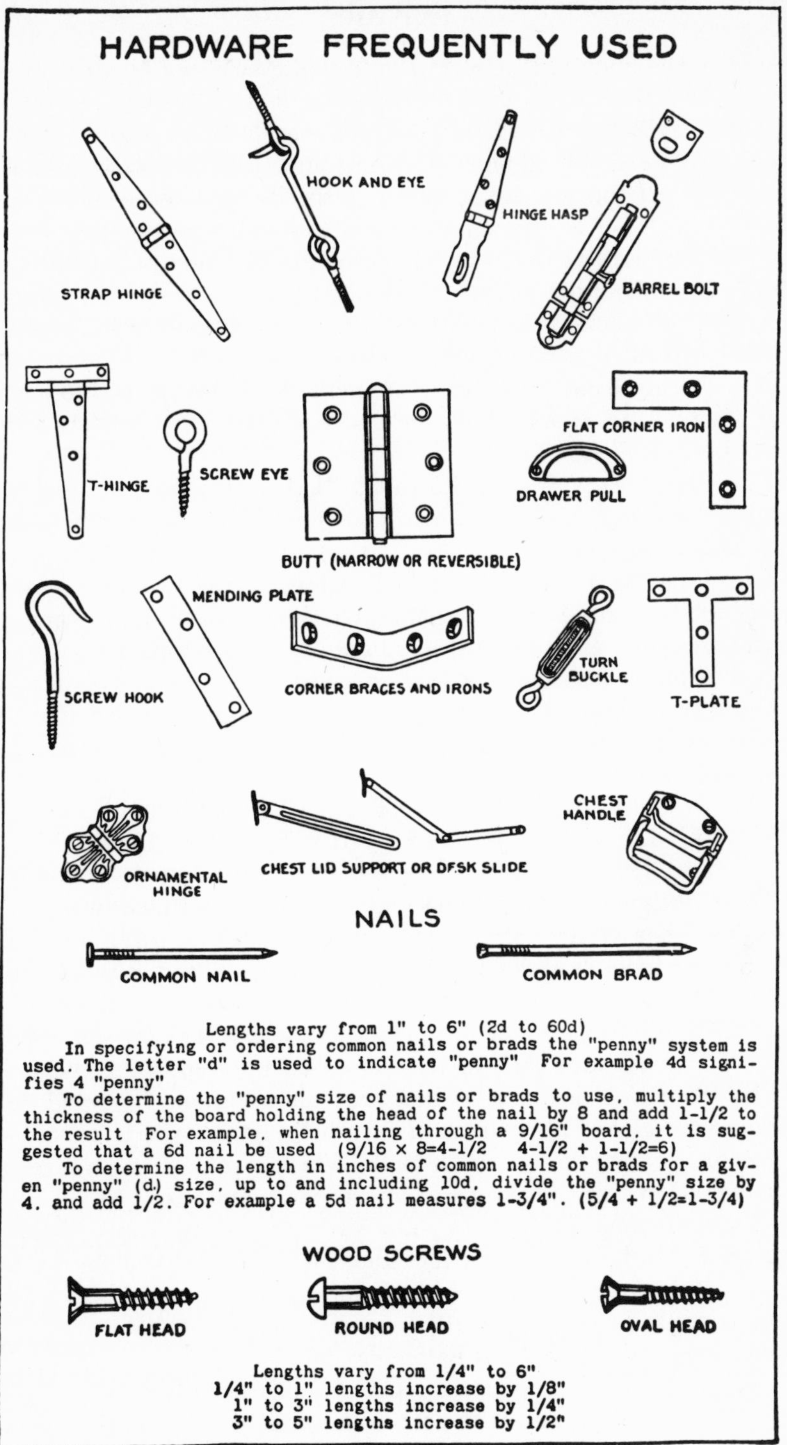
HARDWARE FREQUENTLY USED

STRAP HINGE
HOOK AND EYE
HINGE HASP
BARREL BOLT
T-HINGE
SCREW EYE
BUTT (NARROW OR REVERSIBLE)
FLAT CORNER IRON
DRAWER PULL
SCREW HOOK
MENDING PLATE
CORNER BRACES AND IRONS
TURN BUCKLE
T-PLATE
ORNAMENTAL HINGE
CHEST LID SUPPORT OR DESK SLIDE
CHEST HANDLE

NAILS

COMMON NAIL
COMMON BRAD

Lengths vary from 1" to 6" (2d to 60d)

In specifying or ordering common nails or brads the "penny" system is used. The letter "d" is used to indicate "penny" For example 4d signifies 4 "penny"

To determine the "penny" size of nails or brads to use, multiply the thickness of the board holding the head of the nail by 8 and add 1-1/2 to the result For example, when nailing through a 9/16" board, it is suggested that a 6d nail be used (9/16 x 8=4-1/2 4-1/2 + 1-1/2=6)

To determine the length in inches of common nails or brads for a given "penny" (d.) size, up to and including 10d, divide the "penny" size by 4, and add 1/2. For example a 5d nail measures 1-3/4". (5/4 + 1/2=1-3/4)

WOOD SCREWS

FLAT HEAD
ROUND HEAD
OVAL HEAD

Lengths vary from 1/4" to 6"
1/4" to 1" lengths increase by 1/8"
1" to 3" lengths increase by 1/4"
3" to 5" lengths increase by 1/2"

PLATE 9. Photographed from a U.S. Government book.

applied to the underside of surfaces where they will not be seen.

Each of these items come in several sizes. It is best to buy the heavy galvanized type for use where unseen. It may later be painted, if desired. That made of brass (thinner) is sometimes used in places where it is exposed. When buying any type for a specific purpose, get a length of screw that will not go through the wood to which it is applied.

One or more of the types are recommended for use in various procedures throughout this chapter, including securing tops to frames, repairing loose joints or cracks, holding formerly warped boards in place, etc.

Some of the examples are as follows:

1—**Corner Irons** (also called "Angle Irons") may be used to join a top more securely to a frame, as on the underside of a table, etc. At least two should be used for each side.

2—**Flat Corner Irons** (also called "L Plates") may be used on flat under-surface near a corner, when a joint is mitred, with or without the joint being glued, etc.

3—**Mending Plates** (also called "Cleats") will reinforce (from the underside) two boards glued together, etc. It is well to install plates a foot to two feet apart, according to circumstances and conditions.

4—**T-plates** may often be used to advantage when a vertical member of furniture contacts a horizontal piece, as reinforcing a leg to a frame member, on a table, etc.

FURNITURE JOINT ILLUSTRATIONS
TYPES OF GLUE JOINTS—JOINTS AND FASTENINGS

Many beginners, and perhaps some experienced amateur workers, have little knowledge of the various types of joints used in furniture construction. Among those most commonly used are butt, mitred, doweled, mortise and tenon, dovetail, tongue and groove and plain edge. Even in these joints, there is a great variety of methods by which they are cut, especially the dovetail type, and each of these is called by a special name.

In restoration work, it is best that all wood joints should be put together with glue. The waterproof "synthetic resin" type is best as it has the greatest holding power and strength. Where greater strength is required, it is advisable to give added support by mechanical means.

The adjoining illustrations show various types of joints. They were taken from U. S. Government literature and are furnished for your convenience and to enable you to better understand joints used and how they are distinguished. (See Plate 10, page 49, "Types of Glue Joints," and Plate 11, page 51, "Joints and Fastenings Adjoining.")

Below are listed the various types of joints headed by letters as they appear in the illustrations, with comments about them as to their uses and the kinds of mechanical support which may be used with some of them.

These are as follows:

TYPES OF GLUE JOINTS

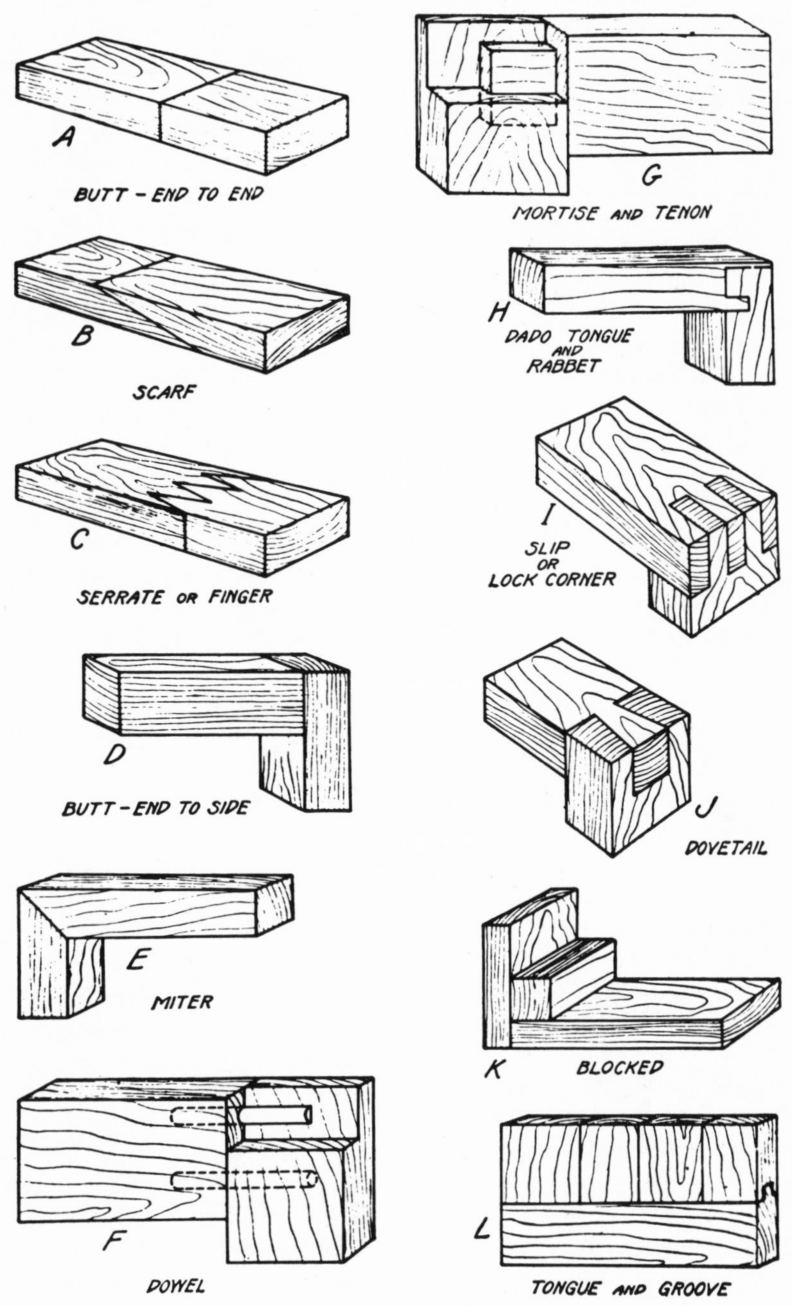

Types of butt-joint construction

PLATE 10. Photographed from a U.S. Government book.

Types of Joints

A—**Butt—End to End** Should have mechanical support, unless otherwise held. If boards are thick enough, "doweling" is best as shown in Joint "P." Can be supported with "mending plates."

B—**Scarf** A simple method of repairing broken boards by cutting them at an angle. Can be strengthened with "screws," with the heads sunk beneath the surface; the holes later filled.

C—**Serrate or Finger** More complicated method of repairing broken boards. Best supported on edges with "mending plates."

D—**Butt—End to Side** Best reinforced with "dowels" as in "F." May be supported with "corner angle" or "flat corner iron."

E—**Mitre** May be supported with "screws" as in "B" or hardware as in "D."

F—**Dowel** Best reinforcement to use wherever possible. This drawing shows corner of upright piece cut away, for purpose of better illustration. See also "P." This joint may be strengthened with "mending plates."

G—**Mortise and Tenon** A joint commonly found in high grade furniture. This drawing also shows the corner of the upright piece, cut away. The "tenon" (as illustrated) is an integral part of the horizontal piece, (above the letter "G") and is shaped to fit closely into the "mortise," a rectangular hole, in the upright piece. A modification of this joint is having the "mortise" cut all the way through the upright piece, and the "tenon" extending the full depth of the hole. The best mechanical means for additional support at the joint is with one or more "dowels," to be installed crosswise through the "tenon," or "mending plates" may be used.

H—**Dado Tongue and Rabbet** There are many modifications of this type of joint. It may be reinforced with "corner angles" and flat "corner irons."

I—**Slip or Lock Corner** A modification of the "dovetail" joint (see "J" and "Keying Common Dovetail" in "Q"). Found often in back joints of drawers and other places in cheaply built furniture.

J—**Dovetail** This is a "true" dovetail, also called a "cistern" dovetail. See "Q" for this type and other modification, some requiring complicated cabinet work. These joints are found mostly in well made furniture and, if they are tight fitting, should require no added support by mechanical means, if properly glued. When the joints are worn and support is needed, it may be supplied by building up each dovetail with small "shims" or with "corner angles."

K—**Blocked** The most common place a "block" is used is for securing tops to frames, as an added strength to screws which pass from the frame into the top. Not only should the "blocks" be glued in place but, for additional strength, holes should be drilled through them in two directions, which will permit screws to go through the blocks into both the frame and top. Thus applied, they will give more strength and holding power than "corner angles."

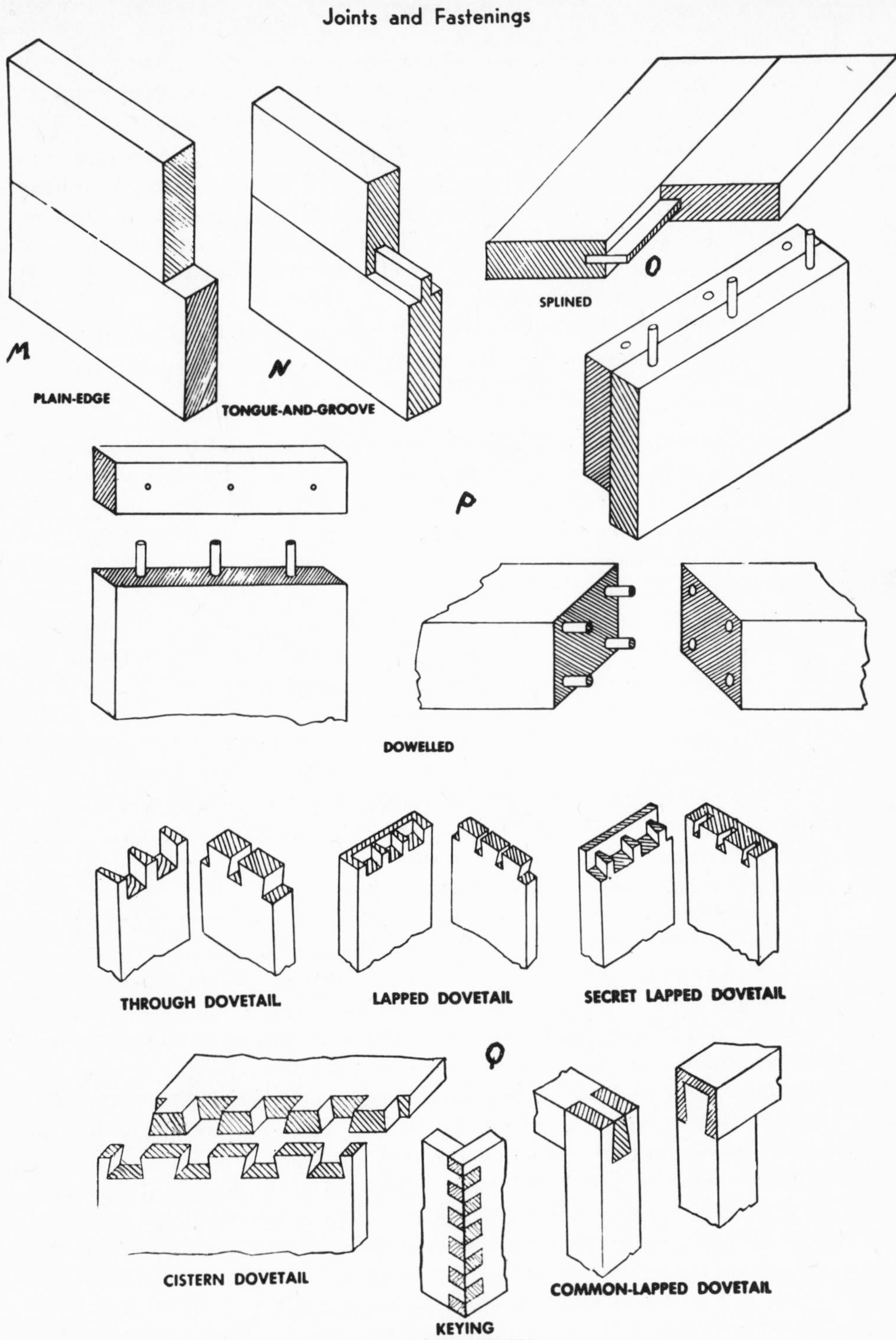

PLATE 11. Photographed from a U.S. Government book.

L—**Tongue and Groove** Not often used in furniture construction except in the cheaper and newer type. Typical joint for flooring. (Also see "N.") The joint may be strengthened with "mending plates."

M—**Plain Edge** The joint most commonly used in furniture construction (new and old) for tops, etc., made of several boards. When the boards are thick enough, the best mechanical strength (in addition to gluing) is with "dowels." The boards may be held to the frame with "blocks" and "corner angles," as directed in "K," and the boards held together with "mending plates."

O—**Splined** A joint mostly found in finely constructed old furniture. May be strengthened with "mending plates."

References

The methods of mechanical support and the materials used for same will be found in the "Items" as follows:

	PAGE
Synthetic Resin Waterproof Glue	21
Using Wood Screws	31
Wooden Dowels	40
Hardware Frequently Used (Mending Plates, etc.)	46
Tightening Round or Square Furniture Joints	below
Securing Furniture Top to Frame (Wooden Blocks)	54

TIGHTENING ROUND OR SQUARE FURNITURE JOINTS

More loose joints will be found in chairs and sofas than in any other type of furniture. Next come stands and tables. Most of these loose joints occur where one member joins another and the joint is either round or rectangular (here called square joints).

Examples of such joints in chairs are the fitting of the back slat or splat into the back post, and spindles fitting into the back slat and seat. Examples in both chairs and tables are stretchers fitting into legs. Most of the square joints (or rectangular) are of the "mortise and tenon" type, while the round joint may be either a solid member, shaped round at the end or a "doweled joint" that fits into a round hole in another member.

Joints become loose through hard usage and abuse, lack of moisture in the place in which the furniture is kept, and from shrinkage in the wood. Joints must be tightened properly to effect a permanent repair. It is sometimes advisable to reinforce a tightened joint with added mechanical means, depending upon prevailing conditions and the type of joint. (See Plate 10, page 49, "Types of Glue Joints," and Plate 11, page 51, "Joints and Fastenings.")

You have been told previously in the "General Rules for Gluing" (Rule "6," page 20), that a joint must fit tightly to hold, and that glue is used merely to keep it in place. You cannot expect to fill a loose joint with glue and have it hold.

The most simple of methods for tightening round and square furniture joints are as follows:

Tightening Joint with "Wedges" Thin, hardwood wedges (maple good) may be used to widen a round piece (rung, stretcher, spindle, chair leg, etc.) or a square or rectangular piece (tenon, slat, etc.) so it will fit against the sides of the hole into which it goes.

To make this repair, cut a slot in the end of the piece, with a saw having a very thin blade (hacksaw good) and apply glue to the slot and hole into which the piece is to fit. Start the wedge in the slot, put the piece into the hole, and drive into place with a mallet. The thickness and length of the wedge must be judged in advance. If the wedge is correct, it will hit at the base of the hole and widen the slot as the piece is driven into place.

When the piece to be widened with the wedge (chair leg, tenon, etc.), is to fit into a hole that goes all the way through the piece, cut the slot, apply the glue and put the pieces together. Then drive in the wedge. Allow the glue to dry, trim off the wedge, and sand to a smooth surface.

Tightening Square Joints with "Shims" A very effective means of tightening square sided joints, such as mortise and tenon. Shims are best made of hardwood, may be of even thickness or slightly tapered, but should be as wide as the hole. Apply glue to the hole and drive the shim into place.

Strengthening Joints with "Screws" Should the joint be one where the hole does not go all the way through a member into which another is placed, as stretchers or some mortise and tenon joints, it may be strengthened by inserting a screw through the base of the hole (into which the second part is placed) and into the end of that part. In such cases, a hole for the screw head should be drilled from the outside of the larger piece, and smaller hole for the screw shank and thread continued through, so that, when the screw is inserted, its head will be beneath the wood surface, later to be plugged with a small piece of dowel, glued in place, smoothed, and finished.

Round Hole Plugged with Dowel When a rounded end of a furniture part has a loose fit in a round hole in another part, glue a piece of dowel of the same size as the hole, into the hole and, when dry, drill a new hole for the part to be inserted. Example—to fit a chair rung into a leg, when there is a "sloppy" joint.

Tightening Joint with Cloth This method may be used on either a round or square joint. Cut some cloth strips narrower than the end of the part to be inserted into the hole.

Put these cloth strips over the end of the piece in the form of a cross. Trim off the cloth on the sides to ½ to ¾ths the depth of the joint, since the cloth stretches when going into the hole. Apply glue and put the joint together.

Should the cloth protrude out of the joint, trim it off closely with a razor blade immediately after the joint is assembled, and wipe off any excess glue with a damp cloth.

SECURING FURNITURE TOPS TO FRAMES

Furniture tops often must be removed to make repairs. They must usually be taken off when warps are to be removed from the boards. Removed tops must be put back in such a manner as to hold them securely in place. When warps in boards have been corrected by application of moisture or steam, they must be secured to the frame immediately, or the warp may return. (See "Removing Board Warps," page 69.)

The method of securing tops to frames is as follows:

1—Should a top consist of two or more boards, scrape any old glue from the board edges and roughen them slightly (knife blade good), so that new glue will have a "tooth" to hold to.

2—Fill any screw holes with wood dough. Pack in well with a match stick and allow to dry thoroughly.

3—Place the boards together, properly matched, up-side-down over wax paper, on a flat surface. Glue the contacting edges (using synthetic resin waterproof glue) and, if necessary, draw the boards together, with a "wedge clamp" (see page 27). On small tops, this may sometimes be done better with "bar clamps," with wood blocks under their jaws. (See "Clamps and Tourniquets," page 24.)

4—Turn the frame up-side-down and place it on the top. Locate its exact former position from marks left at the edge of the frame.

5—Replace any screws that held the top to the frame and tighten securely (best done with a brace and screw-driver bit). The screws usually go through slanting holes in the frame.

6—Install "glue blocks" (see "K," Plate 10, page 49) at the joint between the top and the frame, at each end of the frame side, also along the sides. The blocks should be of hardwood (or semi hardwood), glued in place, and also held with screws, one screw going into the frame and the other into the top. Prior to installation, drill clearance holes through the blocks, so that the screws will not bind in them, countersink the holes and use flat head screws, so as to take advantage of the pull against the head to tighten the screw.

7—It is advantageous to use small "corner irons," at the corners, and, on small pieces where there is but little strain, they may be substituted for the blocks. It is also well to install "flat mending plates" across the contacting edges of the boards of the top about a foot apart, if the boards have been warped. (See Plate 9, page 47.)

REPAIRING DRAWERS

Furniture drawers get hard usage and often become shaky and loosened in the joints, more quickly than other parts of the piece. Usually, they must be taken apart completely in order to effect a repair.

To accomplish this, use the following procedure:

1—Remove the drawer bottom. It slides into a groove from the back of the drawer and is usually held in place with a small nail driven through the bottom and into the end piece.

2—Care must be used in removing the sides if they are connected with each other by dovetail joints. Pound against a small, flat board held against the side, and next to the joint to release the strain.

3—Clean any old glue thoroughly from the joints; apply heavy glue to both members, and reassemble. A small brad, driven into joints will hold them in place. The drawer bottom acts as a square when reassembling, but be certain that the drawer will fit properly. Try it in the opening before the glue sets.

Note 1—If the drawer drags along its sides, it may have to be planed or sanded. A slight drag may be relieved by rubbing on talcum powder, soap, or soapstone.

2—If the drawer drags on its slides (bottom), the slides must be planed or sanded. If the drawer is too loose vertically, build the slide up by gluing to it thin strips of wood. (An effective but incorrect method of doing this is to put a few thumb-tacks on the slide.) If a drawer does not slide easily, it may often be made to do so by applying furniture wax to the slides.

MAKING AND INSTALLING NEW CHAIR PARTS

Whenever it becomes necessary to replace a part of a chair which is difficult to make or install, have the work done in a professional shop, unless you are fully qualified to do this work and have the necessary equipment and tools. Such work includes the shaping of arms or carvings, bows and combs for chair backs, the turning of rungs, spindles, banisters, finials, etc. (Also see "Lengthening Legs," page 57.)

The only instructions given here are for the type of work which should be within the ability of those with limited experience. Simple methods of work are given as follows:

Round Chair Rungs

Rungs which are rather large in diameter may be made from an old rake or hoe handle. Those of smaller diameter are best made from a proper hardwood to match that used.

It is not usually well to taper replacement rungs for any length toward the ends. It is better to reduce the size of the new rung at the ends only to fit the hole, leaving a slight slope or shoulder on the rung at the edge of the hole. The joint must have a tight, or drive fit. Therefore, the end beyond the taper should be round and straight.

This may be done with a sharp jack-knife. Make test for size, by first whittling to the proper diameter at the end of the new rung. When it will fit tightly in the hole, twist the rung, thus marking for continued reduction in size. Then glue and clamp in place or use a tourniquet.

Spindles for Chairs

When complicated turned chair spindles must be replaced, it is best to have them made. The type of round spindle with a bulb and taper toward both ends, such as are found on many Windsor chairs, are rather easily made with a "draw-knife" and a "spoke-shave," (see Tool 6 on Plate 25, page 187), or a short "block plane."

Shape the spindle roughly with the draw-knife and finish it with the spoke-shave with the wood held in a vise.

When the block plane is to be used for the finish, hold one end of the shaped spindle in one hand, place the other end against a very thin block nailed to a work bench, and force the spindle to bend, while using the plane with the other hand. By bending the spindle outwardly, the bulge of a bend may be shaved off and, in this manner, it may be shaped inwardly on both sides of a center bulb. (Be sure to shape the ends of the spindle to fit closely in the holes in the "top back rail" and the "chair seat." Test before installation.)

A spindle of this type may be installed by bending it. A turned or thick spindle which will not bend may be installed by drilling the hole in the top back rail a little deeper. The spindle is first pushed up into the back rail and then let down into the hole in the seat. Apply glue to holes before installation.

Odd Shaped Back Pieces

Many of these pieces which are not turned, may be easily shaped with the same tools used for making spindles, by a worker handy with tools. Such parts include arrow-head slats, splats (sometimes also called slats), which can often be made from the rim of a large spinning wheel. However, such pieces as a "banister back" slat, which is turned and then sawed in half lengthwise, should be made and installed by professionals.

Corner Blocks for Added Strength

Occasional chairs, dining room chairs, etc., which have a padded cloth covered seat, are subjected to much greater strain than chairs with solid wood seats. They must depend almost entirely upon the strength of the joint in the frame of the seat to hold them together. The padded seat should always be held in place in the frame with screws to give support to the seat frame. Screws often do not give sufficient support and the front legs become loose, or the side members of the seat frame loosen at their juncture with the back posts. The same condition may often be found in the frame of over-stuffed chairs, sofas, or other types of furniture.

The best means of repairing and strengthening such loosened joints is with hardwood (birch good) "corner blocks," glued in place and held with screws. (See drawing adjoining.)

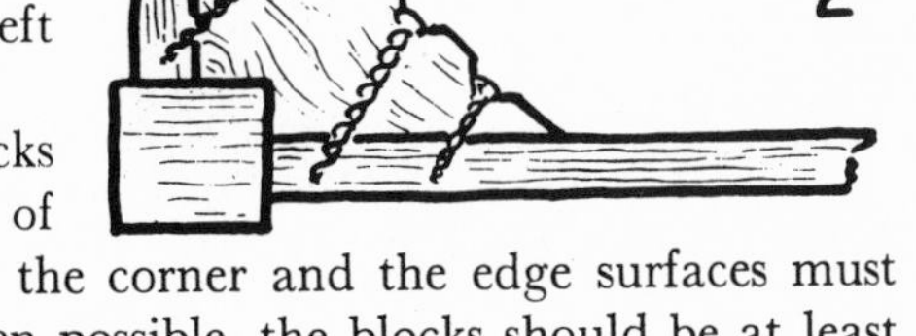

The procedure is as follows:

1—Take out the padded seat by removing the screws (underside) that hold it to the frame. (Working with over-stuffed furniture is difficult, as padding, and sometimes the springs, must be removed, so if you are not qualified to do that work, it is best left to a professional.)

2—Cut triangular shaped blocks to fit into the four inside corners of the seat frame. They must fit into the corner and the edge surfaces must contact the seat frame evenly. When possible, the blocks should be at least 1½″ thick and the side edges over 3″ long.

3—Drill clearance holes through the hypotenuse edge of the triangular block, at an angle, for screws to go through it into the seat frame, and countersink for the screw heads. The holes must be larger than the screw shank diameter so they will not bind.

4—Apply glue and screw the blocks in place.

LENGTHENING LEGS

You may sometimes wish to lengthen the legs of Antique furniture, when the lower ends have been rotted away, due to a damp floor, as happens on tables and chairs, or when legs have become shortened by years of hard usage. Also, the bottom of a leg may have been split or damaged beyond repair; perhaps it may have broken off.

A repair can be made by adding a piece to the bottom of legs. Two methods of doing this follow:

1—If the bottom of the leg is straight (round or square), the easiest method is to dowel a new piece to the bottom, after the leg has been cut off squarely. (See "Wooden Dowels," page 40.) The new piece should be a little thicker and longer than the original. When the glue has dried, the added section may then be shaped by filing and sanding and cut off to proper length.

2—If the bottom of the leg is turned, a new turning should be made to match an existing one. This turning can be shaped at the top, with a straight shaft, to fit into a hole to be drilled in the leg bottom, after it has been sawed off even. (This replaces the use of a dowel pin.)

It is best to have the turning made a bit larger at the top, than the leg into which it is to fit, so that, after it is installed and the glue is dry, it can be shaped down to size. This is a precautionary measure, for, should the hole in the bottom of the leg not be drilled in the exact center, and should the turning to be added be of exact size, there would not be a perfect fit.

Note The repair should be made with hardwood and, if possible, of the same kind of wood. After it is shaped it may be stained and finished.

CORRECTING UNBALANCED FURNITURE

Often a piece of furniture may wobble or be unsteady, because one or more of the legs is longer or shorter than the others. There are two rather simple procedures for correcting this condition.

Adding to Legs If the variance in the legs is slight, a "felt chair tip" (screwed in place), or metal "chair guides" (in the shape of a dome with claws, to be pounded in place), may be added to the bottom of the short leg or legs. The former may be available only in furniture stores but the latter are commonly found in "ten cent" and hardware stores.

Cutting off Legs This method of correction is a little more difficult. The problem is not only to cut off the correct amount from the leg bottoms, but also to have the cut parallel to the floor, so that the cut end touches the floor evenly at all points.

Proceed as follows:

1—Put a small block of wood, of the proper thickness, under the short leg, to correct the balance. This must be done on a level surface.

2—Place another block of wood, of the same thickness as the first, on the level surface, close up against each of the longer legs. Move it around the circumference of each leg, in turn, marking the leg with a sharp pencil, so that there is a circular line on the leg at the exact level of the top of the block.

3—Saw off the leg (or legs) along this mark, on its lower side (leave the line), and if the marks and saw-cuts are true, all legs will touch evenly at all points.

4—Bevel off the edges of the saw-cuts slightly with a file, and put a small amount of stain on the bottoms of the newly-cut leg bottoms. (If you find that you still do not have a perfect balance, because of an error in drawing the line or in cutting, this may be corrected by a little filing on the bottom of the leg.)

Note 1—If the furniture to be corrected has a flat top, it is well to place a "spirit-level" on it, before doing any of the work, to make certain the top is level.

2—The line around the leg for the saw cut may sometimes be made better with a sharp chisel, provided the block used as a gauge is large and thick enough. (Place the back of the chisel on the block and move it around the leg.)

3—When it is desired to cut a considerable length off the legs, and balance them to the floor level, first mark each leg with a pencil (measured with a rule), at the desired point where the legs are to be cut off. Choose a block to be used as a gauge, and measure its thickness. Then saw off all legs, at a distance below the pencil marks, of the thickness of the block and at an angle you believe to be correct, to have the leg bottoms fit flat on the floor. Then proceed with the steps, as related above, to mark with the block as a gauge, saw off the legs at the mark, correct any error in balance, and taper the edges with a file, and stain.

OLD WOODS FOR REPLACEMENT

Wherever possible, in restoring old furniture, use old wood for patching or for replacement of a part. A surface patch must match the surface into which it is inserted and a part replaced (or added) must match the rest of the piece in texture and color or it will be conspicuous.

New wood used for replacement is difficult to treat so that it will resemble the old wood exactly. Even when stained and finished to agree in color and feeling with the old wood, there will nearly always be a difference in its appearance, due to the variation in grain and texture, which age alone can give it.

Old wood will often take color, merely from the finish applied to it. The natural oils in woods dry out with age and leave them more porous than new woods. A porous surface of old wood has a different texture than a new wood of the same species and grain. When a clear liquid finish (such as varnish or shellac) is applied to old wood it results in a much darker color than the new wood. (See "Wet Test for Color," page 105.)

A proper wood for replacement part (particularly for a surface patch) may sometimes be gotten by using a piece from the furniture to be repaired. In well made furniture, such a piece may often be found in the frame or in places as the parting-rail between drawers, or other places normally out of sight. Before removing such a part, make certain it is of the same species and grain of wood.

It is a good plan to accumulate old woods and keep all scraps, if large enough. Old pine boards, maple bed sides or ends, tables (or just tops and leaves) of walnut, cherry, oak, mahogany, etc., may often be picked up at reasonable prices from Salvation Army, Good Will, and second-hand furniture stores; also from cabinet shops. It is worth while having a supply on hand, whether or not it is needed for immediate use. Keep the old wood in a special place away from new wood and guard it carefully.

PATCHING SURFACES

A small dent or hole, in a wood surface, can often be repaired with stick shellac of the correct shade and color, or with stained wood-dough, so that the repair will not be noticeable. However, when the grain of the wood shows through the surface finish, neither of these materials will be practical for a surface patch.

Such surface damage should be repaired by a wooden patch. In order to secure satisfactory results, the wood used for the patch must be correct as to specie, texture, grain, and age, and one which will take a finish that will blend it into the surrounding wood and thus be invisible. If such wood is not available, use a wood of similar grain which you can stain to match the color of the adjoining wood.

Any wood used for a patch must be thoroughly seasoned or the color will lighten greatly while seasoning, unless deeply stained. It should also be cleaned thoroughly to remove any former finish or accumulated dirt and then should be smoothed with a fine abrasive paper.

Shallow Patches and Plug Patches A "shallow patch" fits into a "grave." This "grave" is a hollowed-out space with vertical edges and level bottom, cut to size and excavated with a chisel. This type of patch is used to repair deep bruises, partly rotted surfaces, broken away surfaces, etc. The depth and size of the "grave" depends upon how much of the injured surface must be cut away, to get into sound wood, and true it up to receive the patch.

A "plug patch" is used when it is necessary to cut a hole all the way through the board, to remove dry rot, injuries, etc., that extend through the wood.

Shape of Patch The shape of the patch is very important. Its grain should match as nearly and as exactly as possible that of the surface into which it is to be placed.

For this reason, the grain in a patch must run in the same direction as the grain in the surface. The side edges of a patch will scarcely be noticeable when they run with the surface grain. The ends, however, should be cut at an angle of 45 degrees with the surface grain. An end edge, if left at right angles to the surface grain, would be very evident.

The following are the recommended shapes for patches, either long or short. The five shapes in the drawings will be adequate for most properly designed patches and show how they should be placed in the surface to be repaired. You will note that where the end edges of the patch cross the grain in the surface, they do so at an angle of 45 degrees (except for the diamond patch) and that the side edges run with the grain in the long patches.

Patch for Small Hole

1—**Square Patch** The best patch for small holes and should be inserted with the grain.

2—**Diamond Patch** This patch is for narrow, long holes where the surface of the patch, and that of the wood into which it is to be placed, are quite smooth. Otherwise use the square patch.

Patch for Long Holes

The best patch to select for long holes depends on circumstances, such as the width or length of the hole, or, perhaps, its location near an end, side, corner, etc. This patch should be inserted with the long dimension parallel to the surface grain.

The various shapes recommended are as follows:

1—**Double Arrow Patch**

2—**Reverse Arrow Patch**

3—**Parallelogram Patch**

Make a Template

1—Measure, with a rule, the length (with the grain) and the width (across the grain) of the place to be patched. Be sure to include all of the damaged or rotted area so that the patch, when in place, will be entirely in sound wood.

2—Choose the type of patch which you believe will be best suited for the size and shape of the hole and the circumstances of its position, etc.

3—Make a cardboard template, following the measurements taken of the type of patch chosen. Draw to size, using a straight-edge and a 45 degree angle (except for a diamond patch). Cut straight, clean edges with a sharp knife or razor blade.

4—Lay the template (lengthwise with the grain) on the surface and over the place to be patched. Mark closely around the edges of the template on the surface with the point of a sharp knife.

Digging "Grave" for Shallow Patch

The work sounds a bit "tricky," as given, but it is not too difficult if care is used.

1—Cut down with a sharp chisel, hit lightly with a mallet into the surface along the lines marked from the template. Hold the chisel with the beveled cutting edge inward and perpendicular to the surface. Cut square corners.

2—The surface included within your lines is to be cut down to the correct depth. Start about one-half inch back from the far end. Place the chisel blade at right angles to the grain of the wood and at an angle of about 45 degrees with the surface. Pound the chisel lightly with a mallet to raise chips. Move the chisel back about ¼″ toward you and continue until you reach the near end. Chisel out these chips until you have reached the proper depth. Be sure the bottom is level and the depth uniform.

Note 1—The depth of the "grave" is important. When a shallow patch is to be glued in place, its upper surface should be slightly higher than that of the surrounding area. This can later be sanded down to make them equal. Disregard chisel marks on the bottom of the "grave." They increase the holding power of the glue.

2—A chisel with deep-beveled sides, as well as having a deep bevel on the blade, is best for this work. The beveled sides aid in cutting clean corners. The deep bevel in the blade makes it easier to cut chips and to smooth the bottom of the hole. The cutting-edge of the chisel should be straight and very sharp. The work is more difficult with a chisel having square sides and only a shallow bevel on the blade, even when equally sharp.

Cutting Hole for Plug Patch

A hole of the correct dimensions and with smooth, perpendicular sides is cut *through* the thickness of the board. Proceed as follows:

1—Bore holes (about ¾″ in diameter) with a brace and a bit through the board and in each corner within the lines. These lines are the ones you drew around your template with a knife point. The holes should be close to the lines, but not touching, at the corners of your outline. (For a smaller patch use a correspondingly smaller bit.)

A sharp auger bit is necessary to produce a clean hole. When possible, a piece of wood should be held firmly against the under surface where the point of the bit is to come through. This will prevent tearing or splintering the under surface. If this is not possible, reduce your pressure on the brace as the bit comes through the under surface.

2—With a "key-hole" saw, cut out the hole for the patch. Keep your saw cuts straight and a little inside of the lines for the patch.

3—Remove the remaining wood with a wood file to the lines. The sides of the hole should be properly squared at the corners and at right angles to the surface.

Making a Patch

The following procedure applies equally to a "shallow patch" or "plug patch."

1—Lay the template on the wood you are to use for the patch, being sure that the long dimension is lengthwise with the grain. Mark around the template with a *sharp pencil.*

2—Saw or cut the patch to approximate size leaving the lines. Test the size by matching it with the hole into which it is to fit.

3—Finish the patch to nearly exact fit. This may be done with a sharp knife on thin patches or with a file or small plane on thick patches. Follow by rubbing the edges with a piece of moderately fine abrasive paper, placed over a flat block of wood. The edges must be clean cut and square.

Note 1—Make the patch after the hole has been prepared. You may experience difficulties in cutting and trimming the hole to the lines of the template or you may find further rot in the wood which could not be seen from the surface. In such case, a new template must be made as the patch cut from the original template will no longer fit.

2—The patch should fit the hole exactly. It can be made to do so with careful workmanship. This is particularly important when the patch is in a conspicuous place or when installed in furniture with a distinctive grain.

Gluing Shallow Patch

Mix some powdered waterproof glue reasonably thin. Apply this glue sparingly to the sides and bottom of "grave" and of the patch, then press the patch in place.

Gluing Plug Patch

1—Mix some powdered waterproof glue, fairly thick, and apply it to the edges of the patch and the sides of the hole. Press the patch in place leaving its surface slightly above that of the surrounding wood.

2—Hold the patch in place by inserting a small brad or pin in the cracks on two opposite sides so that it will not slip too far into the hole. Remove these fastenings when the glue has begun to harden.

Note (These notes apply to both kinds of patches.)

1—Wipe off excess glue and allow the patch to dry for 24 hours.

2—Sand the patch down to the level of the surrounding surface. Sand with the grain and use 8/0 abrasive paper. Take plenty of time as a careless rush job will show up under a finish in the completed work. You cannot avoid rubbing the edges of the surrounding surface. (See "Sanding and Smoothing," page 97.)

3—If glue is permitted to remain in the cracks at the surface level it will show through the finish. When the glue has thickened, but before it has hardened, scrape it out with a pin for a short distance down into the crack. This can be filled later with wood dough (which will take a stain) or with stick shellac of proper color. (This is important if the patch does not fit the hole exactly.)

Staining Patches

1—Stain is usually necessary to match the color of the patch surface with that of the old surface surrounding it. This will require a little experimenting. It should be done on a surplus piece of the wood used for the patch. (See "Staining Woods," page 108.)

2—A paste filler may be needed on the patch to secure the correct surface texture. (See "Paste Fillers," page 117.)

3—If the patch was made of old wood, the proper color may often be obtained by using linseed oil without a stain. Often this may be determined by making a "wet test." (See "Wet Test for Color," page 105, and "Coloring with Linseed Oils," page 106.)

4—It is almost impossible to match the color of the patch exactly to that of the surface. If the match is not exact, it may be necessary to stain the entire surface.

Note 1—If the patch material has been taken from a part of the furniture being repaired, it may match exactly in color by the application of the correct finish alone, providing the woods are of the same specie.

2—A sealer coat should be applied before and after a paste filler.

Finishing Patches

When the patch alone is to be given a final finish, it is best to use the same materials that were used for the original finish of the piece. The two finishes will then match more exactly. Usually when you have to patch furniture, you intend to refinish the entire piece. In such cases, you can use different materials for the new finish than those which were originally used, especially when it is planned to stain the entire surface. (Information on various finishes and their application can be found in Chapter 5, page 122.)

VENEER

Veneer is a very thin layer of wood, usually cut from the more expensive hardwood species, and chosen for its beauty of wood patterns or grain. The veneer may be glued to a thicker board base of another species (and usually less expensive), which does not have the cherished patterns or grain. In considerable of the Early American furniture, pine was used for the base.

The wood patterns in veneer often match, as on table and dresser tops, or as in old Victorian drawer fronts, where two pieces have been cut out of the same grain pattern (often a crotch), and butted together in reverse position. The effect, as you may have seen, is one of beauty.

Veneered furniture is more apt to be damaged by hard usage, age, dampness, etc., than solid wood. You may often find marks as a result of flower pots or hot utensils having been placed upon them. Any of these may break or mar the veneer, or cause the glue to loosen, resulting in defects such as raised edges, cracks, blisters, or waves. Often sections of the veneer lift from the base.

The furniture you are to repair will, most likely, be veneered with mahogany, walnut, or rosewood, as these are the woods most commonly used for veneer. They show beautiful figures when the veneer has been cut from the proper angles of the grain and from selected sections of the tree trunk, as limb crotches, stumps, or abnormal growths in the trunk.

REPAIRING VENEER

General information on this special type of repair and the methods used are as follows:

General Information 1—When there is a choice, use that method of repair which will permit you to glue the old veneer back in place without cracking it. Such cracks will leave lines in the surface that will show through the finish.

2—If any lines do show, fill them. Use stick shellac of proper color and shade. (See "Stick Shellac," page 36.)

3—When it is necessary to replace a part of the veneer, use material of the same color, grain and thickness, as the old. If you do not have any on hand, take a small sample to a cabinet shop from the furniture to be repaired. You will usually find them most obliging. Use an old piece of veneer whenever possible.

4—When a piece of veneer is cut to the size for a patch, it is best that the edges be trimmed on a bevel slanting inward, so that it fits tightly when clamped. This makes a closer fit when sanded.

5—Veneer darkens with age. Therefore, new material will be lighter in color and must be stained. This should be done before it is trimmed as the stain may expand or warp the veneer. After the patch has been trimmed its edges must be stained, but, before staining, sand the edges lightly to get them smooth.

6—New glue will not stick over dirt or old glue. Both should be removed with the blade of a knife which is sharp, thin, and pointed.

7—Powdered waterproof glue is the best kind to use for this type of repair. Apply glue thinly to the hole or patch, insert the patch and cover area with wax paper. Clamp a flat block of wood over this place or place a weight on it. Allow glue to dry for 24 hours; then sand with an 8/0 grade of abrasive paper to level the patch to the adjoining surface. (For use of abrasive papers, see "Sanding and Smoothing," page 97.)

8—Small veneer repairs are not difficult. If the surface effected is large, it might be best to take the work to a cabinet shop where they have special equipment. You may be able to hold a newly glued piece of veneer in place, on a small curved surface, by using a sand bag, but larger curved area will require a special mold. Also, an extensive flat surface may require a large press.

Small Defects A great variety of small defects are often found in a veneered surface. Among these are bruises, dents, chips, etc.

"Stick shellac" should be used for the repair of such a defect, whenever it is away from the edge of a surface. (See "Stick Shellac," page 36.)

Should the defect be at the edge, use "wood dough." Sand smooth, when hard, stain, and apply a finish. Stick shellac is quite brittle and should not be used on corners or edges as it may be broken off easily. (See "Wood Dough," page 35.)

Note Small, shallow depressions from bruises may often be repaired by the same method as that given later for plywood. This involves raising the surface with moisture. It may not be successful with very thin veneer but is worth trying. If it fails, use stick shellac. (See "Repairing Plyboard," page 76.)

Loose Edges There are two methods for this work, their selection depending on the conditions you find. They are as follows:

Method 1

If there is no dirt under the loosened veneer and there is life left in the old glue, this method should work. At least, it is worth trying because of its simplicity. Proceed as follows:

1—Lift the veneer slightly with the blade of a small spatula, being careful not to break or injure the veneer. (The same spatula used for applying stick shellac will do.)

2—Work a little water under the veneer or spray it under with an atomizer.

3—Heat the spatula blade over a spirit lamp (wipe off any carbon deposit if you use some other method of heating) and run the spatula back and forth under the loosened veneer to heat the water and soften the glue.

4—Cover the veneer with wax paper, a block of wood and clamp, or use a weight in place of the clamp.

Method 2

If there is any dirt under the veneer, proceed as follows:

1—Scrape out the dirt and old glue carefully.

2—Spread fresh glue on the end of the spatula blade. Lift up the loosened veneer slightly, insert the blade under the veneer, and press down the veneer. Withdraw the spatula, leaving a thin deposit of glue under the veneer.

3—Squeeze out the excess glue and wipe off with a damp cloth or the veneer may bulge. For this you can also use a roller similar to that used in photographic work, rolling it toward the edge. Clamp the veneer or hold it with a weight. (Over wax paper.)

Note 1—The tool used for this work should have no sharp corners on the blade as they might tear the veneer. (The type of spatula recommended has a rounded end.)

2—If you do not own this type of spatula, a piece of heavy paper, cut with rounded corners, may be used for inserting the glue.

Blisters and Waves These are places on a surface where the veneer has raised and are much like blisters on the skin, as from a burn. They are caused by an excess of moisture, either from the air or because a liquid has been spilled on the surface and allowed to remain until it has penetrated through the veneer to the glue beneath. This results in the glue softening and the veneer swelling.

The proper method to use for repair depends upon the circumstances in each case. These methods vary according to whether the surface is "unbroken" (Method 1), "broken" (Method 2), or "cracked" (Methods 3A, 3B, and 3C). The procedures are as follows:

1—Unbroken Surface

This method is simple. Whether it will work depends upon the condition of the old glue and whether there is enough moisture in the wood below the veneer. (Under U. S. Government Standards, most seasoned woods contain 12% moisture in climates of average humidity.) If this method fails, use Method 3B. Proceed as follows:

Place a moderately heated flatiron on the raised veneer surface gently enough so that it will not cause a crack. The iron should not be so hot that it will ruin the finish. The heat should draw out sufficient moisture from the base wood to soften the old glue and make it stick. Leave the iron in place for 24 hours.

2—Broken Surface

When the raised veneer is broken and a piece missing, it is usually best to cut out that section and repair with a patch, as follows:

If you have the broken piece or pieces and they still are in good shape, a very satisfactory job can often be done by flattening the edges that are intact with a moderately hot flatiron over a damp blotter. Next, glue in place the loose piece or pieces, being careful not to show the edge lines. Clamp or hold with a weight for 24 hours (over wax paper).

Cracked Surface—Method 3A

If there is *no* dirt under the surface, use this method. If it does not work because the old glue will no longer hold, use Method 3C. Proceed as follows:

1—Fill the air pocket with hot vinegar and keep the piece in a position which will prevent its running out. Let it stand from 8 to 12 hours and then drain off any vinegar that has not been absorbed. The vinegar is not to remove the glue but merely to soften it.

2—Dry the area with a moderately heated flatiron over dry blotting paper. The heat will shrink the veneer back to a flattened position and the blotting paper will absorb the moisture.

3—Lift the edge of the crack with a knife blade and insert glue through the crack under both sides with an eyedropper. Rub the surface, away from the crack, to spread the glue. Then rub it toward the crack and wipe off excess glue with a damp cloth. Clamp or hold with weight for 24 hours (over wax paper).

Cracked Surface—Method 3B

When there *is* dirt under the veneer and this dirt *can* be easily removed, use the following method:

1—Make a cut with a razor blade, directly *across* the crack, down to the flat surface on both sides. If necessary, cut the *crack* to the surface through the center in both directions, thus leaving four attached flaps.

2—Scrape the old glue off the bottom surface and from the underside of flaps. Scrape any glue from the edges of the cut or flaps to permit the edges to return to their original positions without interference. (If necessary, dampen with a wet cloth to make the veneer pliable.)

3—Insert glue under the veneer and press the flaps down in place. Wipe off any excess glue with a damp cloth and clamp or hold with a weight for 24 hours (over wax paper).

Cracked Surface—Method 3C

When there *is* dirt under the veneer and it is *difficult* to remove, use the following method:

1—Make a cut along three edges of the raised veneer with a razor blade. Two of the cuts should be with the grain and the third across the grain. This makes a flap.

2—Raise the flap and scrape away the dirt and old glue from the bottom surface and the underside of the flap. Glue, clamp, or hold with weight for 24 hours (over wax paper).

Veneer Inlays If any of the veneer is missing, it will have to be replaced with an inlay that should be of the same thickness and grain pattern as the surface into which it is to be placed. Proceed as follows:

1—Trim the place in the veneer to be repaired so that it will have straight and vertical edges. Two sides of this "grave" should run with the grain and the other two sides directly across the grain, or at an angle to it, depending upon how conspicuous the patterns in the veneer are and how closely the inlay pattern should match the sound veneer. For this purpose use a straight-edge and razor blade.

2—Make a template from a piece of paper. To do so, lay the paper over the "grave," rub a finger around the edges, producing lines on the paper. Cut on those lines to fit the hole.

3—Place the template over the veneer to be used as the inlay and mark along the edges with a sharp pointed pencil. Trim the inlay with scissors to size and check it for correct fit into the "grave."

4—Glue and clamp or hold with weight for 24 hours (over wax paper).

Collecting Old Veneer It is advisable to have on hand a supply of old veneer if you plan to do any considerable amount of restoration work. This stock may be obtained from old furniture which may usually be found in second-hand stores at low prices.

The method of removing veneer from its base is as follows:

1—Remove any old finish from the veneer and sand with 3/0 or finer abrasive paper to open the wood grain.

2—Soak the surface with a wet cloth for about 12 hours, moistening the cloth frequently.

3—Lift the veneer at an edge with a knife and remove. (If it does not come off easily, continue soaking.)

4—Place the veneer on a flat surface while still wet, with the underside up. Remove remaining glue by scraping with a knife blade. When dry, sand carefully with 3/0 or finer abrasive paper, until thoroughly clean.

5—Store in a dry place between flat material of sufficient weight to keep the veneer from curling.

REMOVING BOARD WARPS

In furniture, the most severe warps are often found in hinged drop table leaves and hinged chest or stand tops, as they are not secured in a flat position from the underside. To a lesser extent, warps often occur in the tops of tables, dressers, chests, or stands. This warping is found most frequently where the tops are not fastened securely enough to the frames from the underside or where there are not a sufficient number of properly placed glue blocks or screws to hold the top securely in place.

One important cause of warping is that the cabinetmaker has failed to apply a proper finish (linseed oil, shellac, varnish, etc.) to the lower surface when finishing the top. This point should be remembered when you are finishing furniture. This neglect allows a greater amount of moisture from the air to penetrate the wood from the under surface than from the top, causing the board to warp.

A board may twist lengthwise with the grain but it warps across the grain only. Furthermore, the board edges of furniture always tend to warp up toward the finished side. This is the "concave" (inwardly curved) side of the warp. The reverse side of the board is the "convex" (outwardly curved) side.

If the top or leaves of furniture are badly warped, you will want to correct this condition. A slight warp is permissible by the standards of the collector. In fact, such slight warpage often adds a note of charm to the piece.

If a wide, one piece-board used as a top for furniture is not too badly warped, it often may be clamped back and properly secured in place. However, this work should be done with great care, with clamps being tightened only a little at a time. A narrow or badly warped board should never be forced to flatten out. Disastrous cracks will result.

It is important that an examination be made of the frame, to see if it is sound and rigid. Any work to tighten a frame should be done before an attempt to remove a warp. (See "Gluing Furniture," page 28.)

Next, examine warped surfaces and select a method for removing the warp. This will be determined by conditions and circumstances, such as the degree of the warp, the thickness of the warped boards, and their location in the piece. Various methods are used for tops, table leaves, etc. as related in the procedures to follow.

All of the procedures call for careful planning of the work. The materials for holding a board in place, after the warp has been removed, should be on hand before any work is started, when using methods employing moisture or steam. Care and prompt action is required to obtain satisfactory results.

There are four methods for removing board warps, as follows:

1—**Removing Warp with Moisture**

This is the most simple method of all. It rarely results in a permanent correction and it is impossible to tell in advance whether it will work or not. That depends upon the ability of the wood pores to absorb moisture or the angle of grain when the board was cut from the log. Therefore, correcting a warp by this method should be followed immediately by securing the board flat by mechanical means, before the moisture dries out and the warp has had a chance to return.

Uses This method is best for boards which may be secured in place, especially from the underside. Examples: furniture tops or table drop-leaves held flat with cleats.

The Method

1—Fill any screw holes on the underside of the board with "wood dough." Pack deeply and allow to dry thoroughly.

2—Lay the board on damp grass in the sunlight or over wet burlap before a heated stove, with the "concave" (inwardly curved) side up. It usually takes from one to several hours for the board to flatten out, the time depending upon the degree of the heat applied, the thickness, width, or density of the wood, and whether of open pores.

3—If and when a board has flattened, secure it immediately to the place from which it came and before it dries. If it was held with screws, replace them. It is advisable to give additional reinforcement by holding the board in place with "corner irons" and "mending plates" whenever it is possible to use them. (See "Hardware Frequently Used," page 46.)

4—If it is necessary to secure a board temporarily in a flat position, do so by clamping rigid strips of wood on both sides near the ends and at the center. Otherwise, the warp may return.

Note 1—It may be necessary to remove paint or finish to permit a board to absorb moisture. Usually the back of a board from furniture has little or no finish and that is the side to be placed downward to absorb moisture.

2—Wide tops and wide table drop-leaves are usually made of more than one board, glued together, side by side. When warped, such pieces usually give way where glued and each board warps independently. Because waterproof glue was unknown when old pieces were made, any glue still holding at such joints may give way when moisture is applied.

3—When cleats are to be fixed to a board to hold it in a flattened position, the work should be done immediately after the warp has been removed (see "Cleats on Drop Table Leaves," page 73).

4—There are many modifications of the above method, mostly complicated and to be avoided. A brief example is where there are several boards, as in removable table leaves. They are stacked with wet sawdust between and around them for days, removed, restacked with cleats between them, gradually flattened with clamps across the boards about a foot apart, and allowed to dry. The clamps are made of heavy wood, wider than the boards, with long bolts through holes near both ends. The bolts are tightened in rotation, little by little, so that the pressure will not crack the boards.

2—Removing Warps with Steam

Warps that are stubborn and cannot be removed by Method 1 will usually submit to this method. With it there is a far better chance that the warp correction will be permanent, than if removed by Method 1, as the penetration of moisture goes all the way through the board. Consequently, narrow and thick boards submit best to this method.

Uses The same as Method 1.

The Method

1—Remove all paint and surface finish to permit penetration of moisture. (Various methods are given in Chapter 3. The most commonly used is that by using "Paint and Varnish Removers," as related on page 83.)

2—Have the board steam-treated in a steam box. (Such boxes are not too common but you should be able to learn where such work is done by inquiry at a cabinet shop or lumber yard.)

3—Follow steps 1, 3, and 4, in the method given for Method 1.

Note If the warped board is extremely dried out or of the type which has open pores, it is sometimes advisable to apply a single even coat of 50% pure white shellac and 50% denatured alcohol, so that the moisture will not be absorbed too rapidly. However, inquire at the shop to do the steaming before applying same.

3—Removing Warps with Grooves

This is a very satisfactory method of removing warps and may be new to some workers. It is done with a power saw. Since the grooves are cut on the reverse side of the boards only, it leaves the face undamaged, a point in its favor.

Uses This method can be used only on parts of furniture which can be removed to be sawed (like a table top) and should never be used on a part where the grooves may later be seen like table leaves, in a hanging position. (For an illustrated example, the warp in the *table top* was taken out by this method, as shown in Plate 12, page 73.)

The Method

1—On the reverse (convex—swelling outward) side of a flat wood surface, saw slots (grooves) lengthwise where the warp occurs, about 3″ apart and to a depth of about ¾ths the thickness of the board, with a power saw. The grooves should run lengthwise with the grain of the wood for the full length of the board, but should stop just short of the ends, so that the grooves will not be visible on the end surfaces.

2—Replace the board (or top) and secure to the frame by the means previously used (usually screws). Reinforce with "corner irons" (see "Hardware Frequently Used," page 46) and "glue blocks" (see "Securing Furniture Tops to Frames," page 54).

Note 1—In cases of extreme warpage or with thick boards, it is well to straighten the warp from the grooved board (or top) before attempting to secure it to the frame, to avoid cracks. (This may usually be done by Method 1 or by laying the board over wet burlap before a heated stove with the grooved side down.

2—This method is similar to that used by carpenters in building construction, where a flat molding is placed around a curved wall surface, by sawing cross-grain slots close together on the reverse side of the molding.

4—Removing Warp by Sawing Board in Strips

This method of removing a warp must be done in a professional shop equipped with large power tools, as boards wide enough to warp require them. The work cannot be atempted on boards too thin to plane level, as a final operation. Usually boards should be in excess of one inch in thickness for this method, but it may be used on boards of lesser thickness, if the warp is not too great. (See Plate No. 12, page 73, for *table leaves* straightened by this method.)

Uses This method is best for such items as table leaves which are hinged to hang down and the reverse side of which can be seen, as the operation results in a smooth finish on both sides. When it is possible to use "cleats" on the reverse side of the board, that method of straightening a warp is preferred by many. (See "Cleats on Drop Table Leaves," page 73.)

The Method

For your information and direction, the work is done as follows:

The board is cut lengthwise with a ripsaw into strips about 3 to 4 inches wide. The cut edges are smoothed on a joiner, alternate strips turned *upside down* and glued together under pressure. When dried, the board is put through a planer and then sanded on both sides. This eliminates the alternating convex and concave curves which were on both surfaces, due to every other board having been turned over.

Note This procedure for removing a warp destroys all evidence of age and wear, and the board is thinner. The new surfaces, when finished, will seldom match the rest of the furniture in color or tone. It is for this reason that many workers object to this method.

WARP REMOVED FROM TABLE TOP

PLATE 12. Underside of table shows grooves sawed in center section and how both leaves looked after each was sawed in 3 sections, glued and planed. Lines of saw marks and glue in repair of leaves were practically invisible. They were marked with black to photograph better.

CLEATS ON DROP TABLE LEAVES

(After a board warp has been removed)

The best method for keeping a hinged table leaf flat, after a warp has been removed by moisture or steam, is to install cleats. The method is relatively simple and is acceptable to most collectors.

The work should be done immediately after the warp has been removed and before the leaf has had a chance to dry out. The cleats should have been prepared previously; the glue, screws, and clamps should be at hand.

Cleats are installed on the underside and across the grain of the leaf. They should be set in from the ends of the leaf, in a position where they will not interfere with the frame or legs, when the leaf is hanging in a vertical position.

Usually, two cleats only are used, one near each end of the leaf. However, if it is possible to install a third cleat near the center of the leaf and still not have it interfere with the frame-arm or brace (which swings out from the frame to hold the leaf in a horizontal position), the additional support furnished by this third cleat is desirable.

Directions

1—The cleats should be of hardwood (oak good) to be effective. On medium width table leaves the cleats should be ¾″ thick and from 1″ to 1½″ wide. Their length should be within an inch of the width of the leaf.

When a cleat is installed, its narrow edge is placed against the board and the wide dimension of the cleat stands vertical to the board surface.

2—To make cleats, saw them lengthwise from a board of proper thickness for the *narrow edge* and of a determined width dimension. When a cleat is made in this manner and installed on its edge, it gives the greatest resistance to bend.

3—Use flat head steel screws of the proper length to go through the cleats and take a good hold in the table leaf. (Brass screws are made of soft metal and, if the leaf is hardwood, they are apt to break off.) Drill holes through the narrow width of the cleats, not more than six inches apart and large enough to give free clearance for the shank of the screw through the cleat, and countersink with a "rose drill" so that the screw head will be flush with the surface. Round off or taper the upper ends of the cleats so that they will have a neat appearance and then sand off the upper edges.

4—Take an accurate measurement of all four corners from the edge of the leaf to the leg or frame. If the table is not too large, it is well to turn it up-side-down over cloth or paper, while doing the measuring. Draw lines from these measurements, representing both side edges of the cleats. Leave enough clearance so the cleats will not interfere with the leg or frame, when the leaf is in hanging position. The lines must be parallel to the board ends The finish must be removed from the surface where the cleats are to be installed to assure the glue holding. Re-check your measurements and marks. It is most important that they be correct.

5—Mix some powdered waterproof glue fairly thick. Apply the glue to the contact side of the cleats. Secure the cleats to the leaves with screws, driven in tight with a "screw-bit" and "brace," being careful to place the cleats in exact position between the drawn lines. Wipe off the excess glue with a damp cloth.

6—Apply clamps over the cleats to hold them firmly to the leaves. Place in a warm room and permit the glue to dry for at least 48 hours. (Should the cleats be installed immediately after the warp was removed, the leaves will contain moisture.)

7—Stain the cleats to match the underside of the leaves.

8—After the leaves are thoroughly dry, seal the underside of the leaves with a coat of 75% boiled linseed oil and 25% pure turpentine or with a coat of varnish or shellac. This prevents absorption of moisture from the air, that was the cause of the warp.

Note 1—Cleats are often applied by this method to the underside of hinged tops of chests, stands, etc. after a warp has been removed. In such cases they are most frequently installed under the extreme ends of the top, when space will permit.

2—Another method of keeping a board flat, after a warp has been removed, is with hardwood dowels. Holes are drilled from side to side through the board edge, dowels are inserted and glued. The drilling requires accurate workmanship, and is best done with a power tool. The boards must not be too wide nor too thin. This method is rarely used but it is well to know about it.

GLUING FELT TO WOOD

You may occasionally wish to glue thin felt to wood, as when replacing it on an old desk top. Other occasions are applying felt to a lamp base or to the bottom of legs of heavy furniture so that floors will not be scratched.

Thin felt for such purpose may usually be purchased in a variety of colors at department stores. The most popular colors are green and brown. Measure the size needed and buy a piece larger than required, as it may shrink somewhat when applied and the glue dries.

Use either the "Synthetic Resin Waterproof Glue" mixed a bit thick (see page 21) or "Old Fashioned Glue" as it comes from the container (see page 23). Follow "General Rules for Gluing" (see page 20).

Proceed as follows:

1—When the surface is prepared, by removing any old glue, scratch or roughen it with coarse abrasive paper and clean off. Then apply a generous and even coat of the glue. Allow this to dry until it becomes very sticky and is not too liquid. Otherwise, it might soak through the felt.

2—Apply an oversize piece of felt to the surface, starting on one side and laying it carefully in correct position with no wrinkles. The felt must overlap on all sides. The hands must be clean and free from dust.

3—The felt must now be rolled or patted into the glue. This is best done with a photographer's roller. If not available, hold a lintless clean cloth around a small wood block and pat the entire surface. It is best not to rub it for fear of moving or stretching the felt.

4—Allow to dry for 24 to 48 hours in a warm room.

5—If the felt goes beyond the edges, trim off closely with sharp scissors. Should it be used on a piece such as a desk top which has a wood border around the surface to which it is applied, the excess felt material is best cut off with a safety razor blade against a straight edge as a guide. (A carpenter's large steel square is good for this purpose.)

Note What is known as "Rubber Cement" is often used by professional workers for this work instead of the glue as mentioned. This is not that type of cement used for patching inner tubes for tires. It is a heavier substance and often hard to purchase.

FURNITURE CASTERS

Casters used for furniture are usually the "stem and socket" type. The stem is the round shaft on the top of the caster. Near the top of this shaft is a slight groove. The socket is the hollow tube made with a beveled top and a plate at its base, with upturned jagged teeth, called the "ferrule."

To Install Casters

1—Measure the outside diameter of the socket tube. This is usually ⅜″ for smaller casters and ½″ for larger ones.

2—Drill holes in the center of the bottom of the furniture legs about ½″ deeper than the length of the socket tube to allow for the stem to protrude through the tube. If the furniture legs are small in diameter, wrap friction (tire) tape around their base to give added strength to the wood while drilling. If this is not done, the legs may split, especially if the bit is not sharp or the wood is very dry. The bit should be the same size as the diameter of the socket tube.

3—Pound the socket gently into the holes until the jagged teeth engage firmly in the wood of the leg bottom.

4—Insert the stem in the socket and hit sharply with the palm of the hand. This forces the stem through the beveled top of the socket, where it is held by the groove. Finally, remove any tire tape.

To Tighten Loose Sockets (3 Methods)

1—Shred steel wool, twist it, and work it into a string. Wrap it tightly around the socket, cover it with plastic type glue, insert it in socket hole and drive it into place.

2—Wrap the socket with tough paper or cloth, glue and insert, or with friction tape or rubber bands and insert.

3—Fill the hole into which the caster fits with wood dough which has been thinned by additional solvent. Assemble the caster with the stem in the socket and drive it to its full depth in the hole before the wood dough has a chance to harden. Twist the stem around several times and work it up and down a bit to make a space at the end of the stem so it will not bind when the wood dough hardens.

Note "Tea wagon casters" are an added attraction to such pieces as light tables or old commodes to make them mobile. The wheels are narrow, usually 3″ high and rubber tired. (See Plate 4A and B, page 13.)

REPAIRING PLYBOARD

Repairing a Hole

Cut from the top layer of another piece of plyboard, a piece of the correct shape to fit the hole but leave it slightly thicker than the piece to be repaired. Put waterproof glue in the hole ("grave"), insert the patch and wipe off any excess glue with a damp cloth, cover with waxed paper, a block of wood, and then clamp or weight. Allow it to stand for 48 hours and then sand down the patch (with the grain) to the correct level. (Follow the same directions as for "Veneer Inlays," page 68.)

Repairing a Bruise

Punch small holes (with the wood grain) along the edge of the bruise and then in the center, with the sharp point of a knife. Wet with a few drops of water and repeat, if necessary. Hold a hot soldering iron over the hole but do not touch the wood with it. This will steam the bruised part and lift it back to its former level. Sand smooth when dry.

FILLING CRACKS

Cracks in the surface of furniture and other articles made of wood should be filled at the time of repair as they are then in view. However, they will often come to light only after an old coat of paint has been removed. In any event, they should be filled, and stained to proper color and shade, before the final finish is applied. Filling cracks adds greatly to the finished appearance of a piece.

Use wood dough, wood putty, or stick shellac for the repair material. (For application, see procedures under those titles.)

CHAPTER
3

REMOVING OLD FINISH

In most cases the surface of old or Antique furniture should be refinished. However, where the original finish on a piece of value is still in good condition, such finish should be left untouched. Such work will destroy the charm, signs of age and usage, and will greatly reduce the value of the piece.

Nevertheless, it is obvious that the old finish must be removed from many pieces of furniture and a new finish applied in order that the hidden beauty of the old wood grain, wood patterns, and natural color may be brought out. This can only be accomplished, after the many coats of varnish or layers of paint of various colors have been removed, under which may be found a stain or a filler.

When the finished surface of a piece of furniture is covered with paint or a clear finish has an undercoat of heavy, non-transparent stain material, as was so often used, the wood grain is hidden. The grain in solid boards can be determined, if it is possible to examine the underside, as wood grain goes all the way through a board. This simple inspection may often show a beautiful grain in wood, which will greatly improve the appearance of a piece, when an old non-transparent finish is removed and an appropriate clear finish applied.

Test Before Condemning Old Finish

Beginners must guard against being over-ambitious. They will often condemn an old finish because of its doubtful appearance when this finish might be revived and made even more beautiful than it was originally. This fault should be excused in inexperienced workers as they have never enjoyed the thrill and delight of seeing the results which can be obtained by following methods used to restore an old finish. Even the experts may sometimes overlook this as they, too, are prone to condemn a finish because their examination of it has been too casual.

It is always possible to test these simple methods of restoring an old finish, by trying them on a small area, and, if the results are not satisfactory, the old finish can then be removed and a new one put on, without any harm having been done.

Some old furniture, such as "Hitchcock" chairs and "Boston" rockers, were constructed of wood which was intended to be painted and these should be restored by painting, although those still carrying their original paint can often be revived.

You will sometimes find furniture made of hardwood, such as mahogany, maple, or walnut, with the varnish in bad condition, due to age or abuse. This may have been marred, dented or scratched. If the condition is not too bad, the finish can usually be satisfactorily revived, but, when it is very badly "checked" or "alligatored," there is no alternative but to remove the old finish and replace it with a new one, suitable to the type of furniture and its use.

Determining Type of Old Finish

It is often difficult for the amateur to determine what kind of an old clear finish was used on a piece of furniture. It may be shellac, varnish, or lacquer, with no definite characteristic to indicate the finish which was used.

A test will show whether the material was shellac, by applying denatured alcohol with a rag to a small area, free from wax, to see whether the finish will soften or rub off, as shellac is always thinned with alcohol.

To distinguish between varnish and lacquer, treat a small area (free from wax) in the same manner, but with lacquer thinner. Lacquer will soften or rub off with this material while it will not be harmful to varnish.

Very often a heavy lacquer finish may be distinguished from one of varnish by the mere fact that lacquer is almost crystal hard as compared to varnish.

Reviving Old Finish

In Chapter 6 on "Reviving Old Finishes," you will find many practical methods which have proven satisfactory when properly executed. The grime and dirt must first be washed off from the old finish so that you can decide whether the finish can be revived. You will often be surprised at the results of your efforts. However, if the old finish is still found to be in a poor condition, it must be removed, the surface prepared, and a new one applied. (See Chapter 4, "Preparing for New Finish," and Chapter 5, "Refinishing.")

Work of Removing Old Finish

There are no "short-cuts" to good refinishing and each step, from removing the old finish to the final rub-down, must be followed in order and each properly completed before proceeding to the next one. With most finishes, the work is not too difficult, if you are willing to follow directions carefully and have the patience necessary and take sufficient time to do the work well. Experience is necessary to develop the proper technique when working on a highly finished piece.

When it is obvious that the old finish must be removed or when you have determined, from tests made, that its removal is necessary, the question then arises as to the proper procedure to follow to secure the best results and cause the least amount of damage to the wood surface.

The best and most harmless method of removing an old finish is with the use of a commercial "Paint and Varnish Remover." Before using this material, estimate the time it will take to complete the entire job of removal. It is poor practice to allow the "remover" to dry on the surface of your work. When you see that cracks and crevices are filled with old paint, or there are places where the finish is thicker than on the surface, it is well to apply the "remover" to those spots first, to allow extra time for softening.

"Lye" should be avoided whenever and wherever possible, as it is destructive, not only to certain species of wood, on which it should never be used, but is harmful to all woods, as well as to the new finish, if the directions for its use are deviated from in the slightest degree.

You have been told in the chapter on "Restoration" that the use of a "cabinet scraper" should be avoided, never to use broken glass as a substitute, and that a "plane" will remove the patina and old surface texture, so greatly cherished.

In the present chapter will be found, under titled procedures, various methods for removing old finishes and complete instruction for their use, preceded by detailed information as to their value, use, and abuse.

However, do not be discouraged. The piece on which you are working may appear to have been ruined by your efforts and the task of getting off all the smeared mess of old finish may seem impossible. Time and patience will produce results worthy of your effort.

Refractory Paints

You may find another disturbing factor in the removal of paint from Antique furniture. This arises when the only coat of paint, or perhaps, the undercoat of many layers, is a "Refractory" (obstinate) type, which has penetrated deeply into the wood pores.

Before the days when linseed oil was used as a vehicle in making paints, many paints were made by mixing a pigment with skim milk or buttermilk. These pigments may have been soot (lamp-black) from kerosene lamps or colors from the earth, such as sienna (brown) or iron oxide (red). "Refractory" paints were used generally on pine, because of the desire to cover knots or other imperfections in the wood. This produced an effect that made cheap woods appear more beautiful. It is said that finely grained and finished furniture was often covered with this paint to make it appear less valuable in the eyes of the tax appraiser. However, we cannot understand why so many fine woods were thus painted. (See page 86, "Removing Refractory Paints.")

General Rules—Removing Old Finish

When removing an old finish or paint from the wood surface of furniture, it is well to abide by the following rules:

COUNTRY DESK (Maine)

PLATE 13A. (*Left*) Checked shellac finish with heavy brown stain was removed disclosing beautifully grained quarter-cut cherry. No repair necessary.

PLATE 13B. (*Right*) Varnish 'polish rubbed' finish applied (surface was smoothed with a filler).

1—Do nothing which will harm the patina or the original surface, unless it is in such bad condition that drastic methods are called for or unless the piece is to be painted.

2—All old finish must be removed so that the new one will hold properly, if you plan to replace the old finish with a new one of a clear type.

3—When removing old paint, it is not only permissible but acceptable to most collectors that the marks of wear through the years be allowed to remain, as well as traces of color from the old paint, so that they will show through the new finish. However, old paint should not be left on in thick patches or blotches. Traces of old paint add interest to the piece by their variations of color and are evidence of age.

4—Usually stubborn paint can be removed down to that which may be satisfactory but it is impossible to remove it all, particularly from open-grained woods. White paint is most difficult to remove, particularly from cherry, mahogany, and walnut.

5—Before attempting to remove an old finish or paint, it is a good plan to scrape off a small area, in an inconspicuous spot, to determine the condition of the finish, the number of coats that have been used, and to inspect the undercoat. If this undercoat is found to be of the "Refractory" type, the necessary materials for its removal should be at hand before the "paint and varnish remover," if used, has had a chance to dry.

CRUDE HICKORY ARMCHAIR

PLATE 14A. (*Left*) Grime and heavy brown stain material removed with a 'commercial remover.' Glued many loose pinned joints. Filled small holes with wood dough, sanded, and stained them.

PLATE 14B. (*Right*) Wood grain and beauty brought out with 'shellac and wax' finish, some orange shellac added to the white for color.

6—After using any kind of material as a remover, the piece must be allowed sufficient time to dry out thoroughly. This usually takes 24 hours or longer. If shellac is to be used as a sealer or for the finish and the wood is not completely dry or traces of remover have not been properly cleaned from the surface, the finish may turn white or discolored. Moreover, many materials (other than shellac) used for a final finish, may not dry hard over some of the old finishes, if any has been left on a surface.

7—Do not attempt to remove old paint from furniture with a blowtorch, as it will burn and ruin the piece.

Note Use a cabinet scraper or knife blade on joints, corners, and angles on flat surfaces for the final cleaning, after using a remover, and steel wool to clean out carvings, turnings, moldings, cracks, and crevices. Some workers make scrapers of hardwood, with a beveled edge and handle, instead of using a metal scraper, as wood is safer and cannot injure the surface. Orange sticks, wooden meat skewers, and sharpened hardwood dowels make good tools for use in small places. The points of such tools should be covered with a piece of cloth. Doweling, of various diameters, which has been cut on the end at an angle of 45°, makes a fine tool for removing softened finishes from grooves or moldings.

PAINT AND VARNISH REMOVERS

Commercial removers are solvents, rather than corrosives. They act more slowly on older paints than on new, but are the only materials to use with safety. They attack the vehicles only, such as linseed oils used in paint, or the resins in shellac, varnish, and lacquer. They will not injure a surface, by burning it, leaving marks, be harmful to glue, or raise the grain of the wood.

These removers may be used on veneered surfaces without causing the veneer to loosen, as they contain no water. When properly applied and then washed off, they leave the surface clean.

Commercial removers are more expensive than other materials which might be used, such as "lye," but, because of the excellent results from their use, they are usually the cheapest in the end. Always read the full directions on the container.

Buying Commercial Removers

Commercial removers are sold under many trade names and are made from various formulas. Some contain paraffin or wax. They may be purchased in containers, from one pint to a gallon, at most hardware and paint stores.

Some professional workers prefer the thin liquid form of remover, claiming it is best for speeding up the work. From my experience, a thicker liquid type (more like syrup) is preferred. It will "stay put" better when applied, will remain wet longer and there is less waste. Also, those removers which are made *without* wax or paraffin are preferred. These substances are added to retard evaporation but it is difficult to remove all traces of the wax or paraffin. If any remover is left on the surface, the new finish will not stick properly.

Removers made in paste form, rarely used, are best for vertical surfaces, such as walls, but may be used advantageously on large pieces of furniture which are difficult to turn on their sides.

Using Commercial Removers

"Paint and Varnish Removers" should be used in a well ventilated room. Drafts and direct sunlight should be avoided to obtain the best results. The reason is that the action of most removers is accelerated by a film which forms on its surface. This retards evaporation; preventing the remover from drying too rapidly. You are, therefore, advised to "flow" a remover on thickly with a brush in one direction only, and not to rebrush it, since that would destroy this surface film.

Equipment

A good grade of remover, small can or jar to hold it; old paint brush (2″ best); dull-bladed putty knife; small scrub brush (about 4″ long);

burlap pieces (cut into 15″ squares, approximately); soft cloths; steel wool (2/0 or finer); denatured alcohol; and some old newspapers.

If there are any turnings or carvings to be cleaned, add an old tooth brush, an orange stick, or a wooden meat skewer. The use of canvas or rubber gloves is suggested if you wish to keep your hands clean. However, this dirt and stain can be removed from the hands with alcohol and a thorough scrubbing with soap and water. Old clothes or a washable coverall is recommended.

Directions

1—Place the piece to be worked on, over layers of old newspapers (on a table if the piece is small), in a good strong light and, if possible, with the top surface in a horizontal position.

2—Shake the remover thoroughly and pour a small amount into the can or jar and apply thickly with a full brush in one direction. Do not rebrush and limit the surface to be covered to not over a two foot square.

3—Let the remover stand, without touching, for a period of from 10 to 20 minutes or until the paint or finish "lifts." This is indicated by a wrinkling of the surface. Do not let the remover dry. If it begins to dry, apply an additional coat, and wait for it to act.

4—When the surface covering has lifted, remove it with a dull putty knife. The corners of the knife should have been rounded off to prevent gouging. From time to time, wipe the knife on a piece of old newspaper, to remove the accumulation of remover and finish.

5—Wipe off as much of the remaining finish as possible, using burlap squares (best) or crumpled paper.

6—Scrub the surface with a small brush, dipped in denatured alcohol.

7—Wipe off with several clean cloths.

8—Rub the surface with steel wool, dipped in denatured alcohol.

9—Wipe with cloths, dipped in alcohol. This not only cleans the traces of remover from the surface but neutralizes its further action. Some professionals use gasoline (not ethyl), benzine or turpentine for this work.

10—Allow the piece to dry thoroughly (at least 24 hours).

For Turned and Carved Surfaces

1—Apply remover, as directed above.

2—When the finish "lifts," wipe off as much as possible with a burlap square.

3—Scrub crevices and grooves with a tooth-brush, dipped in remover, and then, with a larger brush, dipped in denatured alcohol.

4—Clean turnings as well as possible by holding a pad of steel wool (dipped in alcohol) in the hand and using a twisting motion. Follow with the use of threads from burlap or steel wool, twisted into narrow strips, for the final cleaning of turnings. Clean crevices in carving with an instrument such as orange stick or a meat skewer, with a piece of cloth over its end.

5—Allow at least 24 hours for complete drying.

Note 1—Circumstances may be found wherein some of the steps given above may be shortened or even omitted. Some experts add another step. They brush the surface lightly with remover before the final clean-up. (After step 5.)

2—If any of the old finish is still visible in spots, this must be removed by repeating the procedure or the new finish may not dry at these places.

3—If any streaks of color are left on the surface, dip a clean cloth in alcohol, wring it out and wipe the surface with long light strokes.

4—If the piece must be repainted, the new paint will adhere better if the surface is sanded smooth. The only reason for removing the old paint is to have an even surface upon which to apply the new.

5—After the upper coats of paint have been removed and it is discovered that the undercoat is of the "Refractory" type, the surface should be kept moistened by applying one or more coats of the remover.

6—If there are several coats of paint and these are found difficult to remove, several layers of the remover should be used, one on top of the other. Cover with layers of wet burlap or cloth and allow it to stand for several hours or even overnight. If this covering is kept wet, the old paint can usually be removed with a putty knife. The action of the remover on old paints is very much the same as removing several layers of wallpaper. They sometimes come off layer by layer.

7—The drawers and doors should be removed from the piece before using a remover.

8—Whenever possible, apply removers to flat surfaces in a horizontal position. This may be accomplished by turning the piece. Put small pieces and parts on a table or work bench, over old newspapers.

9—A large piece sometimes cannot be turned over or moved to a position which will permit applying remover to all surfaces in a horizontal position and it will have to be applied to a vertical surface. In such cases, tilt the top of the piece towards the surface to be worked upon, by placing blocks under the opposite surface, so that the remover will not run on to unfinished horizontal surfaces. Example: When using a remover on the front surface of a dresser or a cabinet from which drawers or doors have been removed.

10—Any remover that has gotten on to bare wood should be wiped off with a cloth dampened with denatured alcohol. Otherwise it will leave a stain on the wood.

11—Get rid of dirty burlap pieces, cloths, and paper on which you have wiped the putty knife or placed the removed finish.

12—Spread out cloths, clean enough to be used again, so that alcohol will evaporate.

13—A paint brush used with removers becomes unfit for other uses. Clean with denatured alcohol and then wash with hot soapy water for further use with removers.

REMOVING REFRACTORY PAINTS

These old paints, which were made by combining a pigment with skim milk or buttermilk (see "Refractory Paints," page 80), are often difficult to remove with a commercial "Paint and Varnish Remover" and cannot be removed by this material, when it is the only paint which was used.

You were told in Note 5 above to keep refractory undercoats moistened with the remover. When the work is to continue without delay, this stubborn paint may often be successfully removed by a method, as follows:

1—Apply a heavy coat of the remover and allow it to stand awhile in an attempt to further soften the old paint.

2—While the remover is still wet, scrub the surface with pads of grade "1" steel wool. Turn a pad to a new surface when filled with paint and remove all paint possible, repeating operations 1 and 2, as long as any paint can be removed.

3—Scrub the surface with a fresh pad of steel wool dipped in denatured alcohol and wipe with a rag.

4—Remove carefully with a knife any paint remaining in joints and corners.

5—Allow to dry for 24 hours and smooth by sanding, followed by steel wool.

When the only coat is a refractory type of paint, it usually can be removed with certain materials, but just which to use is difficult to determine in advance. You will have to learn by trial which may be successful. It is, therefore, a good plan to start with the least harmful and then try the others later.

The first suggestion is to use "Denatured Alcohol." Next try "Sal Soda" or "Tri-sodium Phosphate," and "Lye" as the last resort.

Refractory paints may be red, black, green, or brown. If you find in advance that the undercoat is black, it is best to remove all coats by scraping, as a liquid remover will drive black deeper into the wood grain. This will leave a grey color that even bleaches will seldom lighten. (See "Cabinet Scrapers," page 102, and "Using Cabinet Scrapers," page 104.)

Using Denatured Alcohol

This method is the easiest because so little equipment is required and it is less messy than any of the others. Try it first. It may do the trick.

Equipment Denatured alcohol, steel wool 2/0 or finer, garnet abrasive paper 6/0 or finer.

Directions

Moisten the surface with alcohol and use the steel wool or abrasive paper, rubbing with the grain of the wood. Wipe off occasionally with a clean cloth, moisten the surface again and continue rubbing. Finally, wipe off with a clean cloth dampened in alcohol.

Note If the paint is well into the wood grain and there is more of it left than you feel is desirable, try the procedure for using shellac. (See "Removing Deeply Buried Paints," page 89.)

Using Sal Soda or Tri-sodium Phosphate

A solution of sal soda should be used while the surface is still wet after an attempt to remove the paint with a commercial "paint and varnish remover." Tri-sodium phosphate (a powerful alkali), often used in water softening, may be substituted for the sal soda. Neither will harm the wood but they should not be used on a veneered surface as the water will soften the glue holding the veneer. You can get sal soda at your grocer's, in pound packages. Tri-sodium phosphate, in the form of small crystals, will be found in most paint and building supply stores.

Equipment Two medium size galvanized or enamel pails; a cotton dish mop with long handle; a large scrubbing brush (8″ to 10″ with handle if possible); hot water, both for making the solution and for washing it off; and a supply of sal soda or tri-sodium phosphate. (2 lbs. is usually enough for a piece of moderate size.)

Glasses or goggles should be worn while doing the work. Use rubber gloves (or canvas with leather palm, treated with waterproof oil) and old clothes with long sleeves. (Either solution will burn the skin.) The work should be done on a cement floor with a drain or outside in the shade.

Directions

1—Dissolve one pound of either sal soda or tri-sodium phosphate in a pail containing 5 quarts of hot water. Have the other pail filled with hot water only.

2—Apply the solution sparingly to one surface, using a dish mop. This surface should be in a horizontal position, if possible.

3—Let it stand less than one minute and then scrub vigorously with scrubbing brush for a few seconds.

4—Dip the scrubbing brush in clear hot water and wash the surface.

5—Continue applications of solution and the scrubbing until you have removed enough of the paint or until you are convinced that some other method must be used.

6—Use clean cold water to flush off the surface and, if you are satisfied with the result, turn the piece so that one of the other surfaces will be horizontal and repeat the procedure.

7—Use a hose to flush all surfaces while *scrubbing thoroughly,* particularly in cracks and grooves.

8—Keep the piece in the shade. Direct sunlight will cause the wood to warp. Let it dry thoroughly. This will usually take several days.

Note 1—Either of these solutions, in hot or cold water, is excellent for cleaning a piece, following the use of "paint and varnish remover," particularly where it has dried and there is considerable paint color in this residue. Scrub with clear water and dry, as above.

2—A method of removing Refractory paints was offered by an expert but its value has not been experimented with in my shop through lack of time before publication. The method involves the use of equal parts of pure turpentine and household ammonia rubbed on the surface with steel wool.

Using Lye Lye is a dangerous substance for anyone to handle. It is a powerful caustic and has a chemical reaction which causes even the most stubborn paints (Refractory type) to powder instead of "lifting" (as do "paint and varnish removers"). Lye should never be used to remove other finishes.

Lye is inexpensive (a few cents per can at the grocer's). Its action is quick and thorough. Knowledge of its properties and great care in its use are necessary. It will burn certain woods, turning them black and must, therefore, be washed and scrubbed off completely and thoroughly, particularly from any cracks and crevices. It will raise the wood grain and spoil any later finish you may apply, unless the *utmost* care is taken in removing all residue.

A strong solution will destroy clothing, burn the skin, and injure the eyes. It is least harmful to hickory, maple, and pine but should never be used on open grained woods such as butternut, chestnut, oak, or walnut. It will ruin cherry or mahogany and should not be used on veneers, because of the water in which it is mixed.

These warnings should not prevent you from using lye when it is necessary. My first attempt with its use was on a chair of little value which had a pine seat. It burned the seat but worked well on the balance of the piece which was maple. The proper procedure was then unknown to me.

Since then it has been used often in my shop without harm. The procedure here recommended was given by a professional with 18 years experience and his mixture is three to four times stronger than that customarily used.

In your first attempt at using lye, select a piece of furniture of little value, either intrinsic or sentimental. If you will use it only on woods suggested and make sure that you have washed off every trace, you should be successful. Do not attempt to use lye unless you have the proper equipment and are willing to spend the time it requires.

Equipment Two cans of lye (13 ounce size); a supply of white vinegar; a 10 quart galvanized or enameled pail (never use an aluminum one); and running water with hose attachment.

You should have a mop, brush, glasses or goggles, gloves, and old clothes. The work should be done on a well-drained cement floor or out of doors in the shade. (See "Using Sal Soda or Tri-sodium Phosphate," last procedure.)

Directions

1—Fill the pail half full with *cold* water. Pour in the lye from the two cans. Dissolve by stirring with mop and then fill the pail with more cold water. (The water should never be poured onto the lye as this will cause it to foam up out of the pail.) Have water running slowly through the hose.

2—Apply sparingly with the long handled cotton dish mop to a horizontal surface.

3—Let it stand for about one-half minute and then scrub vigorously with the brush.

4—Wash off with the hose and continue scrubbing.

5—Repeat until enough of the powdered paint has been removed from all of the surfaces, turning the piece so that you always work on a horizontal one.

6—Scrub well with water from hose and a brush, working deeply into cracks and crevices, until all of the slippery film of the solution has been removed.

7—Wash with vinegar on a clean cloth to neutralize the caustic action of the lye.

8—Place the piece in the shade and allow it to dry thoroughly for 24 hours or longer. Direct sunlight may warp the wood.

Note 1—This solution is very strong. The secret in removing the paint without burning the wood lies in not letting the solution remain on the surface long enough to injure it. The more often and more quickly you apply the solution and wash it off, the less danger there is to the wood.

2—It is nearly impossible to apply the solution to one horizontal surface and not have it get on an adjoining vertical one. Therefore, these other surfaces should be scrubbed off at the same time as in step 3 above.

3—Should there be spots of paint which are stubborn, let them remain, rather than to continue the use of the solution, for fear of injury to the wood. These may usually be removed easily with a cabinet scraper after the wood is thoroughly dry, as much of the life has been taken from the paint by the lye solution.

REMOVING DEEPLY BURIED PAINTS

A deeply buried paint may often be removed entirely or partially by a simple procedure. This paint is usually that which is left after you have removed the previous coats with remover or by light scraping. Because of its simplicity, this procedure is worth trying.

Equipment High grade white shellac (thinned with 25% to 35% denatured alcohol); a clean paint brush (2″ best); commercial "Paint and Varnish Remover" with old brush for application; and the equipment suggested for removing the remover. (See "Paint and Varnish Remover," page 83.)

Directions

1—Apply a liberal coat of the shellac with a brush and let it dry for at least 24 hours.

2—Use the remover as previously directed. All or part of the buried paint may come off with the shellac.

PAINT WITH DIRT, HARDENED BY HEAT

Heat from the sun or a hot stove will often soften a finish and when it has cooled again, dirt and dust will be found imbedded in a finish which has again hardened. A commercial remover will often fail to remove it, particularly in those cases where another coat of paint has been added over the dirt.

This paint can often be removed by applying a mixture made of equal parts of linseed oil and turpentine. This is rubbed into the surface, allowed to stand and then cleaned off with fine steel wool dipped in turpentine. If necessary, followed by a light scraping.

REMOVING OLD VARNISH WITH A SCRAPER

Very old varnish will, at times, be found to be so "flaky" that it can be removed easily with a cabinet scraper, or the sharp blade of a large knife (hunting knife good), without injury to the wood surface or destruction of the patina. This should be attempted only by those familiar with the use of such tools. (See "Cabinet Scrapers," page 102, and "Using Cabinet Scrapers," page 104.)

STENCILLED CHAIRS

You may, at some time, wish to remove old varnish from a Windsor, Hitchcock Chair or a Boston Rocker, without injury to the paint or the stencil design with which they are so often decorated. The stencil may have been covered with paint which you want to remove but leave the stencil intact.

The removal of old varnish is more simple than the removal of paint. However, both require careful and delicate handling. Either may often be removed in part by light scraping and the balance by the method given below.

If you suspect that a stencil has been painted over, first experiment at the spot where you might expect a stencil to be. There is usually one on the front of the top back. Use a scraper with care to remove only the hard outer coat of paint so that the materials for removing (to follow) can penetrate the undercoats more easily.

The decoration of furniture, by painted or stencilled designs, is a specialty and hence beyond the scope of this book. Some such pieces can be restored if the condition of the outer surface is not too bad. They must then be refinished by a fresh coat of shellac and wax or with varnish and a rub-down. (See Chapter 5.)

Following are the methods to use in removing an outer coat of varnish or paint:

Removing Varnish

Apply denatured alcohol on wads of cotton to small areas, in an attempt to soften the varnish. If successful, wipe off the varnish. If this does not work, try a mixture of equal parts of benzine and alcohol. Finally, try a mixture of equal parts of pure turpentine and alcohol. These solutions are given in the order of their strength.

If none of these will soften the varnish, clean off a small area and apply a light coat of a commercial remover. (See "Paint and Varnish Removers," page 83.) When the varnish starts to "lift" stop the action by washing off the remover with alcohol and start again, using alcohol on a wad of cotton. Repeating this process may bring results. The great difficulty is in knowing when to stop, in order to save the stencil.

Removing Paint

Use fine steel wool dipped in alcohol and a sharp knife blade or delicately use a scraper, as in the procedure for removing "refractory" type paints. (See "Removing Refractory Paints," page 86.)

CHAPTER
4

PREPARING FOR NEW FINISH

This is the turning point in the work. Thus far you have been given general instructions for repairs and the removal of old finish. Now you are ready to prepare the surface for a new finish. This requires careful workmanship and full knowledge of the necessary procedures and methods, as the quality of the final finish depends directly upon the carefulness of this preparation. Except for handling a scraper, which is not often used, the work is not too difficult, but at times it calls for careful selection, judgment, and forethought.

Before starting the work, make a thorough inspection of the piece, especially after you have removed an old, heavy paint. You may find dents, holes, cracks, etc., which were not before visible in the surface and which will require repairs. This must be done before preparing for the new finish. The method will be found in the index or included among the most commonly used procedures, as follows:

	Page
Gluing Cracks	29
Filling Cracks	77
Wood Dough—using	35
Wood Putty—using	36
Stick Shellac—using	37
Removing Dents—with water	39

You may often be agreeably surprised to find a wood of beauty after an old paint has been removed from a surface. When it is sanded and smoothed, you may see how the piece is going to look with a clear, new finish, by making a simple "wet test." Should the wood have a drab appearance, the color can often be restored, but, if discolored, it may require a bleach. You may find a piece made of many kinds of woods of various colors which you may wish to stain a single color, or you may wish to stain the piece (or a "nude"—new unpainted piece), to match other pieces, or, perhaps, an inserted patch must be stained to match the surface into which it is placed. Finally, if the piece is of such utility, quality of workmanship, fineness, or it is customary that it have a "Polish Rubbed Finish," the surface must be prepared with a paste filler.

Some of the procedures in this chapter are seldom used but all are described so that you may have a full knowledge of them. The number and choice of those to be used for a single job is determined by the condition of the wood, after a former finish has been removed, and whether it must be bleached, stained, or the surface filled for a final finish of extreme smoothness.

With each procedure you are given information as to when and why it is used. Some are necessary, according to conditions, and some are a matter of choice. They are listed below, in consecutive order, as they would be used if all were necessary, with brief comments as to their use:

BLEACHING

After the old finish has been removed from a surface, any darkened or discolored spots which may remain can be lightened or entirely removed by the proper use of a bleach. Although you may feel justified in wishing to remove all traces of old stain and marks of discoloration from antique furniture, these, in most cases, add to the charm of the finished piece and may be left when they do not show too plainly through the new finish. Some collectors prefer that a certain amount of this evidence of age and usage be left. However, when working on pine or maple, it is best to remove discoloration and freshen up the surface.

Bleaches are of different kinds and each have their special place in this work. The bleach most commonly used is a solution of oxalic acid. In my shop it has been found that other bleaches will, in some cases, do as good a job. Where the nature of the material, which has left the discoloration, is unknown, you may often have to experiment with several bleaches before finding the one that gives best results. One will work where another will not.

Other bleaches which have been used satisfactorily are pure household ammonia, "Double X" (available at paint and hardware stores), Purex, Chlorox, or Gold Dust Powder. This last is a good mild bleach for freshening a surface. If none of these give satisfactory results, the discoloration may require considerable sanding or even the use of a scraper. In some cases it may even be necessary to plane the surface to remove a stain which has penetrated deeply into the wood grain. Such harsh methods as sanding, scraping, and planing will ruin any patina and should be avoided whenever possible, if you have any regard for that beautiful old finish that age, care, and usage can give to a piece.

The following procedures will tell you how to use bleaches to freshen a surface and to remove stains left by grease. It is important that the old finish be removed from a surface and the wood pores opened so that the bleaching solution can get into the grain.

Important A surface having oil or grease on it should be washed with alcohol or benzine before applying a bleaching agent.

Note Prior to World War II there were many excellent liquid bleaches on the market which are again being produced, although they are still scarce. Bleaches of this type come in two containers marked No. 1 and No. 2. They are used in that order. The first does the bleaching and the second neutralizes the action of the first when it has proceeded far enough. Some manufacturers produce a third (No. 3) solution for use on mahogany and this is applied after Nos. 1 and 2. These are expensive but well worth the cost.

Using Oxalic Acid

This should be your first choice when you need a bleach. If it will not do the job, try one of the others. Oxalic acid is not expensive. It can be purchased at a drug store in either crystal or powder form. It is also sold by some paint stores.

Equipment Oxalic acid; household ammonia; hot water; clean paint brush (2″ or larger for extended areas and an artist's small one for spots); and Clean Cloths.

Directions

1—Prepare a solution of oxalic acid by dissolving 1 ounce of the powder or 2 ounces of the crystals in 1 pint of very hot water.

2—Apply the solution (hot) with the large brush, to the entire surface, from which the finish has been removed, or to a spot with the small brush. In the case of the spot, work the solution carefully to the edges with the brush.

3—Let the solution remain for 10 to 20 minutes and then wipe it off with a damp cloth. If the discoloration has not been bleached sufficiently, repeat until you obtain the color you are after.

4—When the proper result has been secured, wash off the solution with 1 part ammonia in 10 parts of water. This will neutralize the bleach and stop its further action. Then wash with clear water and allow the piece to dry for at least 24 hours.

Note 1—It is recommended that you bleach an entire surface rather than to remove a spot only. However, you may be very successful in spot-bleaching where the outline of the spot is clearly defined. If your efforts to remove a spot are unsuccessful, no harm is done as the entire surface can then be bleached.

2—Some woods, maple in particular, respond more readily to a solution of one-half oxalic and one-half tartaric acid, used as above.

3—Some workers recommend the use of white vinegar (full strength) as a neutralizing agent following the use of oxalic acid.

Using Household Ammonia This material is best for spot work only and should be applied, full strength, with a fine brush to the spot and then allowed to dry. Further applications may be used, if necessary.

Using "Double X," "Purex," and "Chlorox" In using "Double X," follow the directions for mixing as shown on the container but using a smaller quantity of the powder for your first solution. If this does not give satisfactory results, increase the strength by adding more powder.

The directions for using "Purex" or "Chlorox," as given on the container, are intended for bleaching cloth and give a very weak solution. For your purpose, the solution must be much stronger. Therefore, increase its strength by greatly reducing the suggested amount of water. The strength of the solution you may need in any particular case will vary according to circumstances. Hence, the exact proportions cannot be given.

These solutions can be used for surface or spot-bleaching. In the latter, a stronger solution is necessary. In both cases, the solution should be allowed to dry.

REMOVING DISCOLORATION

Gray or Faded

You may find that the surface of a piece, particularly pine or maple, has a gray or faded appearance. It may be freshened and brought back to a more satisfactory color by the following procedure. This is recommended for a surface that has just been cleaned with a "paint and varnish remover" and before it has again dried.

Equipment Detergent type of soap powder; oxalic acid; hot water; neutralizer (ammonia or white vinegar); clean paint brush (2″ or larger); scrubbing brush; and clean cloths.

Directions

1—Scrub with the soap powder in water that is just under the boiling point. Wash off with hot water and wipe with cloth.

2—While the surface is still wet, apply a hot solution of oxalic acid. Let this stay on for about 10 minutes and then wash it off and neutralize its action with the ammonia or vinegar. Let it dry thoroughly. (See "Using Oxalic Acid," page 95.)

Note 1—This treatment will raise the grain of the wood but it usually removes the fine particles of colored pigment. The grain will settle down again when dry and can be later sanded.

2—The surface will not have the appearance of new wood but, if circumstances are favorable and the work has been done properly, it should have an even mellowness.

REMOVING GREASE STAINS

A grease stain from animal fat may usually be removed by an application of benzine or other commercial cleaners, such as come in small containers for removing spots from clothing.

If the grease spot is of vegetable origin, it will usually respond to the use of acetone. This may be purchased at a drug store.

In both cases the remover should be applied to the spot with an artist's small brush, and then worked around with the brush and removed with a piece of absorbent tissue paper, such as are sold for use in removing cosmetics. The operation should be repeated until the spot has been removed.

SANDING AND SMOOTHING

Any surface on which a new finish is to be applied requires smoothing, an operation which brings a surface to a fine silky condition, without destroying the patina and evidence of age and usage. Many pieces are free from any finish or paint and need no repairs. However, these must go through the smoothing operation as well.

The smoothing of a wood surface, free from a finish, is done with "abrasive papers" and is called "sanding," by first working with relatively coarse papers, followed by those of finer grit. "Steel wool" is often used for final smoothing and at times it is necessary to use a "scraper" (to be avoided if possible) to smooth a surface that is to be followed with fine abrasive papers and steel wool.

The degree of smoothness a piece requires, depends greatly upon the type of the article and the wood of which it is made, as well as the type of final finish which is to be used. For example, a crude piece of pine furniture does not call for as smooth a surface as a well designed piece made of hardwoods, nor would the final finish be smoothed to the same degree. (See Chapter 5, on "Refinishing.")

When smoothing a surface, all work must be done with proper materials of the right grade of fineness and with great care or result will be disastrous, as scratches show through any kind of a final finish. You must remember that you are working with wood surfaces, for which you must have regard and respect, regardless of whether the woods are rare or common, old or new.

In the following procedures you are given brief information about the uses of abrasive papers and emery cloth.

Abrasive Papers and Emery Cloth

The so-called "sandpaper" (off-white), made of "flint" as the abrasive agent, breaks down under usage; is the cheapest of all abrasive papers to buy but the most expensive to use. However, use it, if preferred, or when other kinds of abrasive papers are not available.

The following are recommended for long wear.

Garnet Paper—Light reddish brown in color, the most commonly used.

Carborundum Paper—Dark gray to black in color and the choice of many users.

Aluminum Oxide Papers—Brown in color and sold under various trade names. This cutting agent is the toughest and most durable.

Emery Cloth—Black in color with "carborundum" grits on cloth.

All abrasive papers come in various grades of fine or coarse grit and "weights" of paper, as well as with an "open-coat" or "closed-coat." All are thus marked by printing on the backs of the sheets. Furthermore, those with medium grade grit are called "Cabinet" papers; with fine grit "Finishing" papers; while those with a "waterproof backing" are used for polishing fine finishes.

Note For complete and detailed information regarding abrasive papers and "emery cloth," their uses and the use of "sanding blocks," see Chapter 8 on "More about Materials" starting on page 172.

Smoothing by Sanding

The sanding of a wood surface is the least difficult of all procedures in restoration work, yet it is one of the most important parts of refinishing and must always be done thoroughly and with great care, regardless of whether it is accomplished by hand or with a power tool. If not done correctly, a surface will be a mass of scratches. A good sanding job is essential to a good finish.

Rules for Sanding

1—Always sand with the grain of the wood—never across grain.

2—Use straight strokes with an even pressure, avoiding a twisting or circular motion.

3—First use a paper of as coarse a grade (grit) as the wood will stand without scratching, then finer ones until the surface is as smooth as the wood will become. (The results will vary with the kind of wood.)

Useful Information

1—**Planing and Scraping** are not substitutes for sanding. When such tools are used, sanding should follow.

2—**Moistening** will often permit of better sanding on old and relatively smooth wood surfaces. Wring out a wet cloth and rub the surface. When dry, the fine ends of the fibers (termed "wood whiskers") will be raised. Sand with fine grade of paper (6/0 to 8/0).

3—**New Woods** (and veneer) are best smoothed by moistening the surface before sanding to raise fibers with a glue water (1 ounce of liquid glue such as LePage's, to 1 pint of hot water). Dry and finish as in "2" in the "Rules for Sanding." Be careful of wetting veneers too much.

4—**Grades of Paper** It is seldom advisable to use a paper coarser than No. 1/2, even on a rough surface. Depend mostly upon grades 1/0, 2/0, and 3/0 for the first smoothing and upon 6/0, 7/0, and 8/0 for finishing the work. The general rule is to start and finish with finer grades of papers on hardwoods than on softwoods. Also, on softwoods it is well to use the "open-grain" papers, especially when using the coarser grades, as these woods respond to sanding more readily than do hardwoods and clog up the paper.

5—**Clean Papers Often** by brushing and you will prolong their life and cutting power. (See "Cleaning and Using Old Abrasive Paper," page 176.)

6—**Sanding Blocks or Folded Paper** may be used to advantage on large surfaces. (See page 177.)

7—When **Paint or Varnish** has been removed it must always be followed by sanding to get rid of any wax that may have been in the remover, otherwise a finish may not harden.

8—**Inwardly Curved Surfaces** may be sanded by wrapping the paper around wood dowels of various sizes, according to the curve. If the paper is soaked with turpentine, it will make it more flexible.

9—**Turned Surfaces** are best smoothed with emery cloth of a fine grade (grit) torn into narrow (½″ to 1″) strips and worked back and forth in the grooves, holding the strip by its ends. Great care must be exercised in smoothing the bulge of turnings, also long cylindrical surfaces (like chair or table legs), or harm may be done. It is best that this work be accomplished with "steel wool" (following), especially on very old Antique furniture, as these parts may have been turned by hand-powered lathes, resulting in slight ridges on the long surfaces which should not be obliterated. This will happen if they are sanded.

10—**Sanding Edges and Ends** of the tops of tables, cabinets, etc. should be done with only the finest grades of abrasive papers, regardless of whether the part is of hardwood or softwood. Unless otherwise designed, the edges must be true and the corners square. Improper treatment of board ends may spoil an otherwise beautiful finish. They should be brought to an almost glazed surface by sanding with no coarser than an 8/0 sharp paper and finished with a worn paper of that grade or finer. Place paper over a "sanding block," when working on square ends, to insure such surfaces being kept flat.

When this work is completed and should the edges or corners be too sharp, relieve them slightly with light strokes of first the sharp paper, followed by polishing with the worn paper.

11—**After Sanding,** and after using Steel Wool, the surface should be cleaned by brushing, wiping with a clean, soft cloth, and finally with a lint-free cloth moistened with turpentine.

12—**Crude Pine Furniture** will be greatly improved in its finished appearance if the top corners of the used surface are rounded down considerably, by sanding and smoothing, as well as the corners of nicks and dents, along the upper edges of the used surface, to make them look as though such rounding had come from usage.

The same is true of other parts or places on surfaces of crude furniture, if such work is not overdone. Examples—

A—A natural crack that runs only a short distance from a surface edge into a top will often look better if it is not filled but widened slightly along its edges and rounded on the upper corners of its outlet, by sanding and smoothing, just as though it had been worn into that condition.

B—Low stretchers on tables (such as the "tavern" type), and often front rungs on crude types of chairs, are worn from shoes. Many unscrupulous professionals fake such wearing, but smoothing surfaces and removing dents from hobnails is justifiable and it certainly adds to the finished appearance.

C—Very often turnings on small parts will be marred by chipped

HORSESHOER'S BENCH (Rare)

PLATE 15. Dirt and grime removed with knife blade and sanded by hand (my first job). Broken partitions in nail tray filed and sanded smooth; corners and edges throughout rounded. Colored with linseed oil; finished with 'varnish and oil' and waxed. Bought in Maine for 75¢; have been offered $75.

places or cracks. These also look better smoothed up than if filled and stained.

D—Many pieces of crude, yet most attractive early American furniture, were fastened together with nails which have rusted or were used in such a manner as to leave holes around their heads. Others will be found with narrow cracks between small partitions or parts (examples—see Plate 15, this page, and Plate 16, next page).

The appearance of these pieces will be greatly improved if such holes and cracks are carefully filled with "wood dough" and then sanded, to expose the top of the nail head and to remove the surplus wood dough from the surfaces around the cracks. The remaining dried wood dough is then stained to match the piece, with the use of an artist's small brush.

The reason for the greatly improved appearance of the piece is that, with this procedure, the surfaces are "tied" together and you would be surprised at the improvement in "eye appeal."

USE OF STEEL WOOL

Steel wool is made of finely shredded steel and is a most important and

PINE COBBLER'S BENCH

PLATE 16. Completely disassembled to remove grime with scraper and portable electric sander, to repair and reglue. Missing drawer replaced; made from door of old commode, old wood for sides, and plywood bottom. Cracks and holes filled with wood dough, smoothed and stained. Finished with 'varnish and oil' and waxed. New leather seat installed.

economical material for use in many stages of restoration. Many finishers ignore steel wool and depend entirely on abrasive paper for smoothing, thereby losing the benefit of this most valuable material. It must be remembered that a poorly smoothed surface is likely to be a poorly finished one.

Grades and Buying

There are only six grades of steel wool which should be used for woodwork. They are as follows:

No. "3"—The coarsest grade, rarely used in this work.
No. "2"—Should be used on rough lumber only.
No. "1"—The coarsest grade that should be used on furniture.
No. "0"—The most commonly used of all grades.
No. "00"—Used for rough smoothing.
No. "000"—The finest grade and used for final smoothing.

Steel wool is commonly carried in paint and hardware stores. It comes in packages of 16 individual pads at an average cost per package of about 50¢. It is well to have a package of each grade on hand.

Note Steel wool may be purchased also in small packages of mixed grades, but it is not economical to buy it that way. It also comes in a large one-piece roll in packages of the same size as those containing the 16 pads. If there is a choice, avoid this type as it is hard to tear and roll into pads, which is the best way of using it.

Uses in Refinishing

1—After **Paint and Varnish Removers,** as an aid in mopping up or cleaning off the messy residue left after most of it has been removed with a putty knife or burlap. Use Grade No. "1" for this work. It will not scratch when the surface is wet and it may be used to advantage when dipped in alcohol.

2—After **Sanding or Scraping** a surface, use the finer grades for greater smoothness. Start with Grade No. "0" and finish with the finer grades in turn. Steel wool is best on hardwoods and is particularly good for smoothing turnings and carvings. On long turned surfaces (like table or chair legs) it will work rapidly and will not disturb marks or ridges left from the old, slow turning lathes. Steel wool will put a smoother finish on end grain surfaces after they have been sanded.

3—When **Stains** are to be applied to a surface, it is well not to smooth the surface too much, so as to allow the stain to penetrate, but a light rubbing with fine steel wool will smooth the surface after the application of the stain without injury.

4—In **Care of Tools,** use the finest grade of steel wool as an aid in polishing and removing rust. (See "Oiling Tools," Chapter 11.)

Note 1—As steel wool is used it disintegrates into minute particles, many of which go into the air. It should not be used outdoors because of danger of its blowing into the eyes and those with tender hands should wear gloves to keep it from working into the skin.

2—The pads of steel wool fill with wood-dust during use. Their life and cutting power may be prolonged if the dust is knocked out by striking the pad against something. New sharp surfaces may be brought to the top by turning the pads inside out, but it is not a good plan to add a new pad to an old one, for steel wool mats as it is used, especially in the finer grades.

CABINET SCRAPERS

This is a difficult tool to use properly. Its sharp, hook-shaped edge removes a very thin shaving from the wood surface. Unless this edge is sharp and smooth, it will not do the work properly but will leave marks which will later show through the final finish. Watching an expert use a scraper is indeed a pleasure. It would be well for an amateur to take lessons from such a person, both in the handling and sharpening of the scraper. Both operations are among the most difficult, in the art of cabinet making, to perform correctly.

Scrapers are used in cabinet shops for final smoothing of surfaces after they have been planed. They are particularly well adapted for smoothing cross-grained boards which are difficult to dress with a plane. Some experienced workers like to use the scraper for removing paint or varnish. One should be sufficiently adept in its use or great damage may result.

One cause of damage lies in a scraper not being properly sharpened (causing scratches) or in gouging the wood with the edge or corners of the scraper. There is less risk in using a scraper on hard woods than on soft. Soft woods are more likely to rip and fuzz. Extensive sanding is then necessary to restore them to their proper condition. A scraper should not be used on old woods (such as pine), which have a beautiful patina as some of this cherished surface is bound to be lost in the process.

Many experts warn against using a scraper on mahogany, walnut, or cherry. Scratches on the surface of these woods will show through a clear finish. It is often difficult to remove color from maple without resorting to the scraper. However, the best rule to follow is never to use a scraper except as a last resort.

A scraper is a very handy and satisfactory tool for many small jobs and as a supplement to other tools, as in removing spots of paint left by a paint remover.

It is also useful for removing paint from angles and crevices or as the only means for removing flaky paint from the legs of chairs, etc.

However, there are many people with experience who understand the proper use of a cabinet scraper and who do not consider their work properly done without it.

TYPES OF CABINET SCRAPERS

There are two kinds of scrapers recommended for use. These are as follows:

Hook Scraper

This scraper consists of a shaped wooden block into which is inserted a narrow curved steel blade. This blade is placed crosswise in a metal groove at one end of the block. The handle end usually has a compartment for storing spare blades. Several manufacturers produce this type of scraper and they are available at hardware stores and tool supply houses. They come with extra blades and additional ones may be purchased, as needed. In the hands of an inexperienced person, this tool can be a dangerous one as the blade corners are sharp and apt to gouge a surface if not properly handled. The edge of the blade is beveled and will retain its sharpness for a longer time, if burnished.

Blade Scraper

These blades are fabricated from flat pieces of hardened tool steel which are about $\frac{1}{16}''$ in thickness. They may be purchased in the stores mentioned above. The type of blade most commonly used is rectangular in shape (in sizes up to 3″ x 6″) while others are available in different shapes or may be ground to any shape required. The edges are squared, then hook-turned and burnished.

Note 1—Several scrapers are shown with other tools in Plate No. 25, page 187.

2—A "Hook Scraper" (Figure 2) should be well made and large, for good use. Small cheap ones are hard to handle and increase danger of damage.

3—"Rectangular-shaped" hand scrapers (Figure 3) of high quality are stocked by most stores selling high grade tools.

4—The two "Odd-Shaped" handmade scrapers (Figure 4) are useful on moldings, turnings, etc. The wider one was made from a rectangular scraper and has square sharpened edges. The longer one was made from a plane iron (blade) and has beveled edges at each end.

5—The handiest of all odd-shaped scrapers, for the same uses, is the "Swanneck," shaped as shown in the drawing. This type may also be purchased at stores.

6—It is a good plan for the inexperienced worker to round off all square corners of the scraper slightly when working on a flat surface. They must be rounded for work on warped boards, as a square corner would gouge the surface.

Other Cabinet Scrapers

There are many other types of scrapers used in professional cabinet work. Some are "Hoe-type" (with a single handle), some have double handles and look somewhat like the "Spoke-shave," while others resemble chunky planes with handles. These are not usually owned by the amateur worker.

Note For complete information regarding the sharpening of various types of cabinet scrapers, see "Cabinet Scrapers," page 196, under the heading of "Sharpening Tools," in Chapter 11.

USING CABINET SCRAPERS

It is well worth while to practice using a scraper (of any type) on pieces of scrap wood before undertaking work on a piece of furniture.

The following general rules are, for the most part, applicable to the use of Hook and Blade Scrapers only.

1—Because of its construction, a "hook scraper" is drawn only toward the worker and is used with one hand. The tool should be tilted at the most advantageous angle and just enough pressure applied to *shave* the surface properly.

2—Most of the work with a "blade scraper" is done on a plane surface, by pushing the tool away from the worker. The scraper is held with the fingers of both hands on the far side of the blade and with the thumbs on the near side. When working on a surface at a corner or adjoining a molding, etc., it is easier to pull the blade toward you. The blade can then be held in one hand. The angle at which the blade should be held is approximately 45 degrees with the top slanting in the direction of the push or pull.

3—On plane surfaces (with either type of scraper) the strokes should be as long as possible and with an even pressure, lifting the tool on the return stroke or you will dull the edge.

4—Scraping with the grain is best although you can scrape across it. You should avoid scraping across the grain or on an end grain. Scrape away from surface ends rather than toward them. With the scraper held at a slight angle to the direction of the push or pull, the result is known as a "skewed cut." This type of cut is smoother and the blade stays sharp longer, but great care must be exercised to prevent a corner of the blade from gouging or scratching the surface.

5—If it is found difficult to secure a smooth surface with a scraper, a light sponging of the surface before scraping will aid in getting more satisfactory results.

6—The use of hand scrapers requires caution since the blades are not held at a fixed angle or position, as are the blades in a plane or other types of tool scrapers. Consequently, on some kinds of woods, hand scrapers tend to follow the contour of the surface, cut more deeply into soft areas and ride over hard ones.

7—When a scraper no longer lifts thin, curved shavings, and shows a tendency to "fuzz" the surface, the blade needs to be resharpened. These same conditions may arise when the scraper is not properly handled or the cutting edge has not been correctly sharpened or "hooked" (turned) by burnishing.

WET TEST FOR COLOR

Make a "wet test" to see whether a change of color in the bare wood will take place, if a clear finish is applied. This test can be made on wood which has had no finish and is the next step after a surface is free from previous finish or paint and after sanding and smoothing. The test will show the approximate color the wood will take when a clear finish is put on.

Merely wet a finger tip with clean water or saliva and touch the surface. The drier and more porous the wood, the greater will be the change in color. The most pronounced difference in color from this test will be found in softwoods like pine, but the change will be hardly noticeable in green or unseasoned woods.

Woods with open-pores, whether they are softwoods or hardwoods, darken more after an application of a clear finish, than do those with closed-pores. Neither type of wood will absorb to a great degree until the sap has dried out. Those which contain more of the natural oils and gums dry out more slowly than those containing these to a lesser degree.

The purpose of this simple test is to determine whether it will be necessary to treat the surface with a linseed oil mixture or stain. (Procedures to follow.)

COLORING WITH LINSEED OILS

Pure linseed oils, applied in a mixture with pure turpentine to a wood surface which has been freshly sanded, smoothed and cleaned, may produce rich colors which are admired by some refinishers and disliked by others.

This color may range from various shades of yellow to reddish brown, depending upon whether raw or boiled linseed oil is used, the number of applications, the condition, age, and whether the wood is open-grained or close-grained. Raw linseed oil is lighter in body than boiled oil, penetrates deeper, and usually results in a lighter color.

The degree of color, from a single application, is often effected by wood's ability to absorb the mixture. That is, whether the wood is old and the sap and natural oils have dried out, whether it is of open-grain or closed-grain, hardwood or softwood.

The colors desired from refinishing change in style from time to time. This is especially true in the case of Antique pine furniture. In the past, the most popular color for pine was reddish-brown, but, now that the vogue is for modern houses and bleached stream-lined furniture, it has influenced the taste, and pine finished in "natural" color is the more popular.

Maple may be given a beautiful golden tone by the application of the boiled oil mixture, while old oak and other porous woods may darken too greatly from either the boiled or raw oil mixture, even though it is applied very lightly. The shade of color may often be judged or predetermined by a "wet test."

The procedure for either the raw or boiled linseed oil mixture is as follows:

Equipment A mixture of 50% pure linseed oil and 50% pure turpentine; a thin, clean cloth about 10″ square for applying; a clean cloth for wiping; a pad of "00" steel wool.

Application

1—Saturate the cloth in the mixture, squeeze it out or apply as is, according to whether a light or heavy application is desired, and rub the entire surface to a uniform color.

2—Wipe off any surplus mixture completely with a clean cloth. (If not wiped off, surplus oil will become sticky.)

3—Allow to dry at least 24 hours in a warm room, or in the sunlight, and until the odor of the turpentine, with the nose held close to the surface, is entirely gone.

4—When dry, rub surfaces with steel wool, even though the mixture did not raise the wood-grain.

Note 1—It is a good plan to use a mixture of *boiled* linseed oil on any *unexposed* surface, regardless of desire for color from its application and also irrespective of the type of final finish to be used on the *exposed* surface, to protect the unexposed surface from moisture absorption and warpage. (See "Removing Board Warps," page 69.)

2—It is a good plan to keep the mixture in a container (paint mason jar good) for future use. Leave the small rag for application, in the mixture. Label the container and secure the lid tightly or the turpentine will evaporate.

COLOR RESTORERS

A wood surface which has been sanded and smoothed will usually appear rather drab. It is difficult to see any grain the wood may have and the color is usually much lighter than when covered with even a transparent finish.

If you have made the "wet test" for color after smoothing (see page 105), you now know the approximate color that will result from the application of a transparent finish. However, at this point in the work, many workers like to use a "color restorer," as a guide in deciding whether the piece should be stained or not. This is especially true if a surface has been repaired with an "insert patch," as the patch may be of newer wood which will not stain the same color as the surface.

The color of a cleaned surface may be partially or entirely restored by either of the two methods, as follows:

1—Brush or wipe on a thin coat of 1 part pure boiled linseed oil and 5 parts pure turpentine. Allow to dry for 24 hours or until the odor of the turpentine has disappeared. With this treatment old pine and maple take on a very nice color. Oak, mahogany, and other woods with open-grain, may darken too much.

2—Brush on a thin coat of 1 part white shellac (4 lb. cut—see "Shellac," page 170) and 5 parts denatured alcohol and allow to dry for several hours. This is primarily a "wash coat" (see next) but is often recommended and used at this point in the work. It brightens a color, shows the wood grain, and may be used on fine or coarse grain woods without fear of over-darkening them.

PRELIMINARY WASH COAT

Some experienced workers advocate that a "wash coat" be used on a wood surface before a stain is applied while others do not. A wash coat is a mixture of 1 part White Shellac to 6 or 8 parts Denatured Alcohol. It is mixed, used, and applied similarly to a Color Restorer.

It stands to reason that no wash coat should be applied if it is going to lessen the penetrating ability of a stain, for, without penetration, a stain will not last. A wash coat may be beneficially used under certain conditions and circumstances, whether softwoods or hardwoods or those with large pores (called "Coarse-grained" or "Coarse-textured") or with small pores (called "Close-grained" or "Fine-textured").

The deciding factor is the condition of the wood. As previously stated, some woods dry out greatly, depending on the amount of natural oils or gums they contain. Some old pine dries to the point where it powders when sanded. It sounds reasonable, and it is my contention that, when woods are considerably dried out, a wash coat is beneficial before the application of a stain. However, this must be judged by the worker according to the condition of the wood and the type of stain to be used.

When making a decision, it must be borne in mind that a wash coat of the type recommended has but a very small proportion of shellac and will be absorbed quickly and deeply into well dried out wood. It should never be used on woods which are not well seasoned. The purpose of the application is to partially seal the pores and to retard the absorption of a stain, but not to prevent its absorption into the pores to such an extent that it will remain upon the surface only. The rate or speed of absorption of a properly sanded and a thoroughly dry clean wood surface, may be judged with much accuracy by making a "wet test" (see page 105).

It is recommended that no wash coat be applied when Water Stains or Spirit Stains (reduced with water) are to be used and it is not needed under a Varnish Stain or a Penetrating Sealer, for these materials both seal and finish. A wash coat is often beneficial when Oil Stains are used and is recommended for use with "Home-made Dry Powder Stains."

Note All brush-work with very thin materials should be done with as few strokes as possible. Three strokes only should be used. One stroke each way to lay the material on the surface and one stroke to "tip" it off (to remove or spread excess material). For this work a full-tipped brush (2″ wide good) is best, but do not overload it. Proceed quickly until the surface is covered.

STAINING WOODS

Stains are employed to bring out the full beauty of the grain or to emphasize the color of woods. They are also used to harmonize the color of a patch with the surrounding surface, or to match pieces of wood of different colors to bring them to a uniform color.

Stain will add color to wood that has no natural beauty of color in itself or if the color has faded. There is a definite need for stains in refinishing, but it is well to pause for consideration and not jump to conclusions before planning for its use.

Such woods as mahogany, walnut, cherry, pine, maple, etc., which have a natural beauty of pattern and color, should be finished to bring out those characteristics and should not be stained. Any type of clear finish will darken a wood somewhat and magnify the beauty of the grain and the wood patterns.

It must be remembered that a stain is not a finish and that a finishing coat must be applied over it, except in the use of "Varnish Stains" and "Penetrating Wood Sealer Finishes" and "Lacquer" containing stain.

The various types of wood stains with brief comments about their qualities and use are as follows:

	PAGE
WATER STAINS Mostly used in factories. True colors.	111
OIL STAINS Penetrating clear type without pigments. Best for amateur use. Widely sold in small containers. Non-fading colors.	112
HOMEMADE DRY POWDER STAIN Cheaply made good oil stains.	114
PENETRATING WOOD SEALER STAINS Excellent newly developed products.	149
VARNISH STAINS Avoid use on Antique furniture but sometimes used on "Nude" (new unfinished furniture). (See "Varnish Finish.")	124
LACQUER STAINS Avoid use on Antique furniture. (See "Lacquer Finish.")	153
SPIRIT STAINS Dyes dissolved in alcohol. Difficult to use and should be avoided. (No further data given.)	
OTHER STAINS Simple materials for coloring.	115

GENERAL INFORMATION FOR STAINING

It takes patience and experience to learn the art of staining, but the general information to follow should be of assistance. Some portions may be repeated from the information about or use of the various types of stains.

1—A surface to be stained should not be too smooth, but should be dry, and free of dust or other foreign matter, before a stain is applied.

2—A surface having a drab appearance may need a "Color Restorer" (page 107).

3—A surface should be treated with a "Wash Coat" (page 107) when the wood is extremely dried out and as a preliminary coat, before the application of some stains.

4—A stain should be tested for color, shade or tone of color to match, by applying it to an unexposed surface of a piece, or to a wood of the same kind and allowed to dry.

5—Stains of similar type may be inter-mixed for shades of color and thinned for a lighter tone.

6—One coat of stain may be applied over another for a darker color and, if a piece is of several colored woods, stain to the darkest.

7—A stain should be brushed or wiped on quickly in an even coat and without overlaps. It is best applied on a horizontal surface as it may be there smoothed out more evenly. If it becomes necessary to apply it to a vertical surface, wipe out sags and runs evenly.

8—After a stain has been applied, all surplus should be wiped off with a lintless cloth to an even color tone. The longer the unabsorbed stain remains on the surface, the darker will be the final effect. Time varies as to when the excess stain should be wiped off, according to the types and thickness of the stain, and the condition or kind of wood.

9—Care must be exercised in wiping the edges and corners of the piece, so as not to remove too much stain.

10—It often requires two coats of stain to get a uniform color. There should be at least 24 hours between coats.

11—End grain surfaces which are porous will soak in too much stain which will often result in too dark a color. To overcome this, the surface should be well smoothed and, if necessary, treated with extra "wash coats."

12—When "insert-patches" are to be stained, it is usually necessary to stain the entire surface into which they are placed.

13—When applying a stain (or paint) to an article like a chair, it is always best to do all the inside of the underpart first. Then do the outside of the underpart and, finally, the upper part of the piece.

14—All stains should be applied in a room or place free from excessive heat or drafts.

15—Allow stain to dry for at least 24 hours unless otherwise instructed. If a stain is not thoroughly dry, it will "weep" (blend) with the "Sealing Coat" to follow and will not dry.

16—A stained surface should not be smoothed with an abrasive until after a "sealer coat" has been applied and dried.

COLORS OF COMMERCIAL STAINS

Color charts are furnished by the manufacturers of the various types of stains and are supplied, without cost, to customers in those retail stores (paint, hardware, and builders' supply) where wood stains are available.

These charts show the various colors available and each manufacturer has his own version of the shade of a color. They vary greatly and often are called by a coined name, rather than by the name of the wood that they represent.

Those most commonly found are oak, maple, mahogany, and walnut. The various colors may be called by those names only, a coined name, or a name that is generally accepted as a shade of one of the colors. The colors and shades are as follows:

OAK—light oak (yellowish); dark oak (brownish-yellow); golden oak (dark oak slightly reddish).

MAPLE—maple (brownish-yellow); honey (reddish-brown); Vermont (brownish-red).

MAHOGANY—mahogany (reddish-brown); dark mahogany (brownish-red).

WALNUT—variation of brown to blackish-brown.

The colors on the charts may vary greatly from the color found in the can, so, when making a purchase, it is well to have the can opened and make a test, by placing a small quantity on a piece of paper into which it is quickly absorbed and dries, because the wet color varies from the dried. All stains should be mixed in the daylight.

CHERRY COLOR stains may be mixed, if they are difficult to buy. For a *dark* cherry stain, use Italian burnt sienna (ground color in oil). For a *light* cherry stain, add Italian raw sienna. Mix with 3 parts of pure linseed oil, 1 part of pure turpentine and ½ part of the best grade of Japan drier.

WATER STAIN

Water stain is considered by most professional workers the best for all-purpose use. It is by far the most universally used stain for mass production in factories. For use in a home shop, it has both advantages and disadvantages.

The principal advantage in its use is that it may be readily mixed by dissolving aniline dye powders in hot water, for a concentrated form, which may be stored in glass bottles indefinitely, and diluted to tints as needed, resulting in low cost dye. Also, with proper materials, colors may be made and intermixed which harmonize with true wood colors of various shades and tones, that do not fade or bleed, and may be applied to a prepared wood surface without a preliminary sealer coat.

The disadvantage in the use of this stain, for an amateur, is that it is better applied with a spray gun than with a brush, for even application. Also many workers do not care to take time or trouble to mix and store water stains when they are able to purchase newly developed non-pigmented oil and other types of penetrating stains which are now available in small containers, ready mixed for use and in colors to match various woods. These stains do not raise the grain while a water stain will. Another disadvantage in the use of water stains is that many paint stores do not carry the powders in stock.

The method of mixing and using water stain is as follows:

Mixing Water Stain

Heat water to just below the boiling point in a vessel other than aluminum. Pour the aniline powder into the water slowly while stirring. Allow to cool and store in a glass bottle. If water is "hard" (containing lime) or not pure, use distilled water. The mixture should be in proportions of 4 ounces of powder to 1 gallon of water. Dilute this solution with pure water to density of color or tint desired.

Equipment A 2″ brush for application; a small scrub brush for use in crevices; a pad of 2/0 steel wool for rubbing stubborn areas; clean absorbent cloth for wiping; and a water stain, mixed for shade of color or diluted for tint.

Application

1—First moisten a surface. Then apply stain with a brush, using long straight strokes. Free the brush from stain on the edge of the container or by shaking it and go over the surface, picking up surplus stain. Continue doing so, using long strokes until the surface is even in color. Remove all excess stain from cracks and crevices with a small scrub brush.

2—When brushing is completed, wipe the surface with a cloth, using light full length strokes, picking up stain remaining on the surface, making the surface uniform in color and without streaks.

3—The end surfaces should be thoroughly wetted before stain is applied to an adjacent surface. Do not let such end surfaces become dry. Stain the end surfaces while wet and wipe off immediately, repeating if necessary. By this method the end surface may be kept from absorbing too much stain and becoming too dark.

Note When spots will not absorb the stain to match with the area to which it is applied, rub them with steel wool to open the pores while the surface is wet with stain.

OIL STAINS

Oil stains are best for the beginner and amateur worker to use whether such stains are purchased ready-mixed or are homemade. (See "Oil Stains," Chapter 15.)

These stains are rich in tone and produce lasting colors. Oil stains are generally available, inexpensive, easily applied and stored. They do not raise the grain, causing "wood-feathers," nor do they conceal the natural wood-grain or wood-patterns, and those of similar type may be mixed together for shades of color.

Oil stains are made of coloring matter with linseed oil as a vehicle, Japan drier to hasten the drying of the oil and turpentine used as a thinner which carries the mixture into the pores of the wood and later evaporates.

There are two distinct types of oil stains, as follows:

Pigment Oil Stains

This type of stain is often referred to merely as an "Oil Stain" or a "Wood Finishing Stain," without mention, on the containers of the fact, that it is a pigment type. The coloring matter is the same as used in so-called "Colors in Oil." The pigment settles to the bottom of the can and must be stirred before using.

They are best on close-grained woods, such as basswood, birch, cherry, gumwood, maple, pine, and poplar. The small and closely spaced pores of these woods will not become clogged with the finely ground color pigment because of the wood's fine texture, if the stain is properly applied and wiped off.

Penetrating Oil Stains

This type of stain is usually referred to on the containers as a penetrating material or described by a "coined" word, indicating that it is of that kind. The coloring matter is in liquid form so that these stains are transparent. They are best for use on coarse-grained woods, such as ash, beech, chestnut, elm, hickory, mahogany, oak, rosewood, satinwood, sycamore, and walnut. These woods, with large pores and coarse texture, will often clog up too much with a pigment stain which is detrimental to the finished appearance.

Penetrating oil stains should be used by preference on woods which are not well seasoned or old enough to have had their natural oils dried out and on surfaces which are quite smooth, as they will penetrate better than stains of the pigment type. Some workers prefer them to other types of stains and use them exclusively, when available.

Their greatest drawback is that when this stain is used on extremely porous surfaces it penetrates deeply and is very difficult to remove, should the occasion arise. If prior tests are made for color, tone or shade, there should be no need for their later removal.

INTER-MIXING OIL STAIN COLORS

Practically all the variation of colors you may need for staining furniture woods may be made by inter-mixing stains of but three basic colors—maple (brownish-yellow), mahogany (reddish-brown), and walnut (true brown). However, if the maple contains too much brown, it will be necessary to add the light oak to the list, and, should the walnut contain too much black, you will need raw umber or burnt umber.

Those who doubt this can satisfy themselves as to its truth by buying all the colors available (including the oaks) and applying them to a clean light-colored wood surface. Write on each the color used, allow to dry, and then brush over with a white shellac or clear varnish finish.

If this test is made, there will be no variation in color, or only one of the slightest degree, between the various oak stains and light maple. The mahogany and walnut, however, will show their own distinctive colors.

A small amount of oil stain goes a long way, especially when thinned with turpentine for lighter color tone. Buy only quality stains of the three colors and intermix for various shades of color. If necessary, you may add to these colors, as directed in the first paragraph above.

Never buy cheap grades of stains. They are off-color, particularly the mahogany stain, which may be much too red. The walnut stain also may not be the true color of the wood it is to represent.

USING OIL STAINS

Equipment The stain and a small piece of cloth or a 2″ brush to apply it; lintless cloths for wiping off excess stain; grade "00" steel wool or worn 6/0 or 8/0 garnet paper for after-smoothing; gloves or protective hand cream worked well around and under fingernails.

Application

1—Brush or wipe on an even and moderately thin coat of stain without overlaps, after having thoroughly stirred the stain, especially if the pigment type.

2—Wipe off the excess stain after it has set a little and you believe it has penetrated sufficiently. Repeat operations to get a deeper color tone.

HOMEMADE DRY POWDER STAIN

Excellent homemade stain may be made with "dry powders" which are usually available at the larger paint stores and from lumber yards. They are easily mixed and come in a great variety of colors. The colors are lasting and, when properly mixed, are easily applied.

Most of the colors, shades or tones, which are found in Antique furniture, made of various species of woods, may be matched with but *four* basic colors of the dry powder. These are—raw sienna (yellow), burnt sienna (red), raw umber (light brown), and burnt umber (dark brown). Other powdered colors include chrome yellow, yellow, and French ochre, Venetian red or Spanish red oxide. One of these might be added in sparing amounts to any of the four basic colors, or a mixture of them, to obtain an off-color, but based on personal experience this is seldom necessary.

A severe test of this material is in matching lovely old pine pieces which range from a mellowed coffee color to light toned brownish-reds or reddish-brown. This has been done most successfully in my shop by the use of raw sienna.

It might be well for a beginner to stick exclusively to the oil stains, but it would be interesting, and perhaps instructive, to experiment with the dry powders.

Equipment A small piece of cloth for applying; cloths for wiping off excess stain; grade "0" and "00" steel wool for smoothing; rubber gloves (or old leather or canvas ones for this work only).

Testing for color Use only about a teaspoonful of the dry color powder you believe to be nearest to that desired and experiment by adding other dry powder colors to get what you believe to be the correct match desired.

These must be thoroughly mixed.

When satisfied with the color, add a little turpentine (which temporarily darkens it greatly), to a small portion of the powder only and, with a rag, apply it to a scrap of clean wood (if possible, of the same kind as that to be stained). Wipe off surplus stain immediately and allow to dry (few minutes) for a positive test of color, shade, and tone.

Mixing Stain When satisfied with the mixture, mix a quantity of dry powders and make a test, as above, to be certain. Add to the mixed powders: 2 parts of *raw* linseed oil, 1 part of pure turpentine, and about 1/8th part of Japan drier. Thin to a consistency of medium heavy syrup.

Application

1—Apply with a rag to a small area, rubbing the mixture into the surface and wiping off immediately with a clean rag.

2—Continue until all surfaces are covered.

3—Allow to stand about 24 hours to dry.

4—Remove any remaining surplus stain with grade "0" steel wool and then smooth with grade "00" steel wool.

Note 1—It is well to apply a relatively heavy "wash coat" (see "Preliminary Wash Coat," page 107) or two thin wash coats to well dried out porous surfaces before applying stain, as this stain penetrates quickly and deeply. The wash coat will enable you to control the application and make it spread more easily without too fast absorption.

2—Some users omit the raw linseed oil and the Japan drier, when it is to be used on fairly smooth and close-grained woods. (The use of linseed oil is to make the stain apply more easily.)

3—The powders average about 20¢ per pound in small quantities and but one pound of each of the basic colors goes a long way. It is so inexpensive that, when mixing a batch for a specific job, it is advisable to have more than needed, than to be forced to make more, especially when mixed colors are used, for it may be difficult to make the same mixture again, unless the quantities of powders used were carefully measured and recorded.

OTHER STAINS

Other materials are often used by finishers as stains, the formulas many times being developed by them. Sometimes, formulas or materials which have been successfully used are printed in a "swap column" or other places in newspapers or magazines.

Examples

Warm Pine Stain was recorded as made from plug chewing tobacco. The plug was broken up and allowed to stand in 1/2 pint of household ammonia, then steeped for 15 minutes. Apply 2 coats, to give varying degrees of light to dark tones, depending upon the strength of the material. Use outdoors when possible.

Brown Stain is often recorded as successfully made from tobacco juice from tobacco soaked in water.

Nut Brown Stain is often made by professional refinishers from "potassium permanganate" which may be purchased in drug stores. It is violet in color but turns brown when applied to wood.

SEALER COAT AFTER STAINS

A "sealer coat" should be applied to a wood surface after a stain has been used, unless otherwise directed. It should also be applied before a wood filler (for an ultra smooth fine finish) and over the filler before the final coat, as later related. (See "Sealer Coat after Paste Filler," page 120.)

Wood finishers have never come to complete agreement as to the type of undercoat to be used beneath succeeding coats, but it is now generally conceded that the sealer material should be a thin coat of whatever is used for the final finish. The reason for the variance in thought is that shellac hardens by evaporation and loses weight, while varnish becomes oxidized and gains weight and neither has an affiliation for the other, when one is placed over the other, but they are often mixed and used for a final finish.

The purpose of the sealer coat is to keep the stain from "bleeding" into the succeeding coats, by sealing the pores, so that the surface may be ready for a filler or smoothed for the final finish. The sealer prevents liquids from entering the wood fibers and reducing the stain material, which often causes a gray cast or light colored area, surrounded by small rings.

Sealer coats should be so thin that they will leave no "shine" and one coat only is applied (with a brush), and later smoothed, according to the final finish to be used, as follows:

For Shellac Finish

Reduce 1 part of pure white shellac (4 lb. cut) with 8 parts of denatured alcohol.

For Varnish Finish (Or Mixtures Containing Varnish)

Reduce 1 part of varnish with 1 part of pure turpentine. A "synthetic" type of varnish should not be used as it may not blend with turpentine. (The 4 hour drying or spar varnish containers usually state thereon that they may be thinned with turpentine while a synthetic varnish may mention *no* thinning material.)

Smoothing With Abrasive

If a filler is to be used on a sealed stained surface, merely "knock" off any roughness by a very light rubbing with grade "00" steel wool.

If the final finish is to be applied over the sealer coat, the surface should be completely smoothed. Do this with worn 6/0 to 8/0 garnet paper or grade "00" steel wool. When using either type of material, great care must be exercised not to go too heavily on the edges or the corners, for fear of cutting through the stain. (Should this be done, the spots will have to be restained, dried, and a new sealer coat applied.)

Note During recent years new types of so-called "sealing compounds" have been developed and are popular with many professional refinishers. They are a varnish-type material, clear in color, which can be thinned with turpentine and may be used as a diluted sealer, as above directed, and for a finish coat in place of varnish. They give a clear protective finish, are tough, waterproof, and dry hard. They are used largely on exposed surfaces of yachts and are often added to "reinforce" paints or varnish, and to increase gloss and durability.

PASTE FILLERS

The purpose of using a paste filler is to fill the pores of the wood in order to have a surface which is extremely smooth for a "Polish Rubbed Finish."

The fact is that all liquid materials which are used for finishing woods fill the pores to some degree so that paste fillers are seldom used, except where extreme smoothness is required. In such cases, the final work lies in polishing the dried finish with mild abrasives to a soft polished surface as smooth as glass.

The wood pores *must* be filled with a paste filler on *all* woods to acquire an extremely smooth surface for a "Polish Rubbed Finish" regardless of the kind of finishing material used, including varnish, shellac, penetrating wood sealer (of the varnish type), lacquer, or enamel.

Paste fillers are made with "silex," a crushed and finely ground rock, crystalline in character, and with no chemical action. It is transparent and similar to glass. When the paste is thinned, the application is a simple, fast operation that greatly enhances the beauty of the wood grain, as it is seen through a smooth glass-like finish (except when enamel is used).

Important A paste filler is used *over* a stain which must be sealed with a "Sealer Coat" to keep the stain from "bleeding" and a "Sealer Coat" must follow the application of a paste filler.

Note 1—The only type of *clear* finish requiring the use of a paste filler is the "Polish Rubbed Finish." To conserve space, this finish is described for the use of varnish only. (Chapter 5 on "Refinishing.")

2—When a varnish type of a "Penetrating Wood Sealer" is to be used for a "Polish Rubbed Finish," do not use a paste filler as directed here. It is used by a special method as related for the use of that material under the sub-title of "For Polish Rubbed Finish." See page 132, in Chapter 5 on "Refinishing."

3—When old furniture is to be enameled, a paste filler should always be applied to surfaces, for otherwise the surface roughness will show through the enamel, regardless of number of coats applied or care taken. See Chapter 7, "Enameling and 'Nude' Furniture Finishes."

4—Note 3 (above) also applies to new unfinished furniture which is to be enameled. See Chapter 7.

Buying Paste Fillers

Paste fillers can usually be bought at stores selling paints and painter's materials. They are made by many paint manufacturers and are often sold under the name "Wood Filler." The usual size container is a quart, which is sufficient for many ordinary jobs as it should cover about 75 square feet. The material is reasonable in price.

Paste fillers are usually found only in neutral (grayish) color. However, sometimes they may be purchased in colors to approximate those of the wood surface to be filled, in which case they do not need to be colored.

Making Paste Fillers

You can easily make a paste filler if it is impossible to buy. To do so, mix the following:

1 part pure boiled linseed oil.
1/3 part "4 hr. drying" type of varnish.
1/3 part pure Japan drier.
1/2 part pure turpentine.

Mix with this enough powdered silex to form a heavy paste. However, when silex is not available, fine "silica" may be used, even though it is not transparent.

The varnish used must be of the type which states on the can that it may be thinned with turpentine, for synthetic varnishes (made otherwise) would not mix.

Thinning Paste Fillers

Paste fillers, as they come in the can, are a thick heavy paste and must be thinned considerably for use, after which they should be colored to match the wood to which they are to be applied.

General directions for thinning and material used will be found on the containers but they may be confusing, as they often seem to be directed to the professional shop. There they are measured by the weight of the base stock, to the gallon of thinner. You will also find various thinning materials or combinations of them recommended by different firms.

Manufacturers of paste fillers and authorities recommend as a thinner pure turpentine, benzine, or naphtha. A good mixture is 1 part of turpentine and 1 to 2 parts of white gasoline (ethyl is poisonous). The purpose of thinning is for ease of application and the medium used must evaporate. You may use any one mentioned above, with good results.

A filler is used for the sole purpose of filling the grain of the wood surface so as to have a smooth finish. It is best that the filler be thinned to various consistencies of thickness, according to whether the wood is close-grained or coarse-grained.

For general purposes, thin the filler to a medium heavy brushing consistency, a little thicker than heavy soup.

For woods with fine pores (close-grained), the filler can be thinner. These woods include birch, cherry, gumwood, etc.

For woods with medium size pores, use the medium heavy filler. These woods include many species, such as beech, mahogany, maple, walnut, etc.

For woods with large size pores (open-grained), the filler should be heavy or thick. These woods include ash, chestnut, elm, hickory, some mahoganies, oak, sycamore, etc.

There is but one rule to remember. It is difficult to handle and remove a filler which is too thick and, if it is too thin, a succeeding coat of the filler may be applied, should there be bare spots, but too thin a coat may be injurious to a stain, if the stain is not properly sealed.

Coloring Paste Fillers

Paste fillers are used *over* stain, rather than depending upon the color of a filler for a stain. When a paste filler is used, it is best that it be approximately of the same color as the surface to which it is applied, except when the final finish is to be paint or enamel. Otherwise, the filler might show through a transparent finish, if the filler is not correctly applied or properly wiped off.

Neutral paste (usually gray color) may be changed to match the wood, whether it be stained or natural color, by the use of "colors in oil" or "colors in Japan," which are available.

"Dry powder colors" mixed in turpentine, and "oil soluble aniline" colors thinned with turpentine, are sometimes used for colors in paste fillers, and a shade of color may often be had by using a "pigment stain" or a "penetrating wood stain" as it comes from the can.

The mixing of colors to match a wood is not at all difficult and may be quickly learned by a little experimenting. Thin the mixed color in turpentine and add to the thinned paste. Before this is applied to furniture it is best to make a test on scrap wood of like color, as the piece, to see if the color is satisfactory. Remember that a color in turpentine will lighten when it dries.

To briefly summarize, a thinned paste filler may be used without coloring if it is applied and wiped off in a manner that will not show the paste in the wood grain, but it is better to have the filler colored to approximately that of the wood and it is best if it is of the same shade of color.

Using Paste Fillers

There is a difference of opinion as to how the thinned paste fillers should be applied. If the following method and the correct timing for "padding" are used, the work should be a success, providing the filler is applied to a surface properly prepared for its acceptance. Have on hand a supply of clean burlap (15″ to 18″ square) and clean rags.

1—Clean dust from the surfaces with a stiff brush.

2—Apply the filler quickly and generously but to a limited area at a time, with an old, short-bristle stiff brush, *with* the grain of the wood, rubbing it in a little. Then brush it smooth, with the grain. Stir the mixture thoroughly before each application.

3—Fold a piece of burlap several times to about the size of your hand. When the surface of the applied filler "flattens" and loses its shine appreciably (usually 5 to 10 minutes), rub the filler into the wood surface with *cross-grain* and circular motion and without changing to a new surface of the cloth. This operation "pads" the powdered silex particles into the wood pores and smooths the surface. The time when this work should start is most important for, with conditions favorable, the filler sets up quickly.

4—Follow immediately by wiping off the surface, *across* the grain only, with clean pieces of burlap squares, followed by fresh rags, until all the surplus filler is removed and the surface is clean and free from smears. Finally, when you look at the surface against the light and it shines, you may stroke the surface with a clean cloth *with* the grain, to remove all traces of surplus filler and fingerprints. This must be done lightly or the filler may be pulled from the surface.

5—Carvings, joints, moldings, etc., should be scrubbed with a small brush packed with the filler. *When* the surface "flattens" wipe with clean burlap, followed by cloths, etc. Hold a bit of cloth over the point of a wooden meat skewer or a sharpened small dowel stick to clean out the depressions and corners.

6—A filled piece should dry at least 24 hours in a warm room but 48 hours or even more would be better. Fillers which have colors added to them take longer to dry.

Note 1—When the work is correctly accomplished by the above steps, the surface should be smooth and ready for a "Sealer Coat." If the surface shows evidence of the filler, remove and smooth it with worn 6/0 to 8/0 abrasive paper dipped in white gasoline.

2—If the surface has blotches or smears not seen until the filler has dried, moisten a cloth with the same thinner as used in the filler and wipe the spots carefully so as not to cause a light colored area. If this will not remove the excess dried filler, the spots or area must be sanded lightly with a worn 6/0 to 8/0 abrasive paper dipped in white gasoline. If the area is then too light in color, dip a rag in the filler and work over that part of the surface until the color is blended. Then allow to dry and use the "sealer coat" on the entire surface.

3—If a filled and dried surface is found to lack a sufficient amount of filler, refill the entire surface again by starting at the beginning of the process.

SEALER COAT AFTER PASTE FILLER

Apply a "sealer coat" to a surface that has been treated with a paste filler. This should be a very thin coat of the same material to be used for clear final coats. Thin shellac with alcohol or varnish with turpentine as previously directed. (See "Sealer Coat after Stain," page 116.)

This coat will penetrate the filler and, being of the same material as the sealer coat applied prior to using the filler, it will have the same adhesion and expanding factors, and assist in leveling the surface.

Sand with 6/0 to 8/0 grade abrasive paper to prepare for succeeding final coats after the sealer coat has dried for 24 hours.

Note Use a varnish sealer coat over paste fillers on wood surfaces when the final coat is to be "enamel," as this product is also thinned with turpentine. When a shellac sealer coat is used, it fails to give proper adhesion between the enamel and the filler, allowing the enamel to chip more easily.

CHAPTER 5

REFINISHING

You were previously advised to plan your work in advance, not only for the type of finish you decide to use, but for which may be most suitable for the piece.

The finish best suited for a particular piece depends upon these factors:

1—The wood from which the piece is made; pine or mahogany, etc.

2—The utility of the piece—that is, for what used; chair, cabinet, table, etc.

3—The quality of workmanship or fineness of the piece; a highboy as compared with a cobbler's bench.

4—The customary finish for the type or period of the piece. That is, the kind and smoothness of a finish which is or should be found on certain types of furniture; as for example, a crude piece of pine furniture as compared to a mahogany dining room table, which has been smoothed with a "paste filler."

It is just as bad to over-finish as to under-finish, depending upon the factors outlined above. There are, however, many cases which are not in the extreme and a worker should use good judgment.

You were also instructed to plan ahead any change of color or degree of smoothness desired, in order to decide on a stain to be used (for color), or whether to apply a "paste filler" (for smoothness). This work must be completed and a "Sealer Coat" applied after each, before putting on a finish coat. (See "Staining Woods," page 108; "Sealer Coat after Stains," page 116; "Paste Fillers," page 117; and "Sealer Coat after Paste Filler," page 120.)

When all these directions have been followed and the work of "Repairs" (Chapter 2), "Removing Old Finish" (Chapter 3), and other work of "Preparing for New Finish" (Chapter 4) has been successfully completed, you are then ready to apply a previously chosen finish material, to be left in a gloss (seldom desired), or rubbed or polished.

The various types of finishes with brief comments on them follow:

1—**Varnish Finish** (Page 124). A finish partially or fully resistant to water, alcohol, heat, and acid. Has been considered the ultimate of all finishes for furniture of high quality, including pianos. Difficult to apply for a "Polish Rubbed Finish."

2—**Shellac and Wax** (Page 139). A finish requiring little skill. Will not resist water stains, etc. About the most universally used of all finishes but should only be applied on certain pieces.

3—**Varnish-Oil Finish** (Page 147). A finish not generally known and, hence, seldom used. Easy to apply, partially or fully resistant to water, alcohol, heat, and acid. May be used advantageously on any type of furniture requiring a "Satin Rubbed Finish."

4—**Penetrating Wood Sealer Finish** (Page 149). A finish little used (except for floors) but which is certain to become popular because of its extreme ease of application (mostly with a rag). It has quick drying qualities, durability, beauty, fineness for rubdown, resistance against injury, stains, etc.

5—**Blond Finish** (Page 151). A bleached finish, fashionable at the moment.

6—**Pickled Finish** (Page 152). A bleached finish, with pores of wood grain filled with paint.

7—**Lacquer Finish** (Page 153). A finish to be avoided in restoration work. Quick drying, durable, and may contain a stain. Mostly used in mass production (by spray-gun), particularly on cheap products.

8—**Oil Finish** (Page 155). One of the oldest finishes known. Easy to apply but requiring hours of rubbing and months to complete. Now seldom used.

9—**French Polish** (Page 156). An old high grade finish with shellac. Exacting and difficult work with long hours of labor. Now seldom used.

Note Most of your finishing work should be done with FINISHES No. 1, 2, 3, 4, or 5, for which full instructions are given. You are given only a brief outline for FINISHES No. 6, 7, 8, or 9, as a matter of interest, information, and instruction.

There are three types (or degrees) of a FINAL FINISH. They are briefly as follows:

1—**High Gloss Finish.** The natural gloss left after the application of several coats of finishing material. A finish seldom desired for indoor furniture.

2—**Satin Rubbed Finish.** A finish secured by smoothing a high gloss finish with abrasive papers or steel wool and then waxing. The most used and liked finish.

3—**Polish Rubbed Finish.** This finish requires a "paste filler" before the final finish. A finish to be used on that type, period, or quality of furniture requiring it.

In the first of the procedures which follow, you are given full and complete information and instruction for the application of a "Varnish Finish."

In the balance of the Chapter, you will be given information, specific uses, and instructions for the other finishing materials, leading up to or for a "High Gloss," "Satin Rubbed," or "Polish Rubbed" finish.

VARNISH FINISH

A varnish finish meets that high standard which most other final finishes lack.

It is usual, in the professional shops and in mass production, to apply varnish only with a brush (never with a spray gun), and it is best applied with a special type of brush, made for "laying" on the varnish. The greatest detriment is dust and foreign particles. It has great lasting qualities, resists scratches, may be revived, and, when properly cared for, will seldom "check" or "alligator."

It is seldom that a "High Gloss Finish" is appropriate for furniture made of wood. The "Satin Rubbed Finish" is used as an original finish and in restoration. It does not require exacting work. The "Polish Rubbed Finish," only used where required, is difficult to complete correctly, requires a wood surface to be smoothed with a paste filler, made free from dust with a "tack rag," exacting brush work, the removal of dust particles with a "pick stick," careful smoothing between coats, and final polishing with a "rubbing block" and powdered abrasives.

The application of varnish (and similar materials) calls for a special technique in "laying" it on and a "chisel" shaped brush for exacting work. However, varnish may be applied with a regulation brush in a satisfactory manner for ordinary finishes, when care in brushing is exercised.

The following will give, first, information regarding types of varnishes, brushes, and their use, methods of brushing varnish, drying, and smoothing between coats. Next the methods and materials used for a "High Gloss Finish," a "Satin Rubbed Finish," and a "Polish Rubbed Finish." Finally, you are given methods, materials, and equipment, only required for a properly completed "Polish Rubbed Finish."

The sequence is followed so that the worker will first have the essential information and then detailed instructions for applying various types of varnish finishes in order that the book may be better used as a bench manual.

Buying Varnish

Varnish may be purchased in many grades or kinds, to fit the pocketbook or for a special use. For best results, use the information as follows:

1—The "4 hour Floor Varnish" made by nationally known concerns is the most satisfactory type to use as a finish for a furniture. The label on the can should state that it is highly resistant to water, alcohol, heat, or acid, and that it may be thinned with turpentine.

2—"Spar Varnish" may be used as a substitute. It has the same proof qualities as floor varnish and can also be thinned with turpentine, but may dry more slowly.

3—Avoid "Cabinet" and "Rubbing" varnishes for amateur refinishing. The qualities of these varnishes and their application varies so greatly that they should be used only in the professional shop.

4—So-called "Interior" varnishes should never be used in this work as they will not resist wear and have little resistance against anything.

5—So-called "Flat" varnishes dry to a dull and rather rough finish. They can be smoothed but are not truly satisfactory for refinishing.

6—"Bar Varnish" (so-called) is fine for use on sinks, etc., for hard usage and is stain, heat (moderate), alcohol, and acid proof. It may be rubbed to a "satin" finish with fine steel wool and is used by many amateurs for furniture refinishing. Most bar varnishes are synthetic, a drawback, since it often cannot be thinned with turpentine and it is difficult to clean the brush, after use.

7—Avoid buying a cheap varnish. A small quantity of varnish covers a large area and a cheap grade will never result in a good or lasting finish.

Varnish Brushes

It is important to have a good brush for varnishing. There are brushes especially made for use with varnish. (For general information regarding brushes and the type to buy, see "Brushes for Single Purpose Use," page 205.)

Varnish brushes should have special attention when cleaning them. They are more costly than ordinary paint brushes and will ruin a surface if they are not clean. (See "Cleaning Brushes," page 206.)

Holding a Varnish Brush

To obtain best results a varnish brush should be held in a slightly different manner than a brush used for applying pigment paints. (See "Using Brushes," page 206.)

Dustless Surfaces

Surfaces to be varnished should be free from dust. Wipe surfaces with a clean, lintless cloth (shaking often), then remove dust from cracks, deep pores, etc., with a clean dry brush, and finally wipe again with the cloth.

The surface is then ready for the first coat of varnish, if preparing for a "High Gloss Finish" or a "Satin Rubbed Finish."

Any dust or particles left on a surface will be picked up by a wet varnish brush and spread elsewhere on the surface, or go into the varnish container, contaminating the clean varnish therein. (A very limited amount of dust, etc., is not detrimental to a "High Gloss Finish," as these may be smoothed down with a mild abrasive, or to a "Satin Rubbed Finish," as the procedure called for smoothing. However, they are detrimental to a "Polish Rubbed Finish.")

In preparing for a "Polish Rubber Finish," the surface should finally be wiped with a "Tack Rag" to remove every last particle of dust, lint, etc., before varnish is applied. (See "Tack Rag," page 137.)

Brushing Varnish

Although brushing varnish is the most difficult of all ordinary brush work this should not discourage the beginner. Varnish should be "flowed" on to a surface, with a brush and with thin, even coats. The process is called "laying" it on and "tipping" it off. Most of your varnish work will not require exacting smoothness or freedom from foreign particles.

If workers, inexperienced in applying varnish, will follow instructions carefully in their first few jobs, they will soon qualify to do precision work.

Instructions for brushing varnish (and similar materials) are as follows:

1—Never varnish in damp weather or on surfaces which are not thoroughly dry.

2—Both the room and the varnish should be 70° F. or warmer. There are times (as in winter) when the work must be done in a colder room. In such cases, or if it is desired to use varnish warmer than the room temperature, place the unopened can in a pan of warm water for about an hour before using it.

3—Never shake or agitate varnish before removing the lid as this will cause small bubbles to form which are detrimental in smoothing out a coat. Hold the can in your hand and rotate it gently back and forth a few times to mix the varnish before removing the lid. When some of the varnish has been taken from the can, immediately place the lid (loosely) back on top so that the vehicle (turpentine) for thinning, will not evaporate.

4—A brush is prepared for use before starting work by dipping it into the varnish and working it back and forth on clean paper to get the varnish evenly through the bristles. Too much varnish on a brush will cause it to drip or run on to the handle.

5—On horizontal surfaces, the varnish is "laid on" with very little brush work. Only "lay on" about 6″ to 8″ area at a time, working from the unfinished to the finished surface, and taking about two strokes. Then "tip off" the varnish, to smooth it and wipe out any bubbles, by holding the brush straight up and going lightly over the surface with the tip of the bristles. Inspect the surface against the light.

6—On vertical (standing) surfaces, the procedure is different, to prevent "curtains" (sags) on the finished work. Use short, quick strokes, working an area of about 6″ square, back and forth across the surface, starting from a corner at the top. Then "tip off" the surface, by brushing down half-way and up half-way, so that the brush is lifted from the surface in the central portion.

7—Start strokes from a center toward an edge, rather than from an edge toward the center, to avoid wiping the varnish from the brush over the edge.

8—On turned parts, such as chair and table legs, brush around turnings but stroke lengthwise on the long plain sections, "tipping off" half-way up and half-way down.

9—When varnishing small furniture (chairs, tables, stands, etc.) which may be easily lifted, turn the article up-side-down, place on a work bench (boards on saw-horses good) and complete all the under-structure first, and then do the upper.

Note 1—Varnish sets very rapidly. When varnish thickens to a point where it does not flow easily from the brush, it should be thinned with pure turpentine. A little thinner goes a long way and it should be thoroughly mixed.

2—The first coat of varnish should be "brushed" on very thin. Later coats should be "flowed" on.

3—A wet varnish should be "picked" free from dust for a "Polish Rubbed Finish." (See "Picking Varnish," page 138.)

4—"Pinholes" often appear when a varnish has dried because of having applied it on a damp surface, having used a poor thinner or one not thoroughly mixed with the varnish.

5—"Crawling" may be caused by coats being too thick, atmospheric changes, or the preceding coat not having dried.

6—"Chipping" or "cracking" may come from using a type of varnish that becomes brittle, or placing one kind of varnish over another, having varying degrees of elasticity.

7—"Sweating" usually ocurs when a varnish is rubbed before it is thoroughly dry.

8—"Brush marks" usually come from using too small a brush or brushing the varnish too long.

9—Better work may be accomplished if furniture is disassembled, wherever practical, before applying a finishing material. This also aids in sanding between coats and before the final rubbing. Remove drawers, doors, back rails, headboards, etc.

10—A "Strike Wire Can" is recommended for removing excess varnish from the brush before applying it to a surface. (See "Strike Wire Can," page 136.)

Drying Varnished Surface

Under no circumstances should a varnished surface be rubbed with any type of abrasive (steel wool, or an abrasive paper or cloth) until it is *completely* dry. If a surface is rubbed before it is thoroughly dried out, the result will be disastrous and, in some cases, it will require a complete removal of the finish and a new one to replace it.

For good results, be guided by the general information given herein regarding the time for drying, making tests for dryness, removing "fatty edges," "curtains," etc., as follows:

1—For high quality work such as a "Polish Rubbed Finish," the first (thin) coat should be given a minimum drying time of three days, a week for the second, and one to two weeks for the third or final coat.

2—When insufficient time is allowed for drying, an abrasive rubbed on a surface will pick up any little particles of foreign matter (dust etc.) imbedded in the finish and cause them to scratch or wear through the hardened face of the varnish. When this hardened face is damaged, the partially dried under-material piles up on abrasive paper or is torn out by steel wool, leaving pinholes or spots on the surface.

3—Make a test with a thumb nail for hardness. If the surface seems hard, then make a test with the ball of the thumb for a print. Wipe the thumb clean and dry. Press it down hard on the surface, wipe the spot with a clean cloth, and examine for a print. If any is noticeable, set the piece aside for further hardening (a warm room is best).

4—It takes a long time for fatty edges, drips, sags, and curtains to become completely dry because of the thickness of the varnish in them. If an attempt is made to sand such a defect before it is hardened throughout, it will cut through to the bare surface, making it necessary that the work be done over, as no later coats would cover such a depression.

5—When such defects have completely dried they may be sanded down with a fine grade of abrasive paper, well lubricated with a white soap, if great care is taken while doing this work. It is best to cut a thick defect (raised surface) down only part way. Then wash and dry it, and set the piece aside to dry for some days. This extra precaution often avoids the necessity of removing the entire finish and starting over again.

Note The drying time suggested above is the maximum which might be required for a "Polish Rubbed Finish." In the case of a "Satin Rubbed Finish," the drying time can often be greatly shortened if you follow the "thumb test" for hardness.

SANDING BETWEEN FINISH COATS

The following information, instructions, and methods, are applicable to such final finish materials as high grade VARNISH, PENETRATING WOOD SEALERS that finish in a high gloss, and LACQUER. For a SHELLAC AND WAX FINISH, the methods should be somewhat modified. (See "Shellac and Wax Finish," page 139.)

Sanding between finishing coats is a most important step in obtaining a smooth finish. There is a dual purpose for this.

1—Careful sanding knocks off dust particles and any foreign matter which may be in the material or accumulate on its surface while drying.

2—It removes the shine from a surface and roughens it slightly as a "bond" for a succeeding coat.

First Coat Sand a completely dried surface with 6/0 Garnet Finish Paper, Open Coat type preferred, as this does not "clog up" so quickly. Use the paper dry or dampened on the back with water.

Between Coats There are two methods for sanding *between* the second and succeeding coats. Each method requires an entirely different kind of abrasive paper. The proper method should be determined by the smoothness desired, for the type of finish planned for. These are as follows:

1—For the standard "High Gloss Finish" or a "Satin Rubbed Finish," follow the same directions as for the First Coat (above), using a like grade and kind of abrasive paper.

2—For a "Polish Rubbed Finish," sand with 360-A, 400-A, or 500-A grade Wet-or-Dry abrasive paper, dipped in lukewarm, soapy water.

3—When it is desired to have a "High Gloss Finish" or a "Satin Rubbed Finish" *extremely smooth,* use the "Polish Rubbed Finish" method (same materials).

Note 1—After a coat has been sanded, dust the surfaces carefully and then wash it with a clean cloth, moistened with clear water and wrung out. Then dry with clean dry cloths. A chamois is even better. Allow a few minutes to dry before the application of a succeeding coat.

2—"Steel wool" may be used for smoothing an applied finish, for purposes later related, but should never be substituted for an abrasive paper in Between Coat sanding. Abrasive papers sand a surface smooth, by cutting down dust particles, etc., while steel wool rides over them to a certain extent.

3—When sanding a large surface, such as a table top, rub with the grain of the wood toward the ends first and then near the sides, taking extreme care not to sand the finish from the edges or the corners. Then sand the center section with the grain, using long strokes, with an even pressure. Never sand cross-grain or in circles.

4—Avoid cross-grain sanding on furniture parts made of several pieces of wood, with the grain running in different directions. For example, it is best to sand a furniture paneled door as follows:

A—First sand panel moldings, if any.

B—Then the panel, in straight lines, with the grain.

C—Then the top and bottom rails, protecting the side members of opposite grain, by holding a piece of stiff paper at the joint, to avoid scratches.

D—Finally sand the side members, protecting the top and bottom rails.

Important When finishing materials are applied for a "Polish Rubbed Finish," follow the same directions for dusting, washing, wiping, and drying the surfaces as related in Note 1. However, immediately before applying a succeeding coat, wipe the surfaces with a "Tack Rag" (see page 137) to remove every particle of lint or dust.

The method of handling finishing materials for a "Polish Rubbed Finish" is also done in a different manner than for less fine finishes and the room in which the work is done should be as free as possible from dust. (See "Strike Wire Can," page 136, and "Dustless Varnishing," page 136.)

HIGH GLOSS FINISH

It is usually preferred that furniture for use in the house be not finished to a high gloss. There are, however, many articles, such as porch and patio furniture, on which you may wish to have a smooth and glossy finish.

Very often a two coat job will suffice, but if a very smooth finish is desired, it may require three or more coats, and perhaps the surface should first be filled. (See "Paste Filler," page 117.)

The final coat of any High Gloss Finish should be smoothed to knock off raised particles, which have settled on it while drying. On extremely smooth surfaces, this can be done best by a very light rubbing with grade 360-A or finer waterproof finishing paper, dipped into lukewarm soapy water. The less smooth surfaces may be rubbed lightly with grade "000" steel wool. Neither should be used until the finish coat has dried completely. If the work is done with a "light hand" and not too much rubbing, it should improve the high gloss, rather than dull it.

SATIN RUBBED FINISH

This finish is the most preferred and used of all the degrees for a final finish. It is a "general purpose" finish which is most satisfactory, from the standpoint of wear and general appearance. It is adaptable to most types of wooden furniture and other wooden objects, and is recommended as a final finish for all Antique furniture, except for those pieces of fineness or quality of workmanship and period furniture, which have been smoothed with a "paste filler" and require a "Polish Rubbed Finish."

The soft, satiny sheen of this finish, which is gained by merely rubbing down a completely dried "High Gloss" finish of sufficient coats and smoothness, may be had on all the finishing materials which are applied in coats, and which dry to a high gloss. These include varnish, shellac, varnish-oil, penetrating wood sealers, blond, pickled, and lacquer finish.

Some workers leave the finish "as is," after it has been rubbed down to the satin sheen smoothness.

This finish is the easiest to accomplish, does not require a high degree of craftsmanship or too much exacting care in the application of the finishing material, looks and lasts well, and is suitable for virtually all woods. It should have *sufficient* coats of finishing material to bring the surface to a *high gloss.*

Final Coat Smoothing

1—Sand the final coat very lightly with 6/0 to 8/0 Wet-or-Dry finishing paper—lubricated with "water," for varnish and similar materials and with a "rubbing oil" for shellac. This is to remove dust particles, etc., that can only be smoothed by sanding.

2—Rub the surface (with the grain) with grade "000" Steel Wool, until the desired sheen has been obtained.

3—It is best and customary to wax this finish (two coats best). (See "Waxing," page 145.)

LATE SHERATON MAHOGANY BANQUET TABLE END

PLATE 17. Old varnish and heavy stain easily removed with 'commercial remover.' No repair necessary. Wood surface was well filled. Finished with 'satin rubbed' varnish finish.

Mahogany mirror frame rubbed with fine grade steel wool; finished with 'shellac and wax.'

Old lemon squeezer on table had been soaked with fruit oils; merely rubbed with fine grade steel wool.

POLISH RUBBED FINISH

This is the pinnacle or acme of all final finishes, except perhaps the "French Finish," now seldom used. The most sought for "Polish Rubbed Finish" is a soft gloss with a high luster. The degree of smoothness of this finish is in direct proportion to the care taken in the application and smoothing of a "paste filler" and the sanding between coats of the finishing material.

The most practical material to use for this finish is a high quality varnish. (See "Buying Varnish," page 124.) However, it may be accomplished with other finishing materials, including some penetrating sealers, lacquer, and shellac, if sufficient coats are applied (over a "paste filler") to secure a hard and smooth high gloss.

A "Polish Rubbed Finish" is seldom used on other than high quality Antique period furniture, or more recently made furniture of fine workmanship and design, made of choice hardwoods. It is customary that such furniture have this finish.

This finish is the most difficult to attain. It requires exacting work in rubbing with powdered abrasives, and the knowledge or judgment of just how far this work should go, for a desired degree of polish, which can only be obtained through strict obedience to directions and practice.

Suggestions for Good Work

There are several things of importance that are done by professionals which should be followed to accomplish good work. They are as follows:

1—**Pumice Stone** is used as the abrasive to rub a surface for a smooth and soft luster, after the final finish coat has been carefully sanded. The best grade for use is "FFF" (triple floated), which should be sifted through a fine cheese cloth into a clean container (small pie pan best), to remove lumps or foreign matter.

2—**Paraffin Oil** (readily purchased) is recommended as the lubricant to use with pumice stone for an oil rubbed finish. No. 10 motor oil, sewing machine oil, or a thin mineral oil may be used as a substitute. Many professionals prefer crude petroleum oil, but it is hard to remove.

3—**Rottenstone** (one grade only) is used for rubbing with water, for a high gloss finish, after a "pumice-oil" rub.

4—**Rubbing Pads** should be carefully inspected before use for glazed spots, grit, bits of steel wool, etc., which might scratch a rubbed surface. They are used with the "Pumice-Oil Rub," the "Pumice-Water Rub," and the "Rottenstone Rub." Rubbing pads used with oil may be scrubbed with a clean "Rubbing Brush" and white gasoline, while those used with water may be washed. (See "Rubbing Pad," page 139.)

5—**Dusting Brushes** used by professionals come in standard widths of ½″ and 1″, with the brush part about 6″ long and a handle extending from one end. They are also used for dusting benches and pieces worked upon. A scrub brush with soft bristles used for the hands will suffice.

6—**An Old Blanket** or padding laid under the piece or parts being

HEPPLEWHITE CHEST

PLATE 18. Removal of varnish stain with 'commercial remover' disclosed inlay in fine cherry. Surface was well filled; 'satin rubbed' varnish finish used. Partitions of plywood for flat silver installed over velvet in top drawer.

rubbed is a great help to avoid scratches. These should be covered with clean, old newspapers, to catch unavoidable splashes and drippings.

7—**Three or More Coats** of finishing material (depending upon kind used) are required for a quality finish. The final coat should have a *high gloss* and be very smooth.

Final Coat Sanding

Use the same method for sanding the final coat, as for a "Satin Rubbed Finish." You were previously given instructions for between-coat sanding. (See "Sanding Between Finish Coats," page 128.)

Rubbing Final Finish

A final polish may be obtained by rubbing the final sanded surface with either "pumice stone and water" or "pumice stone and oil." Expert finishers often have a preference, but sometimes both are used for a desired effect. The highlights of their advantages or shortcomings are briefly as follows:

Water Rubbing requires more skill, closer inspection, and better judgment. If any defect shows up, the surface can be easily cleaned, dried, and touched up or recoated. The work is faster and cleaner. It leaves a brighter gloss when oil polished as a final operation.

Oil Rubbing is best for use on a "shellac finish." The mixture of "oil and pumice" may be removed from a shellacked surface with soap and water, or gasoline, without injury to the finish. If all is not removed from a hard finish, like varnish, and it became necessary to touch up, or apply a new coat, the material would slow up in drying or not dry at all. "Oil rubbing" is best for a soft, satin sheen.

Rottenstone is used for final rubbing to attain a highly polished finish. This operation is not necessary with a WATER RUBBED finish when full directions are followed.

Equipment For Rubbed Polish

Pumice stone (FFF); rottenstone (occasionally used); rubbing pads (distinctive ones for "water rubbing" and "oil rubbing"); 2 flat containers, for abrasive powder and fluid (small pie pan good); paraffin oil (or substitute); white gasoline; 1″ wide rubbing brush; white cotton waste (better than rags for purpose); clean cloths; clean old newspapers, and water.

Water-Pumice Rubbing

1—Place some sifted pumice stone in a clean, shallow container. Dip a rubbing pad in water, and then in the powder, OR, sprinkle the powder evenly over the surface to be rubbed, and use a pad dipped in water only.

2—Rub the surface with the grain of the wood; use even pressure; take fairly long strokes; avoid a twisting or circular motion.

3—Start on an end of a surface (at a side), working next an adjoining space until the entire surface is covered, trying not to overlap the rubbing.

Then go over the entire surface again in the same manner, without the addition of more pumice stone.

4—Inspect the work by pulling the side of a thumb toward you, at a spot with a quick, snappy motion.

5—Continue the rubbing until the entire surface has an even sheen, without any highlights, or cutting through in any place. Add water to the rubbing pad, if necessary.

6—When you are satisfied that the surface has the degree of smoothness and sheen desired, wipe it off with damp cloths, and polish with a dry one.

7—Then inspect the surface by looking at it against the light. Should there be any dull spots remaining, rub them with the rubbing block, *without* using any more pumice stone.

Note 1—Pumice stone grinds finer and finer as it is rubbed. When it is desired to have a high gloss finish, no more pumice should be added to the original amount put on a surface. The addition of pumice stone during the operation results in a much duller sheen.

2—A soft and satiny sheen may be had by leaving the water-rubbing sludge on a surface. Then dip a pad of white cotton waste in water, squeeze it out, and dip it in a rubbing oil. Use this for rubbing the sludge, instead of a rubbing pad, working in lines with the grain, and occasionally making thumb tests.

Oil-Pumice Rubbing

1—Place a mixture of equal parts of paraffin oil (or crude oil) and white gasoline in a clean shallow pan. Put some sifted pumice stone into another pan. Dip a rubbing pad first into the liquid and then into the pumice.

2—Rub the surface, adding more of the liquid and pumice as necessary, following the same procedure as directed for "Water-Pumice Rubbing," to produce a soft, satin sheen.

3—Wash the surface off with lukewarm, soapy water, or with white gasoline, if necessary. A final cleaning with a cloth slightly dampened with "Carbon Tetrachloride" (non-burning cleaning fluid), will remove the last traces of oil. Then give the surface a final polish with a soft cloth (chamois better).

Note 1—A better sheen may be had by leaving the oil-pumice sludge on the surface, rubbing it with cotton waste dipped in a *rubbing oil* (instead of water), squeezing it out, and otherwise following the same directions as given in Note 2, in the directions for "Water-Pumice Rubbing."

2—Plan to let the final finish season and harden before polishing with oil and pumice stone.

Rottenstone Rubbing

A high polish may be attained by rubbing a surface with rottenstone, after the completion of a "Water-Pumice" or "Oil-Pumice" rubbing. Dip a clean rubbing pad, first into water and then into rottenstone. Rub carefully in one direction, as already directed. (A high gloss finish is not usually desired.)

Note Plan to leave a week between the completion of an "Oil-Pumice" rubbing, before rubbing with rottenstone. The finish will soften slightly with the oil rub and needs time to harden well. The effect is much better than following one after the other immediately.

Rubbing Turnings and Carvings

It is advisable to delay the finish rubbing of turnings, carvings, beads, moldings, etc., to avoid marking the slightly softened flat surfaces, already finished.

1—The work should be done with the same mixture (Water-Pumice or Oil-Pumice) that was used on the flat surfaces.

2—Dip a rubbing brush into water (or oil) and shake out the fluid a little. Then dip it into sifted pumice stone and rub carefully, without much pressure, into detailed surfaces and on turnings.

3—Rub the surfaces with thin rubbing pads, moistened with the medium used. The high portions of carvings, etc., may be carefully rubbed in any direction but turnings should only be rubbed lengthwise.

4—Wash off, as previously directed (according to the mixture used) and inspect for highlights. Rub these with the pumice already on the pad.

Strike Wire Can

Professional refinishers use a "strike wire" in a small can (or tin cup) when brushing varnish. Surplus varnish can be wiped from the brush after it has been dipped in the can, by "striking" (wiping) the brush on the wire, rather than against the side of the can.

A strike wire may be installed in a small can (or tin cup) by punching a hole in each of the opposite sides, just below the rim. A wire is then run through the holes, cut off about an inch from the outside of the can and the ends turned down. The holes should be spaced in such a way that the wire will be off center and closer to one side of the can than the other.

It is always good practice to varnish from a small can rather than from the container in which it was purchased. The greatest detriment to successful varnishing is dust particles (etc.) which must be avoided by every possible means. When the job is completed, any varnish left in the small can should be thrown away, as it may contain dust, or be damaged by exposure to the air.

The greater the pains taken when varnishing, the more success will be attained in the final finish.

Dustless Varnishing (For a "Polish Rubbed Finish")

A good varnish job requires that the room in which the work is done and the clothing worn be as dust-free as possible. For best results proceed as follows:

1—A work shop is, of necessity, a rather dusty place. Before applying varnish, it is a good plan first to sweep the floor thoroughly and then dust the shelves, tools, work bench, fixtures, etc. Allow the dust to settle and then mop the floor.

2—Do the work over spread clean newspapers.

3—Keep the piece being varnished in fresh air but not in a draft. A good circulation of air will help the drying. When through varnishing, do not leave the piece in a corner or along a side wall of a room where there is dead air, as the drying will be slower and wet varnish will pick up more dust.

Note The necessity of keeping a varnish job completely free from dust is not so important in other types of finish.

Tack Rag (For a "Polish Rubbed Finish")

A "tack rag" is used for the final wiping of a piece to be varnished. Dry brushing and wiping with a clean soft cloth will not remove all foreign particles and dust. A tack rag must be used for a smooth finish and will save much sanding and rubbing. These rags may usually be purchased in paint and automotive parts stores.

It is well to know how to make and keep a tack rag. Proceed as follows:

1—The best material for this purpose is a piece of finely woven cheesecloth about two feet square. This should be washed in several changes of tepid water and wrung out slightly to prevent drip. (The back panel of a man's shirt, hemmed to turn in raw edges, also makes a tack rag.)

2—Apply pure turpentine to the moistened cloth and shake it out loosely. Then sprinkle varnish freely over the cloth, fold all edges to the center and twist it into a tight roll to force out the water and flow the varnish and turpentine so as to saturate the cloth fibers. Refold the cloth and wring it as tight as possible. Then unfold the cloth, wave it in the air a few moments and refold it, being sure all raw edges are turned inward to avoid threads leaving it. Enough varnish should be used to make the cloth quite yellow. It should be sticky enough to pick up dust but dry enough so as not to deposit moisture.

3—A tack rag, when properly cared for, may be used almost indefinitely. It should never be allowed to dry out—even for a few minutes. It should occasionally be unfolded, sprinkled with a few drops of water and turpentine, refolded, and wrung out. Under this treatment a tack rag improves with age and is kept soft and flexible.

4—Store a tack rag in a mason jar, sealed tight with a rubber washer. Never store the rag in a metal container as the water in the rag will rust the metal. Always add some turpentine and water to the rag (as above outlined) before storing it. A tack rag left in the open air for some time becomes a fire hazard through spontaneous combustion.

"Picking" Varnish (For a "Polish Rubbed Finish")

A varnished surface should be "picked" free from dust and other foreign particles as soon as possible after the varnish is applied. No matter how much care has been taken to free the room (in which varnishing is done) from dust, and even though all the necessary precautions are strictly adhered to, it is impossible to avoid having foreign particles on a newly varnished surface.

"Picking" is best done with a "pick stick" which consists of a very thin wooden rod with a pear-shaped ball of "burnt" varnish on one end. As a substitute, a small artist's sable brush (No. 3 or 5 good) may be used for picking lint or dust.

A "pick stick" is used by touching a freshly varnished surface with the ball of burnt varnish and "lifting" the speck of dust, lint, etc., *upward* with the stick. Before using, tap the ball against your hand and the burnt varnish will become sticky.

An artist's brush is used by inserting the tip between the lips and withdrawing it, so as to have a fine point on the bristles. This point is used by *slipping* it under a particle, and lifting it out.

If this work is done when the varnish is fresh and before it has a chance to set, the varnish will immediately flow together over the spot, from which a particle was removed. When varnish has set, it is too late to remove specks, etc. Then allow the varnish to harden a bit and test the raised spot for hardness with the surface of a finger nail, as it might be an air bubble. All spots which have no give will have to be sanded or rubbed out when the varnish is thoroughly hard.

Foreign particles causes fresh varnish to pile up around them in a small mound by capillary attraction. The type of foreign matter may be recognized as follows:

1—*Dirt* will show as a dark speck.

2—*Bubbles* show a light colored top.

3—*Varnish specks* are soft and transparent granules. They may be removed by the rubbing operation.

4—*Lint* will show a crooked line. It may be removed or rubbed out later, if not too large.

Pick Sticks can be made as follows:

1—Swab sticks used by doctors and sold by drugstores are the best for this purpose.

2—Place 1 part of liquid varnish (less than a teaspoonful) and about 6 to 8 parts of dry brown varnish (crushed) in a small, clean tin can. Place this can in a larger one, filled about ¼ with water, and then heat.

3—Stir and cook until a drop of the melted mixture will form a stiff pill when cooled on glass and rolled between fingers.

4—Dip a stick end into the melted mixture and, with fingers, moistened with saliva, form a small pear-shaped ball.

5—For use, as directed above, tap the ball on the hand and, if the consistency and cooking is correct, the ball will become sticky.

6—It is a difficult problem to store pick sticks for future use. They may sometimes be softened by heat but, as they are easy to make, it is best to make fresh ones for each job.

RUBBING PAPERS, BLOCKS, AND PADS

"Abrasive Papers" of fine grade (grit) as used for rubbing and smoothing final finishes, should be cut and handled in a different manner than those used for sanding. (See "Abrasive Paper and Emery Cloth," page 172, for complete information and chart on types and grades.)

Preparing an abrasive paper for sanding may be done by cutting it to ¼ size and using it with a "Sanding Block," or it may be folded to ⅛th size for use alone. (See "Tearing and Folding Abrasive Papers," page 172, and "Sanding Blocks," page 177.)

When fine grade abrasive papers are used for rubbing and smoothing final finishes, they should not be folded too many times for, if folded in this manner, some of the edges may be thicker than others, causing greater pressure at that point. Some of this work may be well done with the paper *cut* to ¼ size (4½″ x 5½″) for use with a "Rubbing Block" on large surfaces, but for general use, a paper cut to ⅛th size (2¾″ x 4½″) and used with a smaller block is more popular.

A **"Rubbing Block"** is best made of flexible material, like sponge-rubber pad, a block (about ½″ thick) of hard "rubbing" felt, etc. This should be cut slightly narrower than the abrasive paper and placed over it for rubbing. Two types of rubbing blocks may be purchased. The first is of a size for a ⅛th cut of abrasive paper and is made of thin sheet metal, with an inverted "U" shaped grip and a padded rubber bottom. It is cheaply made but good. The second is made of an aluminum casting about 2″ x 6″, with springs holding a rubber padded bottom, and with a coil of abrasive paper attached, that may be drawn out as needed. Naturally, this tool is more expensive. Both may usually be purchased in paint and hardware stores.

A **"Rubbing Pad"** is used for the final smoothing or polishing of a finish, with the use of abrasive powders (pumice stone or rottenstone), and oil or water. Professional shops seem to prefer a block of hard rubbing felt about 1″ thick (of the type recommended for a "Rubbing Block"). One may be made of several layers of an old felt hat or several pieces of felt padding sewed together, of the kind that is used under rugs and carpets; or a blackboard eraser, even though it has a handle. (For uses of this tool, see "Polish Rubbed Finish," page 134.)

SHELLAC AND WAX FINISH

For many years the "Shellac and Wax" finish has, without a doubt, been the one most used and is the most popular of all finishes. The reason for its extensive use is the ease of application and satisfaction, from the standpoint of beauty.

This finish is perfect for chairs, settees, benches, desks, display racks, picture and mirror frames, clocks, etc. It is well not to use it on such items as tables, stands, chests, cabinets, bureaus, etc., on which there may be placed articles which are hot, contain water or alcoholic beverages, as shellac stains easily and white rings develop when wet glasses, vases, etc., are placed on it.

Almost any kind of wood may be finished with shellac, but it is most complimentary to pine and the lighter colored woods, particularly when white and orange shellacs are mixed to just the right shade to do justice to the wood involved, in which case it intensifies the wood colors.

The main reason why a shellac finish is so easy to apply is that in a correct mixture it is greatly thinned with alcohol. Many amateurs (and some professionals) attempt to hasten the work by applying shellac which is too thick. The result is a "botched" job, unsightly in appearance. Also, many people apply a succeeding coat before the previous one has dried thoroughly, fail to rub surfaces between coats, and often leave the last coat glossy, instead of removing the shine and applying wax.

General Information

1—**Shellac** should be the best grade. The so-called "4 lb. cut" is best for general use (4 lbs. of shellac to 1 gallon of alcohol). This cut must always be thinned further for all uses. The best shellacs come in either white (clear) or orange (really orange brown). Cheap orange shellacs are orange or red (or a blend) and should never be used. When shellac becomes sticky and will not dry, it is either too old for use or has been thinned with an inferior grade of alcohol. (See "Shellac," page 170.)

2—**Only Denatured Alcohol,** of the pure type, should be used to "cut" (thin) shellac. The type which is used in car radiators contains kerosene and causes shellac to become gummy. (See "Alcohol," page 170.)

3—**Corn Starch** may be used in the mixture as a filler for pieces to which a "Paste Filler" has not been applied. The corn starch does not completely fill a surface, as does a paste filler, but it will aid in filling the pores. Corn starch added to thinned shellac gives a milky effect, but this will disappear when applied. The mixture must be agitated while it is being used to keep the corn starch from settling to the bottom of the container. Use about 2 heaping tablespoonfuls of corn starch to a quart of the mixture.

4—**Orange Shellac is Added to White Shellac** for color. Add a very small amount of orange to white shellac to enrich the shade and bring out the highlights of the wood color. Use white shellac for "Blond" and light finishes.

5—**A Pint Mason Jar** is a perfect container for a shellac mixture. Most mixtures may be made by eye rather than by actual measurement. First pour in the white shellac, and, if color is desired, add orange shellac. Then add the alcohol. Seal the top and mix by rotating the jar, rather than shaking it, as shaking will cause bubbles to form.

GROUP OF SMALL ANTIQUES REFINISHED

PLATE 19. Greatly improved appearance of various small and attractive articles can be obtained by refinishing them. Follow methods appropriate for the materials from which they are constructed.

However, when corn starch is to be added, first pour some alcohol into a separate container, add the corn starch, mix it, and then pour it into the shellac. Then add the balance of the alcohol.

6—**Brushing Shellac.** Use a good quality 2″ wide brush and keep it for that purpose only. (See "Selection of Brushes" and "Brushes for Single Purpose Use," page 205.)

Take a rather long stroke with the grain of the wood and carry the brush back over once to pick up sags and runs, using the tip of the brush only. It is a good plan to shellac edges first, then the surface. Work around turnings first, then stroke lengthwise.

ODD-SHAPED MAPLE CHAIRS

PLATE 20. Chair on left had been newly recanned and had little finish; smoothed with fine steel wool. Chair on right was painted brown, in flaked condition; finish removed easily with scraper; seat of heavy cord stiffened by many coats of greatly thinned white shellac. Both finished with 'shellac and wax.' Each cost $7.00 in Maine (back country).

Replace the lid loosely on the mason jar, after each time the brush has been dipped into it, so as to keep the alcohol from unnecessary evaporation. When there is to be some delay between coats, or the jar is to be stored away, wipe the threads in the cover and on the jar carefully with a cloth dampened with alcohol, so that the cover will not stick when tightened.

7—**Wash the Brush in Alcohol** before it has had a chance to dry. (See "Cleaning Brushes," page 206.)

Satin Rubbed Finish

This finish is ideal for most furniture or other wood articles. It is perfect for the cruder type of furniture and pieces made of pine and other light colored woods on which it is advisable to use a little orange shellac in the mixture for added color.

Equipment

A mixture of 60% shellac (4 pound cut) and 40% pure denatured

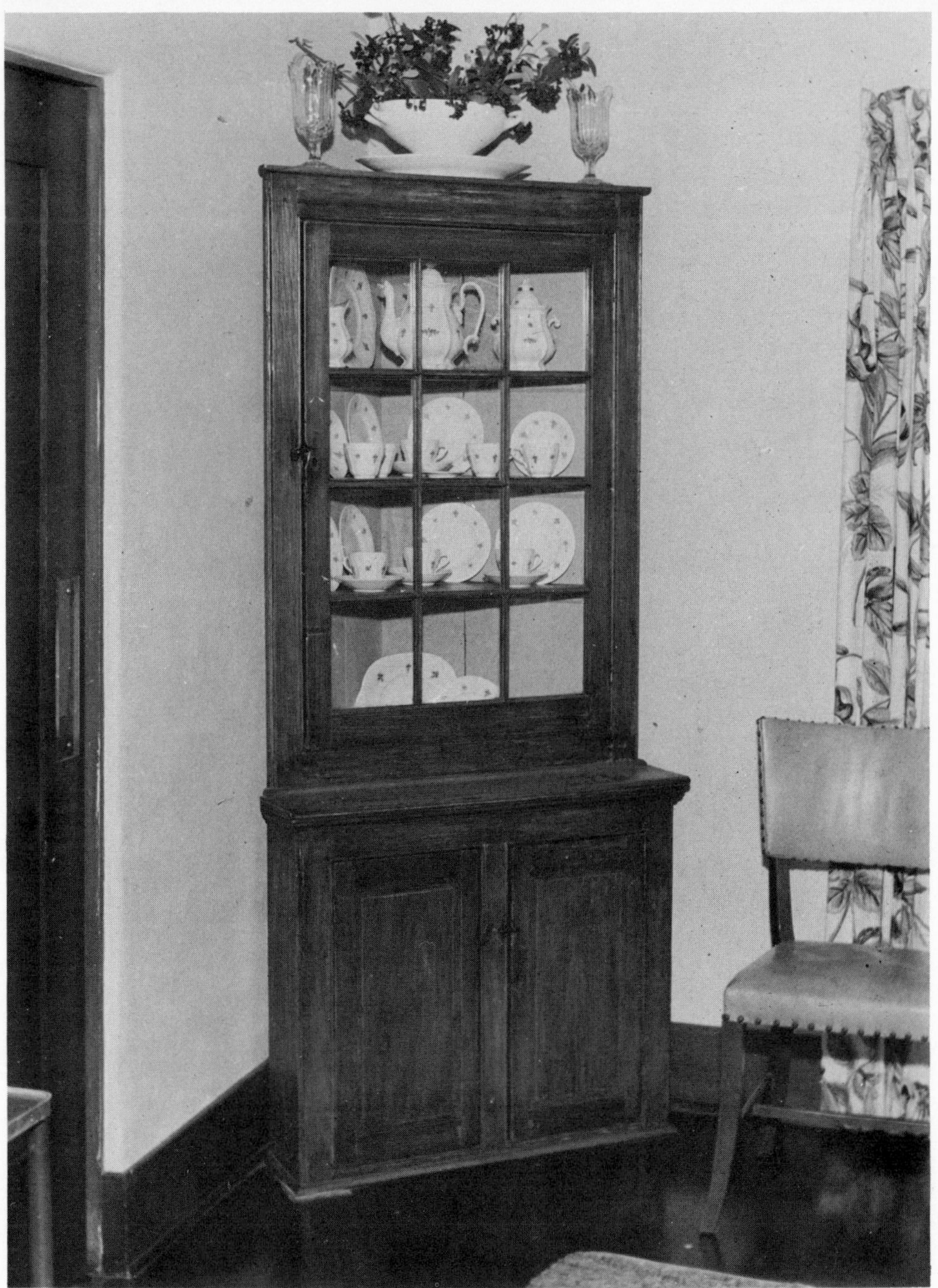

PINE CORNER CUPBOARD

PLATE 21. Cream paint over brown and shellac were easily removed with a 'commercial remover'; refinished with 'shellac and wax'; inside background of water paint (wiped off to give appearance of age). Grooves were cut near back of shelves for plates to stand in. Two missing glasses replaced with old hand-cast glass.

alcohol; a fairly stiff 2″ wide brush; grade 7/0 or 8/0 Garnet finishing paper (open coat preferred); grade "00" or "000"' steel wool pads; a soft dusting brush and cloths.

Method

1—Apply enough coats (usually 4 or more) of the shellac mixture so that the last one shines. Allow time for each coat to dry thoroughly (the first will dry much faster than the later ones). Test for dryness by trying to make a thumb print.

2—Rub the surface (with the grain) between coats, using the *abrasive paper*, whenever roughness is felt with the finger tips. Dust with a brush and wipe the surface with a cloth after each coat.

3—Allow several hours for the last coat to dry completely (overnight preferred) and then rub it with the *steel wool* until there is absolutely *no* shine remaining.

4—Dust and wipe off the surface. Then apply at least two coats of wax. (See "Waxing," page 145.)

Note 1—It is important to shake the shellac dust from the pads of steel wool and refold them, as steel wool becomes dull with use. Too much rubbing in one spot causes heat from friction, softens the finish, and tends to roll it up. Use great care at corners and edges, so as not to cut through the finish.

2—When there still remains many minute bright spots on a surface, after the gloss has been removed by rubbing it with steel wool, sprinkle the surface with dry "FFF" (triple floated) pumice stone and brush it lightly. Use a small hand scrub brush with soft bristles, on flat surfaces, and an old shaving brush (held by the bristles) on carvings, angles, etc. When the spots have disappeared, again give the entire surface a light rubbing with steel wool.

Polish Rubbed Finish

This finish is for high grade furniture and that type which calls for extreme smoothness and high polish. Surfaces should be completely smoothed with a "paste filler" before this finish is applied. (See "Paste Fillers," page 117.) Add orange shellac to white shellac for additional beauty, especially on dark colored woods, as has already been described. No corn starch should be used in the mixture.

Equipment

A mixture of 50% white shellac (part orange shellac if preferred) and 50% pure denatured alcohol; a fairly stiff 2″ wide brush; worn 7/0 or 8/0 Garnet finishing paper (open coat preferred) or grade 360-A wet-or-dry finishing paper; a mixture of 50% raw linseed oil and 50% pure turpentine; grade "FFF" (triple floated) pumice stone; grade "000" steel wool; a rubbing pad; lintless cloths.

Method

1—Apply enough coats (usually 8 or more) of the shellac mixture or until the last coat shines. Allow each coat to dry thoroughly. Test for dryness by trying to make a thumb print.

2—Rub the surface (with the grain) between coats, using the abrasive paper dipped in the linseed oil mixture, whenever the slightest roughness is felt with the finger tips after the first few coats. When you can notice the finish beginning to build up towards the final coat (or to shine), rub the surface between each coat.

3—After each rubbing with the linseed oil mixture, wipe the surface clean with rags and allow a few hours for it to dry completely.

4—When the last coat shines, first rub the surface (with the grain) with grade "000" steel wool dipped in the linseed oil mixture, taking only a few strokes and gradually working across the area, until you believe the entire surface is completely dulled. Then sprinkle the surface with dry pumice stone, dip the rubbing pad in the oil mixture, and rub the surface lengthwise (with the grain) taking long, even strokes, until the entire surface is polished. Wipe off and examine for shiny spots. These should be rubbed without addition of more pumice. When the entire surface has been completed, wipe it off with soft rags and allow to dry completely.

5—Apply at least two coats of wax. (See "Waxing," below.)

Note 1—Rub carvings and moldings lightly with a small hand scrub brush with soft bristles, dipped first in the oil and then in the pumice. Turnings may first be rubbed with the steel wool dipped in the oil mixture and then with the rubbing pad (if flexible) or with a cloth, dipped in the oil mixture and then the pumice.

2—When a high polished finish is desired, it may be obtained by a final rubbing with "rottenstone" and the oil mixture after the surface has been completely cleaned, following the use of the pumice.

WAXING

A thin film of polished wax over all final finishes (except the varnish "Polish Rubbed"), is applied by most finishers, and desired in most homes, yet there are some who never use it or desire it. Many such people depend upon furniture polish, which may be a detriment to a finish. Waxing gives a soft pleasing luster and, if it is renewed before the underlying coat is harmed, the finish will last indefinitely.

Waxing is neither difficult nor involved. However, if it is not properly done, especially on a surface that is not completely smooth, or over dark woods, light yellow waxes may sometimes show white in cracks and pores. In such cases, it is best to use a brown wax.

Never use anything but a *paste* wax on furniture or other wood articles. Those commonly available in grocery stores are satisfactory, but there are carnauba-type waxes obtainable. These may usually be bought in furniture, hardware, or paint stores. Some waxes come in yellow only, while others are colored brown, reddish brown and red, to blend with different woods.

Under *no circumstances* should any type of wax be applied to bare wood. Wax should always be applied over some kind of finishing material. Most professional shops will not accept a piece for refinishing if wax has been applied to bare wood. Grime works into it and it is almost impossible to remove the wax if you wish to refinish the piece.

For good results, directions are as follows:

Equipment

Paste wax; a piece of heavy linen or closely woven cloth about 10″ square for applying the wax; a dusting brush and cloth; a brush with reasonably soft bristles (shoe brush good); a soft cloth (cotton flannel good) for primary polishing; and a very tightly woven or hard cloth such as a clean grain bag (old worsted from legs of man's pants good) for final polishing.

Method

1—Remove dust deposited from air and that left after smoothing the piece with an abrasive. Use a dusting brush and then a dusting cloth.

2—Lay the 10″ square cloth flat and place in its center about two heaping tablespoons of paste wax. Fold the cloth over the wax into a pad. Rub the entire surface of the piece with a circular motion with the pad, thus leaving thereon a thin coat of wax.

3—Allow time for the wax to dry as per directions on container.

4—Then brush all surfaces briskly with the soft bristle brush; then rub thoroughly with the soft cloth and finally with the hard cloth. The brushing aids in removing any surplus wax from the pores and grooves in a surface. A thorough rubbing with the soft cloth removes surplus wax and smooths it out, while a brisk rubbing under pressure with the hard cloth polishes the wax.

5—Follow the same directions and apply at least two coats. Three coats are often required for best results.

Note 1—Under no circumstances "pile up" the wax by applying too much, for then it is next to impossible to brush or rub it out to a smooth, satin finish. The application through the close grained cloth prevents lumps of wax from being applied.

2—For final test attempt to make a "thumb print." If any can be seen, the surface should be rubbed again briskly with the hard cloth until none is visible. This rubbing creates friction and tends to heat the wax, causing the polish desired. Each surface should have an equal luster with no dull spots.

3—A surface thus finished may be brightened from time to time by rubbing with the soft cloth, and then a hard one, without the addition of new wax.

4—Store the polishing brush and cloths for future use in a clean covered container (shoe box good). Do not wash them until they become grimy or contain too much wax; then use gasoline.

5—Store the wax pad in the container on top of the remaining wax, with the top securely tightened.

6—Should you have applied too much wax through the pad or when using a type of paste wax which dries extremely hard, it is well to brush it immediately after application, instead of after it dries.

7—Should none of the especially prepared waxes for furniture be available and it is desired to use a brown wax, it can be made as follows:

Place the contents of a one pound can of yellow paste floor wax on a smooth board and work into it (with a putty knife or spatula) about ¾ teaspoonful of powdered burnt umber.

VARNISH AND OIL FINISH

It is my belief that this is the best of all mixtures of commonly used materials for a "Satin Rubbed and Waxed" finish. It is a finish which will give excellent and lasting results, is applied with a rag very easily and requires little labor. When quality materials are used according to directions, and sufficient time is allowed between coats, the result is always successful. Yet, for some strange reason, this finish is little known.

The addition of varnish to boiled linseed oil and turpentine fills the wood pores and causes the mixture to dry quickly. It is especially well adapted to open-grained woods, such as walnut, mahogany, oak, and chestnut, but may be used with equal success on close-grained woods as well.

The varnish and oil finish will lessen the risk of damage from heat, water, alcohol, and many acids. The degree of proof depends upon the quality and kind of materials used, sufficient coverage of the surface, and the preparation of the surface with a "sealer coat."

If an extremely smooth finish is desired, the mixture may be used over a "paste filler" for a "Satin Rubbed Finish," but it should not be considered as a substitute for varnish in a "Polish Rubbed Finish." (See "Paste Fillers," page 117.)

Equipment

"Spar" varnish (best grade), pure boiled linseed oil, pure turpentine, and a container (pint mason jar good); soft rags without lint; grades "00" and "000" steel wool; worn or new 7/0 or 8/0 Garnet finishing paper and soapy water, if needed for final rubbing.

Method

1—Apply with a small rag a "Sealer Coat" of 50% spar varnish and 50% pure turpentine. Allow to dry thoroughly and lightly smooth the surface with worn abrasive paper.

PEMBROKE-CHERRY TABLE

PLATE 22. Meager old finish lightly sanded; smoothed with fine grade steel wool. Wood surface was well filled. Finished with 'varnish and oil' and waxed.

2—Mix in a container, 25% spar varnish, 25% boiled linseed oil, and 50% turpentine. Apply generously with a small rag, rubbing for several minutes over one surface at a time until the turpentine has had a chance to evaporate some, but stop before the mixture becomes sticky. Then wipe the surface thoroughly with a clean and dust-free rag. Continue with other surfaces. (After dipping the rag in the mixture, always replace the top of the container loosely so as to prevent the turpentine from needless evaporation.) When the whole piece has been covered, wipe off the threads on the container and its top with a cloth dipped in turpentine, place the rag in the remaining mixture and seal the top tightly.

3—Set the piece away to dry in a room where there is good circulation of air and as free from floating dust as possible. Should weather permit, set it out-of-doors and in the sunlight. Allow the piece to dry until you can no longer detect an odor of turpentine, with the nose held close to the surface. (This usually requires 48 hours.)

4—Rub the surface with grade "00" steel wool until it is smooth and

SCHOOLMASTER'S DESK

PLATE 23. Old, checked coat of shellac and heavy stain removed with 'commercial remover.' No repair; legs tightened. Finished with 'varnish and oil' and waxed.

free from small lumps caused by dust particles. (Sometimes it is necessary to use grade "7/0" or "8/0" Garnet finishing paper for this purpose.)

5—Repeat operations 2, 3, and 4, until three or more coats have been applied. After the last coat, rub the surface with grade "000" steel wool (instead of grade "00," as above), or, for still greater smoothness, rub the surface with worn "8/0" Garnet finishing paper (open-coat preferred) dipped in lukewarm water.

6—Wax the piece. (See "Waxing," page 145.)

PENETRATING WOOD-SEALER FINISH

In recent years new types of materials have been developed that are destined to become most popular for refinishing furniture. These are the penetrating type of wood-sealers, thus far experimented with but by a few professional or experienced amateur refinishers.

Most penetrating wood-sealers have been primarily developed for use on floors, though they have been extensively used on panel work. They are easy to apply (with rag or brush), penetrate deeply into the wood, seal the pores, and give a lustrous long-lived finish. They dry quickly, most of the types do not collect dust (as does varnish when drying), do not scratch easily, are for the most part proof against heat, alcohol, stains, and acids, may be used on new or old woods (when all the old finish has been removed), and come clear or contain stains in popular shades (maple, oak, walnut, mahogany, etc.).

Practically all the leading and nationally known paint and varnish manufacturers make some type of a penetrating wood-sealer. Thus far very few of them seem to realize the extent of market there is in the refinishing field, for there is but little literature available advising how to use these products on furniture.

When inquiring for this material at a paint store, it is best to ask for a floor sealer and literature. You will find that many of the names of various products, and "coined" ones for Trade Mark purposes, contain the word "seal" or part or all of the word "penetrate"; others include the word "floor" or "wood." Most of the sales people have not yet been trained to explain that some of these products may be used for furniture.

The available literature on these products generally states that they are made from a base of synthetic resin or tung oil (obtained from the tung trees in China but grown in some Southern States, and valuable for quick drying, penetration, and hardness). Some of the mixtures contain varnish; others plastics. Read the label and literature and ask the sales person for the best type for your use. Buy a heavy type for open-pored wood.

Sealer finishes are of two general types: those that contain wax and those that do not. For furniture, it is preferable to use those which are free from wax and contain varnish, to bring the surface to a high gloss, which is then rubbed down for a "Satin Rubbed" or a "Polish Rubbed" finish.

The mixtures containing wax harden to a soft luster and, if enough coats are applied properly (by smoothing between them), they are ideal and give a lastingly satisfactory finish on most furniture. They may be applied with a rag and completed with little effort. It is recommended that a hard waterproof wax be applied over most of the penetrating wood-sealer type of finishes.

The types of penetrating sealers that contain wax result in a soft sheen which is pleasing on simple Early American pieces requiring a rich mellowness rather than a high gloss. The types that dry to a high gloss are especially fine for a finish with a high degree of luster, on such pieces as mahogany Empire style and most modern pieces.

Special attention should be paid to the plastic type of clear finishing materials that are now being experimented with to a great degree, but as yet seem to be for limited use. Some types dry quickly to an extremely hard elastic finish, which completely seals an object, making it impervious to water, alcohol, most acids, etc.

There seems to be no doubt but that there will soon be a great number of various types of penetrating wood-sealer and plastic finishes on the market, available in small containers, with complete and comprehensive instructions, which may have been prepared especially for use on furniture and other items. It is believed that these materials will take the place of those which have been used in the past for both new and refinishing work. It is well to make periodical inquires from paint dealers, to keep posted on new developments.

Only a limited number of these new finishing materials were experimented with in my shop before the completion of this book. There may be a great many more on the market before it is published.

Follow the instructions on the containers for using these new types of finishes. Brief general instructions, with a few angles discovered by experimenting with them, which may not be mentioned on the containers, are as follows:

For Satin Rubbed Finish

For wax type materials, apply with a rag, rubbing it well into the surface. If the material soaks into the wood at once, apply more until the wood has taken all that it can at a time. Wipe off any surplus before it sets. Allow to dry completely, sand, wipe clean, and continue applying coats until a satisfactory sheen is obtained. When dry, smooth with abrasive paper, then steel wool (both fine grades), wax and polish.

For Polish Rubbed Finish

The surface must be sealed with a proper material and a "paste filler" used. When a material is mentioned for a sealer coat, thin the paste filler with equal portions of the filler and turpentine, apply, allow to "flatten," wipe off, dry, and smooth with an abrasive paper. Then apply two or more coats of a varnish type material with a brush and finish by smoothing with wet-or-dry abrasive paper, then polishing with pumice stone (both wet with water), following the same directions as used with varnish. (See "Polish Rubbed Finish," page 132.)

Note For both above finishes, it is best that the work be done in dry weather and in a warm room. When desired, the woods may be stained prior to the application of the finish, or finishes may be used which contain stains.

BLOND FINISH

The Blond finish, for stream-lined furniture, is in vogue at this time and extensively used in the recently developed modern design homes. The finish is acquired by using a strong bleach to greatly lighten the color of the wood and then a clear suitable finish is applied.

This finish is not recommended for most old woods, as the bleach is injurious to the wood fibers and it removes the natural wood colors. It is more successful on relatively new, light-colored, close-grained hardwoods, and is popular for the transformation of the so-called "Mission" type of furniture (mostly of oak) which had a semi-modern design.

The finish is very popular for use on "Nude" (unfinished) furniture of modern or stream-line design. (For details, see Chapter 7.)

Equipment

A very strong bleach is required to lighten the wood greatly. A type may be purchased in many paint stores and which comes in bottles marked No. 1 and No. 2. (This is the best kind to use.) Rubber gloves, goggles, and old clothes should be worn; bleach applied with a long-handled, cotton dish mop; a large scrub brush for washing; varnish or a suitable finish material.

Method

1—Apply the bleach as directed on the bottles until desired color is obtained. Wash off with water from a hose while scrubbing with a brush. Allow to dry for at least 48 hours. Smooth with a fine abrasive paper.

2—Varnish is the best all-purpose finish. If available, use a new type of varnish that dries as clear as water, as all regular varnishes have a slight yellowish cast. (See "Varnish Finish," page 124.)

Note 1—Use great precaution when applying bleaching materials not to get it on the skin or in the eyes.

2—Never use the "Varnish-Oil Finish" after a bleach as the oil in the mixture will darken the wood.

3—Should the bottled bleaches not be available, other types may be used. (See "Bleaching," page 94.)

PICKLED FINISH

The pickled finish is a very pleasing effect for renewing tables, chairs, dressers, etc., especially those built in a "heavy" manner, like the "Mission" type of furniture. The pickle effect may be properly obtained only on open-grained woods, like oak and chestnut, by rubbing white lead or white paint into the grain after the wood has been bleached. Much of the fad for this finish has for the present passed in favor of the "Blond Finish," but its popularity may be revived at any time.

Equipment

Bleaches, etc., the same as for the blond finish. (See "Blond Finish," preceding.) Also needed is a thick white paint, or make a thin paste of equal parts of boiled linseed oil and turpentine (in small quantity) with enough white lead to thicken it; cloths for wiping; grade "0" steel wool; varnish or other suitable finish material.

Method

1—Bleach the piece, dry, and smooth, as directed for the "Blond Finish."

2—Apply a suitable "Sealer Coat," of a type used after stains, dry, smooth with fine steel wool, and brush off. (See "Sealer Coat After Stains," page 116.)

3—Apply either the white paint or white lead mixture to the surface with a rag and rub it crosswise into the grain of the wood. For doing this work, fold a piece of closely woven cloth (about a foot square) into a pad, dip it into the paint (or mixture) and wipe off all surplus material on the side of the container, so that it will be evenly and thinly spread on the pad surface. Then apply it sparingly, as only enough white is required to fill the grain.

4—Allow the white paint (or mixture) to dry. Then rub the surface crosswise to the grain with the steel wool until all the white has been removed from the surface, except that which remains in the wood pores and grain.

5—Apply a suitable finish. (See Step 2 under "Method" in the "Blond Finish." Also, follow the same "Notes.")

LACQUER FINISH

Practically all new factory made furniture offered for sale today is finished in lacquer, which is applied with a spray gun. When the finish is "polish finished," the polishing is done with power tools.

Lacquer is a most satisfactory finish, from the standpoint of mass production, as it dries very quickly; faster than any other product. Thus it speeds up production on the assembly line. Lacquer gives a fine coverage, and one thin coat may be sprayed over another, usually without the necessity of smoothing by rubbing between coats. The work is done in a spray-booth or room, free from dust and fumes, where exhaust fans expel the contaminated air. High grade furniture, which is finished in a polish, is covered with many coats of high gloss lacquer, and then polished. Practically all cheap furniture, finished in clear or with a stain mixed in lacquer, has only a few coats which dry to a smooth and soft luster without waxing.

A properly applied lacquer finish is also satisfactory from the standpoint of the furniture buyer. The finish is hard, without being too brittle; it has fine wearing qualities but is subject to scratches; it is generally proof (depending on the quality and type of material used) against water, alcohol, most acid stains, and heat; it polishes and has a fine appearance.

However, lacquer is scorned, from the standpoint of its use on Antique furniture, both by dealers and professional refinishers of good repute. It cannot and does not give the soft, satin sheen produced by the other types of finish, commonly acceptable and used for the refinishing of Antiques made of wood.

Should you be interested in using lacquer, the materials to purchase and method of use, are as follows:

Materials

Purchase materials which are made by a well known manufacturer. If you have a spray gun with compressed air, use a spraying lacquer. Brushing lacquers can be purchased, should be applied with a typical varnish brush, but are difficult to put on correctly. Both types require a special "filler" coat, and usually both types of finish material come in a gloss, flat, or semi-gloss (equal parts of gloss and flat). When stains are applied before the lacquer, acid or water stains should be used. Spirit stains are soluble in the lacquer solvent (a special type), that must be used for thinning lacquer, cleaning spray guns, and washing brushes. There are many makes of good lacquer on the market.

Satin Rubbed Finish (Brushed)

1—Apply a clear "filler coat" over a clean surface and sand after 30 minutes to an hour. (Should a separate stain be used, it should be applied, dried, and sanded prior to the sealer coat.)

2—Apply two coats of lacquer in one day. Allow to dry overnight, sand, and apply a third coat. If gloss lacquer is used, and a "satin finish" is desired, remove the gloss by rubbing with grade "00" or "000" steel wool, and then wax. If flat or semi-gloss lacquer is used, it may be left as it is and should be smooth if the second undercoat was sanded. (A lacquer containing stain may be applied, if desired.)

Polish Rubbed Finish (Brushed)

1—The surface must be smoothed with a "paste filler" for this finish. (See "Paste Fillers," page 117.)

2—Follow directions No. 1 above, regarding application of a "filler coat" and separate stain.

3—Apply only clear gloss lacquer (or that containing a stain) for the final coats. Enough coats should be applied to secure a high gloss. However, if there is the slightest roughness felt with the fingertips when a coat has dried, it should be smoothed with a fine abrasive paper dipped in soapy, lukewarm water. The final coat must be rubbed with pumice stone and water, after it has dried over night, and polished (if desired) with rottenstone and water, using the same directions as for varnish. (See "Polish Rubbed Finish," page 132.)

Note 1—Lacquer is the most volatile of all finishing materials. Working with it should be done in front of a spray-booth or in a thoroughly ventilated room in which there is no fire or smoking.

2—Professional refinishers often use a "shellac mixing lacquer" and "shellac" reduced with denatured alcohol for refinishing recently made furniture. This mixture helps to keep water spots off furniture that are so easy to get when finished in shellac only.

A mixture used often is as follows:

1 part pure white shellac; 4 lb. cut. (Part orange shellac if desired.)
4 parts denatured alcohol.

Mix and add to—

4 parts shellac mixing lacquer.

OIL FINISH

An oil finish is one of the oldest and most satisfactory of all finishes on hard or close-grained woods, if you have the time, patience, and willingness to do an endless amount of rubbing. It produces a rich color that is considered by many to be the most beautiful of all finishes. It is particularly good for tables and furniture which may be easily spotted or scratched. When this finish is properly applied, the wood is impervious to water, heat, scratches, and most stains. Furniture may be used during the process of finishing (which may take months or even a year to complete). The finish requires no waxing, when sufficiently oiled and rubbed. It should not be applied to carved woods, as it is difficult to develop into a polish and keep clean.

Equipment

A mixture of ⅔ boiled linseed oil and ⅓ pure turpentine; a small rag for application; soft rags without lint; hard grained polishing cloths (linen grain bag or closely woven hard cloth from men's old suits good).

Method

1—The wood must be free from any old finish, repaired, sanded, and dusted.

2—Apply the mixture (hot or cold) generously with a rag and rub into a limited surface for 10 to 20 minutes. A hot mixture penetrates more quickly but produces a darker color. It should never be applied hot to carvings or grooved parts as it sets too quickly. (When applied hot, the mixture should be heated in a double boiler, to prevent danger of ignition.)

3—Wipe off all excess oil with the soft lintless cloths, taking care to get it out of all crevices or carvings, as excess oil becomes sticky or hardens quickly. It must then be removed with alcohol or a commercial paint and varnish remover.

4—Rub each surface vigorously (one area at a time) with a hard polishing cloth for 10 to 20 minutes. This rubbing with a hard cloth develops heat by friction and is essential in bringing out a luster.

5—From 5 to about 20 coats of the oil mixture are applied as directed above. The process is repeated until no dull spots remain. It should also be repeated once or twice a year to keep the furniture in good shape. Allow at least two days between the first two coats (in warm weather), and from a week to a month between later coats. Each coat must be dried before another is applied. If it is not dried out, the following coat will become sticky. Test a surface by holding a hand on it for several minutes. If the surface is then oily, it is not dry enough for the next coat.

Note 1—For quicker results than the application of a great number of coats, complete the work with "Varnish and Oil Finish." (See page 147.)

2—Should the grain of the wood be raised by the oil mixture, it may be smoothed by rubbing with Grade "00" or "000" steel wool.

3—To prevent warping of surfaces, apply several coats of the oil mixture to the underside of the wood, during the process.

4—It must always be remembered that oiled rags are easily combustible. To prevent fire, they should be burned or washed soon after being used. Should there be any delay, spread them out flat or hang them on a line. If left too long they will harden.

5—The oil finish does not look well on cherry and it should not be used on walnut as it will turn the wood black.

6—Place the rag (that was used for applying this mixture) for storage in the container with any unused portion of the mixture.

FRENCH FINISH

The French Finish dates back at least three centuries and is the finest finish known and probably the most beautiful of all. This finish is acquired with shellac and raw linseed oil, building up coat after coat. The work is painstaking and tedious. It requires time, patience, and skill. You are given but a brief outline of how the work is done, from the standpoint of knowledge, rather than for practical use, as most refinishers look up to this finish with high regard. It is sometimes called the "Lost Art" of finishes.

The finish must be applied to woods which are extremely smooth, whether or not they are filled, and over a water stain.

Shellac is thinned with alcohol to the consistency of water and applied with an old silk stocking made into a ball, squeezing out a little of the material at a time.

The pad is dipped in the shellac solution and applied with straight strokes. As soon as dry, continue to apply more coats until a sheen or gloss is acquired. If cracks appear on the surface, sprinkle on a little pumice stone and apply more coats of the shellac until the cracks are filled.

Allow time for the surface to dry completely. Then put only a few drops of raw linseed oil on the pad, and rub with a circular motion over the entire area, adding a few more drops of the oil, as needed. When a high polish is seen, add no more oil, but continue rubbing until the surface is thoroughly dry. Allow to stand over night, and repeat the rubbing with the oil.

This hard and rugged process will give a high polish. (It cannot be had by rubbing a surface with so-called "French Polish".)

CHAPTER
6

REVIVING OLD FINISHES

Amateur refinishers often assume that an old finish must be completely removed and a new one applied. The condemnation of the old finish often results from jumping to conclusions too quickly after a casual inspection, but such condemnation results more often from inexperience and the lack of knowledge that the existing finish can be revived. (For additional information, see the beginning of Chapter 3 on "Removing Old Finish.")

Old finishes often become dull and drab in appearance merely from an accumulation of dirt and grime from long usage. Both shellac and varnish finishes will take on a milky effect from dampness while varnish will "check" or "alligator" where the atmosphere is too dry. Under normal conditions, this could have been avoided if the furniture had had the proper care. (See Chapter 14 on "Care of Furniture.")

The finish on furniture is subject to scratches and marks from carelessness or accident. It may become stained by acid and ink, or may have white spots or rings left by hot dishes, water, or alcohol.

Methods and materials to be used for reviving the entire finish, or for spot work, are described in this chapter. The effort to revive an old finish is well worth a trial. Should it not be a success, little time and material will have been wasted. The old finish may then be removed and a new one applied.

Commercial Products

There are a number of products made for reviving old finishes. These are often sold in grocery, hardware, and paint stores, but it may be best to inquire at a furniture store for special types of products.

Most of the commercial products are for general cleaning of dulled surfaces. When this work is completed, as directed on the container, the piece should be finished with a good furniture polish or waxed.

Some products will do a much better job than others in the complete elimination of foggy, cloudy, milky, or faded conditions, while others will usually remove white spots or rings, etc.

No harm will be done to a finish which is basically in good condition, by the use of a good commercial product made for the purpose, providing it is used correctly. It should be tried on a small space to see how it works.

In the balance of this chapter are given treatments for various ailments on finished surfaces, and in some cases special products are recommended.

Reviving a Clear Finish

The condition of an old clear finish may often be such that it can be revived satisfactorily with a single coat of the same kind of finishing material which was originally used.

Any wax should be removed (see "Removing Wax," below). If none was used, the piece should be washed with a solution in the proportions of 2 heaping tablespoonsful of "sal soda" to 1 gallon of hot water to remove traces of grease, etc. Rinse with clear water, wipe with clean dry cloths, and allow to thoroughly dry. On veneered pieces, use the solution sparingly, wash, rinse, and dry each surface independently and quickly, so as not to loosen the veneer.

When the piece is dry, sand it lightly (for the new material to have a "tooth"), apply the finish material and allow it to dry. Then complete the finish to the smoothness desired (as directed in Chapter 5) for the type of finishing material used. (Should the type of finishing material on the piece not be known, see "Determining Type of Old Finish," page 79.)

Washing Soiled Furniture

Method One—Commonly used for mild cleaning.

Wash the piece thoroughly with a soft clean rag and warm water to which a small amount of pure white soap has been added (Lux or Ivory good). Wipe dry with clean cloths.

Method Two—For badly soiled pieces. Especially suitable for varnish finishes.

Wash the piece with a mixture of 1 quart of hot water, 3 tablespoons of boiled linseed oil, and 1 tablespoon of turpentine. (Turpentine aids in cutting dirt; oil lubricates, feeds, and polishes.) Use an old double boiler to keep the mixture hot, as it is inflammable. Rub the wood with a soft cloth which has been wet with the solution and then polish with a soft dry cloth. Repeat if necessary.

Method Three—For removing butter, finger marks, syrup, etc. Recommended by U. S. Dept. of Commerce, in book titled "Furniture, its Selection and Use."

Use green soap, available in drug stores. Soak a soft cloth with warm water, put a teaspoon or more of the soap on the cloth, fold it into a pad, and rub the surface of furniture with a circular motion, until it is covered by a lather. Then remove the soap with a cloth dampened in tepid water, and finally dry and polish with a dry, soft cloth, rubbing with the wood grain.

Note 1—Great care must be taken when washing veneered surfaces to prevent the water from getting into the glue and loosening the veneer. When the veneer is not broken or cracked, wash only a small area at a time and quickly wipe it dry. Should the veneer be in poor condition, the surface is best cleaned with a commercial product made for the purpose.

2—After cleaning, use furniture polish or wax, if desired.

Removing Wax

Dirt and old wax may be removed from surfaces with a cloth dampened with turpentine or a product especially made for the purpose. Wax should be removed before attempting to revive surfaces.

Reviving Waxed Surfaces

A scratched or spotted waxed surface may often be revived by rubbing it with a little turpentine on a soft cloth and then rewaxing it.

Reviving Foggy, Cloudy, Milky, or Faded Finishes

It is difficult to state just what materials and methods to use to revive extensively overcast or faded finishes. It may at times require a bit of experimenting. Any wax on the surface should be removed. Sometimes this will remove an overcast, especially when turpentine is used as the medium.

1—**Shellac** finishes may often be revived with a mixture of 2 parts paraffin oil and 1 part white shellac. Apply and rub with a cloth for mild cases, but with a pad of grade "000" steel wool for severe cases, rubbing with the grain. Wipe dry with a clean cloth.

2—**Varnish** finishes can generally be revived with a mixture of ½ raw linseed oil and ½ turpentine. Apply as in Step 1.

3—**A Foggy** appearance should be treated with a mixture of 1 quart of clear water to which has been added 1 to 2 tablespoons of vinegar. Dampen a clean cloth and rub with the grain.

4—**A Milky** effect on varnished surfaces, particularly in damp climates, is probably due to an inferior grade of varnish. A good rub with a mixture of 50% raw linseed oil and 50% turpentine will sometimes improve or entirely remove the defect. Use a closely woven cloth of hard texture. If the piece is not improved, it will need to be refinished.

5—**Commercial** materials are made for the purpose of reviving old finishes.

Note 1—For carvings, etc., use a small hand brush, dipped in the mixture. Then dry with a cloth. Use a pointed stick under the cloth for depressions.

2—After cleaning, use furniture polish or wax, if desired.

Removing White Spots

Most white spots or rings on a furniture finish may be removed. The method employed depends more upon the depth of the damage than upon using a particular method for various types of finishes. However, finishes which are very thin must be treated by a less severe method than those which are thick.

It is best to attempt to remove the white spot first by simple methods with mild abrasives. If not successful, it will then be necessary to use more drastic means. The methods listed run from the mildest to those requiring special materials or coarser abrasives.

1—Rub with cigarette or cigar ashes and butter on a cloth.

2—Rub with rottenstone and butter, or some light oil (sewing machine oil, paraffin oil, raw linseed oil, or grade 10 motor oil) on a cloth.

3—Rub with a flannel dampened with spirits of camphor, essence of peppermint, or a few drops of ammonia on a damp cloth. This method is especially good for a varnished surface.

4—Rub with a thick paste, made of grade "FFF" pumice stone and raw linseed oil, using a rag. Wipe the surface often for inspection, using turpentine on a rag, if necessary. This method also is especially good for a varnished surface.

Note 1—If the white on a surface is successfully removed, follow with an application of furniture polish, after a slight interval, to permit the cleaning materials to evaporate or harden.

2—If the white cannot be removed, it will be necessary to refinish the surface or the entire piece.

Removing Ink or Dark Spots and to Freshen Wood

1—**Ink Spots** are difficult to remove. Ink penetrates deeply into wood, especially when the surface is not finished, as is often the case in old desks. The stain may usually be minimized and sometimes removed by the application of pure household ammonia, or a saturated solution of oxalic acid. It is often necessary to use repeated applications. (See "Bleaching," page 94.)

When an ink stain is only on the surface of a finish, it may usually be removed with a mixture of pumice stone and light oil made into a paste. Rub with the grain of the wood, using a soft cloth. Clean off with turpentine on a clean cloth.

When ink spots are over a finish and do not completely bleach out with treatment, they may often be completely removed by scraping the surface. However, this is useless to attempt for stains on bare wood. (See "Using Cabinet Scrapers," page 104.)

2—**Dark Spots** may often be bleached out with ammonia or the oxalic acid solution, as above outlined. If not, they may have to be scraped.

3—**Faded or Greyish** appearance may usually be revived with a mild bleaching solution. (See "Removing Discolorations," page 96.)

Note If a spot is successfully removed, revive the finish with furniture polish or wax.

Removing Scratches

1—**Light Scratches** may usually be removed by rubbing them with a little raw linseed oil, or with a piece of oily nut meat, such as walnut or pecan.

Commercial scratch removers are available (many very good), some of which may be purchased in grocery stores. Some types, such as those used by the professional trade, are more difficult to find, but may be purchased in paint or furniture stores.

2—**Moderately Deep Scratches** may be treated so as to be invisible by two methods not difficult to use, as follows:

A—Apply a penetrating oil stain, that matches the wood, to the crack with a very small brush or a toothpick. Wipe off surplus and allow to dry for 24 hours. Then apply one or more coats to more than fill the crack, of the same kind of finish material as originally used. (See "Determining Type of Old Finish," page 79.) Allow to dry completely. Then rub the spot down with pumice stone and oil or water, according to the finish material involved. (See "Penetrating Oil Stain," page 112, and "Polish Rubbed Finish" for varnish, page 132.)

B—This treatment is the same as above, except that color in oil is added to the finish material used, instead of applying it separately. This method is used when the proper colored oil stains are at hand. (See "Intermixing Oil Stain Colors," page 113.)

3—**Deep Scratches** should never be filled by Step 2 above. For satisfactory results they must be filled with "stick shellac" of a color shade that matches the finish. (See "Stick Shellac," page 36.)

Note When scratches have been removed, revive the finish with furniture polish or wax.

"Checked" and "Alligatored" Finishes

Many different terms are applied to those finishes which have dried out leaving shallow or deep grooves, that look like the skin of a snake or alligator. Those with very fine lines are here termed "checked" while those with deep lines are called "alligatored." The fine lines (or grooves) may usually be corrected with a product known as an "amalgamator," so as to be scarcely noticeable.

It is usually considered a hopeless task to correct an "alligatored" finish satisfactorily. However, methods are given that have sometimes been satisfactory to professional finishers. It is advisable to take the time in an effort to remove this "alligatored" condition. If it is unsuccessful, no harm will be done. It may aid in the removal of the old finish, preparatory to applying a new one.

Correcting a "Checked" Finish

1—Fold into a pad a piece of closely woven, smooth textured, clean cloth 12″ to 15″ square. Wet this pad with "benzol" or a commercial product that may be used as an "amalgamator." Gently rub a limited area at a time, to soften the finish, and to smooth it out. Rubbing is done best with the wood grain. These liquids evaporate rapidly. Keep the rag wet at all times. When a finish begins to smooth, complete the area by extremely light rubbing, so as not to roll up the finish.

2—Allow a smoothed finish to dry over night and then polish with wax or furniture polish.

Correcting an "Alligatored" Finish

Method One—Especially adapted to varnished surfaces.

Apply either "benzol," or a commercial "amalgamator" to an "alligatored" surface in a liberal quantity with a paint brush. Keep the surface wet with the material until the finish softens and flows. Then allow the finish to dry completely and smooth by rubbing with a pad and grade "FFF" pumice stone. Use water as a lubricant with the powder for a varnish finish and oil for a shellac finish, as previously directed in the procedures for those finishes.

Method Two—May be successful with shallow grooves.

Apply a very limited amount of a commercial "paint and varnish remover" to a small area at a time with a dauber made of a soft, lintless cloth. Rub lightly to soften slightly and spread the finish, thus filling the cracks. The action of the remover may be stopped by wiping the surface with a lintless, soft rag, saturated with turpentine. This method is slow in action and hard to complete. It is used best on that part of furniture which has been "alligatored" from heat or sun.

Note "Paint and varnish removers" are extremely inflammable, while "benzol" or commercial products capable of use as an "amalgamator" are extremely volatile. They should be used with care in a well ventilated room in which there is no flame or spark.

Spot Worn Through Finish

This work is the bane of refinishers. There is nothing difficult in the procedure, except that it takes time, and much care in selecting or mixing a stain that will ultimately match perfectly with the surrounding color. Applying a finish over the stain and rubbing down is the simplest part of the work.

There are mixtures in many colors sold in small bottles that are made especially for this work. Some of the products which have been put on the market have not been successful. Make inquiry at a paint store for a good product. Should an improper product be used, it might cause damage to the spot applied, especially if of the wrong color when dried out.

The following method is for the use of standard products.

1—Prepare the spot and feather the edges, by rubbing lightly and carefully with #400 wet-or-dry finishing paper. Use water as a lubricant on the paper for a varnish finish and a light rubbing oil (paraffin good) for a shellac finish. Clean off and allow to dry completely.

2—Apply a thin wash coat to the spot, using the same material as was used for the original finish. This is to keep the stain from penetrating into the wood pores, so that it may be removed if not the proper shade. (See "Preliminary Wash Coat," page 107.)

3—The spot is then stained. Check for exact shade of color after the stain has dried by applying (if possible) to an unexposed part of the piece. When satisfied with the color, thin the stain considerably and apply coat after coat until you have obtained an exact match, allowing each coat to dry thoroughly. Each coat of stain adds color. Sand lightly with used 7/0 or 8″0 Garnet finishing paper between coats.

4—Apply enough coats of the same kind of finishing material as was used for the original finish to produce a smooth and high gloss. Allow each coat to dry completely. Sand lightly between coats with worn, fine paper, as used for the stain.

5—The last coat of finishing material on the spot must then be rubbed down to match the surrounding finish in texture.

For an ordinary SEMI-GLOSS finish, use grade "00" or "000" steel wool, rubbing carefully with the grain. For a smoother grade of this finish, use #400 wet-or-dry finishing paper. Follow the directions in Step 1 above.

For a POLISH-RUBBED finish, smooth the spot with grade "FFF" pumice stone and a rubbing pad, using water on varnish and light rubbing oil on shellac.

6—Complete the finish by waxing or using furniture polish over the entire piece.

Note 1—It is advisable to use an oil stain for this work, as it may be more readily removed than any other type of stain material, should the color not match properly. (See "Using Oil Stains," page 114.)

2—Complete information may be had regarding the application and rubbing down of various materials for final finish by referring to the Index.

CHAPTER 7

ENAMELING AND "NUDE" FURNITURE FINISHES

Enameling

The so-called "4 hour drying" enamels are used as colors for a non-transparent finish on furniture, instead of paints, such as were used in days gone by. The semi-gloss enamels are usually selected for furniture to be used indoors. These should not be applied on furniture used outdoors as it will disintegrate when exposed to the outside atmosphere.

The high-gloss enamels, primarily for outdoor use, are sometimes preferred for indoor use, and should always be used for an extremely smooth "Polish Rubbed Finish" when such finish is applied over a "paste filler." (See page 117.)

"Glazing" and "Antiquing" solid colors give a tone (with an over-color) that causes furniture to blend more nearly with clear-finished pieces and furnishings. (For further information regarding paints, enamels, etc., see "Paint Facts," page 169.)

The surface of furniture (or other articles) to be enameled is one of three classes, namely:

1—Bare wood which has never been painted.

2—An old finish in good condition.

3—An old finish which is cracked or damaged.

Surface Preparation

1—Surfaces on which there is dust or dirt are best cleaned with soap and warm water. Those on which there is oil, grease, or furniture polish usually require washing with "sal soda" and hot water (see "Reviving a Clear Finish," page 158, for use of "Sal Soda"). In either event, surface should be rinsed, wiped with clean cloths, and thoroughly dried.

A rag saturated with mineral oil or turpentine will be sufficient under some circumstances. Allow a few minutes for the oil to penetrate the surface. Then dry with a clean cloth, turning it frequently to a fresh portion.

2—Most waxes can be removed with turpentine on a rag, but if the coat is heavy or you find it to be a type that is obstinate, it is best to use a commercial wax remover. (See "Removing Wax," page 159.)

3—It is not necessary to remove an old clear finish or one of paint or enamel, if the surface is smooth and is not scaled or cracked. If such a surface has foreign matter on it (dirt, grease, wax, etc.), clean off as directed in Steps 1 and 2.

4—An old finish (regardless of type) should be completely removed when it is cracked, scaled, or rough.

When old paint or enamel has dried out and flaked, most of it may usually be removed with a scraper or blade of a knife. That remaining can be smoothed, and the edges of the patches feathered, by sanding with grade 1/0 Garnet paper. (See "Using Cabinet Scrapers," page 104.)

Any type of old finish which has not dried out or flaked, but is rough, is best removed with a "commercial remover." When entirely dry, the surface should be smoothed with grade 1/0 Garnet paper. (See "Paint and Varnish Remover," page 80.)

5—When a surface has been freed from any foreign matter or prepared as above outlined, sand it carefully with grade 2/0 or 3/0 Garnet paper. A slight amount of roughness caused by sanding gives a binding "tooth" for the primer coat.

Note 1—All surfaces must be fairly smooth before using enamels. If not, a certain amount of roughness will show in the finish. It is best not to use steel wool as it leaves the surface too smooth.

2—If a surface is not completely freed from grease, wax, and oil, the drying of the undercoat will be slowed down or it will not dry.

3—Patch or fill all defects with "wood dough" or "wood putty" and, when dry, sand smooth. (See "Wood Dough," page 34, and "Wood Putty," page 36.)

Primer Coat

1—It is best to apply a coat of shellac mixture (about 75% pure shellac and 25% denatured alcohol) to knots and *end* surfaces, when the piece is of bare wood, whether new or old. The shellac keeps the resin in the knots from being softened by the turpentine in the primer and bleeding through into the enamel. It also stops too much of the primer from being absorbed into the end grain.

2—Read the directions on the container of the enamel for application of a primer coat. This will specify a material (usually white), either made or recommended by the manufacturer, or a coat of the enamel. The same brush (2″ wide good) may be used for the primer and for the enamel. Apply a thin, smooth coat.

3—Allow primer coat to dry over night and sand lightly, until smooth, with grade 4/0 Garnet finishing paper (open coat preferred).

Note Enameled surfaces often flake or chip off, primarily because there was not a good bond between the old finish and the primer coat. A better bond is obtained if the old finish (which is free from foreign matter and smoothed by sanding) is softened slightly, prior to the application of the primer coat, with "Benzol" or a "commercial mixture" especially prepared for that purpose. Usually both may be purchased in stores carrying paint products, are clear and water-thin, can be applied with a rag or brush, and are highly volatile, hence they should be used with caution and in a ventilated room. After their application, the surface dries in a few minutes and should then be painted with the primer.

Mixing Colors

Most manufacturers of enamels produce them in a great variety of colors, both in the semi-gloss and high-gloss finish. These colors may be modified by mixing them as they come from the can.

Add white enamel to the solid colors for pastel shades. Use a semi-gloss white for lightening a semi-gloss solid color and a high-gloss white with a high-gloss color. A semi-gloss finish may be obtained by lightening a high-gloss enamel with a "flat" white primer.

Some manufacturers specialize in making enamels in pastel colors. These may be intermixed or white added, for a greater variety of color, as directed by color charts.

Semi-Gloss or High-Gloss Finish

1—Apply one coat of enamel or two, if needed, as it comes from the can, or mix for color, as directed. Two light coats look better and wear longer than one heavy coat. Paint evenly with a relatively full brush, picking up runs and sags, before again dipping the brush in the enamel.

2—When using enamel which has been left in the can, strain it (to free it from particles of dirt or a skinned top) through cheesecloth or a sheer stocking. Most enamels may be thinned with turpentine. (Read label for directions. See "Storage of Paints," page 204.)

3—The so-called "4-hour drying" enamels do not dry hard in that time. Dry one coat over night before applying another one. Sand lightly between coats with grade 4/0 Garnet paper.

Satin Polished Finish

A beautiful enameled finish may be obtained by rubbing down the last coat to a fine and soft polish with pumice or rottenstone and water. This is accomplished by the same method as used for varnish. (See "Polish Rubbed Finish," page 132.)

This finish may be obtained only after several thin coats of enamel have been applied and sanded lightly after each coat, except the last, with a worn 6/0 or 8/0 garnet paper, and the use of a "paste filler" before the primer coat. (See "Paste Fillers," page 117.)

Antiqued Finish

Antiquing over enamel is a *glaze-coat* which is used to obtain a mellow or soft appearance rather than to simulate great age. It gives a pleasing effect when applied in a delicate manner and when it is not too noticeable.

1—Prepare a mixture of 3 tablespoons of turpentine, a teaspoon of Raw Turkey Umber Oil Color, a tablespoon of varnish or a tablespoon of boiled linseed oil. A trace of lamp-black may be added for dark colored enamels, while Raw Sienna may be used in place of the Raw Umber for a warmer or reddish tone.

It must be mixed thoroughly and very small amount goes a long way. It is a good plan to prepare the mixture in a small tin can and discard any portion unused.

2—Apply with an old paint brush to a thoroughly dried enamel surface, finishing one surface, or one small member of a piece, at a time.

3—On flat surfaces, start at the center and work towards the edges, wiping away the glaze material with a soft cloth and using a circular motion. Turn the cloth to a fresh portion after each wiping. Leave the center of the space lightest, with the color gradually darker toward the edges. Blend further by patting the surface with clean cheesecloth and finish blending with a dry paint brush, working it from the center towards the edges, and wiping off the brush on a cloth often. When the glaze is completely dry, the piece is ready for use.

Wiping off and blending is not at all difficult when only a very small amount of the glaze material remains on the surface, and it gives a slightly noticeable but most effective appearance.

4—On carved surfaces, turnings, moldings, etc., proceed as for flat surfaces. Remove excess glaze material from depressions with a dry brush, wiping it off on a cloth. "Highlight" all raised areas by wiping off most of the glaze, leaving the background dark. Dampen the cloth with turpentine if the glaze does not come off easily.

Note It is a good plan to protect the glaze coat from wear by brushing the entire piece with the new type of water-clear varnish. Ordinary varnish should not be used as it has a yellowish color, nor should a thinned coat of white shellac be used, as water will mark shellac.

If the water-clear varnish is used, it may be rubbed (when dry) with grade "00" or "000" steel wool, to produce a satin effect.

When this varnish is not available, it is well to finish by waxing. (See "Waxing," page 145.)

Glazed Finish

Beautiful effects, if the work is delicately done, may be secured by glazing with white over furniture enameled light opaque colors, resulting in a "frosted" effect.

White primer material or enamel is used in the glaze mixture in place of the Oil Color. This is applied, wiped off, and finished in the same manner as for Antiquing.

Note 1—When applying a primer coat for enamel, the Antique or Glazed finish to such furniture as chairs, etc., turn them up-side-down and do all the underpart first.

2—Spread clean newspapers over the place where the work is to be done.

3—Clean brushes immediately after use as all these materials set quickly. (See "Cleaning Brushes," page 206.)

"Nude" Furniture Finishes

"Nude" furniture is that type which is unfinished and newly made in a cheap manner of softwoods or is constructed in a better manner (often well done) of semi-hard woods (like red alder) or a hardwood-like maple.

Very often those who are not familiar with the use of finishing materials, do not realize that "Nude" furniture, although cheaply made of softwoods (especially pine), may be stained and finished beautifully with a clear finish and waxed.

Most such furniture has been enameled, generally without a filler, which results in a poor finish, regardless of how many coats of the enamel have been applied.

For Clear Finishes

1—The grain of all softwoods should first be raised by the application of water, in which there is a little glue, and then dried and sanded. (See Note 3, "Smoothing by Sanding," page 98, under "Useful Information.")

2—For staining woods (see "Staining Woods," page 108).

3—For smoothing by the use of a filler (see "Paste Fillers," page 117).

4—For various types of clear finishes and waxing (see Chapter 5).

For Enamel Finishes

1—The wood grain does not need to be raised by the water application when surfaces are to be enameled as any grain raised by the Primer Coat is sanded off.

2—Apply the primer coat, enamel, Antique or Glaze, as directed in this chapter.

CHAPTER 8

MORE ABOUT MATERIALS

This chapter contains further pertinent information about materials referred to in the preceding chapters, and especially those about which additional information or knowledge may be helpful. By placing this data here, space in the preceding chapters was saved, and will not be a burden to those who are already familiar with the information given herein.

PAINT FACTS

A few brief facts about paints and the materials used with them may be helpful. Those in which we are interested are used as a protective coating.

House Paints

The better grades of house paints were made in the past from a pigment of titanium white, white lead, and zinc oxide. To these were added linseed oil as a vehicle, turpentine as a thinner, and a Japan drier. Today the finer grades of paints may contain many new types of materials, often synthetic in structure, which are added for the purpose of longer life and better coverage.

Casein Paints

Casein paint is one of the oldest types of decorative coloring. The Romans combined earth pigments with skim milk. Our Colonial ancestors painted houses and furniture with such ingredients. The early settlers commonly used skim milk or buttermilk, and records show they also used salt, boiled rice, coffee, and egg whites in making paints. (See "Refractory Paints," page 80.)

Casein paints are thinned with water for use. They are today made durable and most of them are made washable by the addition of oils, synthetic resins, etc., to the colored pigments. They are sold in great quantities to the professional trade and home owners, under various popular brand names, particularly for the refinishing of interior walls.

Shellac

An attempt has been made to impress upon you that only high quality materials should be used in restoration work, for the test of value is not the cost, but the results obtained. This is particularly true with shellac, of which there are many grades. The more dependable brands state on the container that the shellac is pure and the cut exact.

It is advisable to purchase only that quantity of shellac which may be used within 6 months, for even the best grades of liquid orange or white shellac can only be kept on hand for 6 months to a year without deterioration. After that, the color darkens and the shellac is apt to lose its quick drying and other important characteristics.

Liquid shellac is sold as a "3 lb. cut," a "4 lb. cut" or a "5 lb. cut." For restoration work the best for use is a "4 lb. cut," and it should be thinned down with a good grade of completely denatured alcohol to any desired consistency. (A "4 lb. cut" means that 4 pounds of bleached gum shellac are dissolved in 1 gallon of alcohol.)

The quality of a liquid shellac is dependent upon the selection of the gum, orange or white, and the alcohol with which it is cut. As yet it has been impossible to produce orange shellac gum synthetically. It is made from the secretion of a small scale insect (parasitic in nature) which lives on the sap of "Lac" trees principally grown in India. Hence the name "shellac." The bug secretes lac, a resin that forms a shell-like crust over the twigs on these trees. The natives in India sift out the bark, dirt, and dust by melting and washing, etc., to produce pure orange gum shellac.

Shellac has been produced in India by natives since the 13th Century, and virtually by the same methods as used today. However, one manufacturer, at least, has modernized the process and is refining the gum by machinery, and thereby producing a very clean and beautiful product. The lac gum is purified, rolled into sheets, converted into flakes, and shipped to all parts of the world.

The shellac-resin gum is orange in color in its original form. It is brought to this country and, by bleaching, is converted into white shellac gum. Bleaching shellac is a complicated chemical process and, unless it is done with great care, the results are poor.

It may readily be seen from the above that, when using shellac, care should be taken, and only the best quality should be used if best results are to be obtained.

Alcohol

Alcohol is a very important product in restoration work. It is principally used as a neutralizer, after the use of a commercial "Paint and Varnish Remover," for thinning shellac, and for cleaning brushes after use in shellac. (See "Paint and Varnish Remover," page 12; "Shellac Finish," page 139; and "Cleaning Brushes," page 206.)

Only "Completely Denatured Alcohol" should be used in this work. In the old days, wood alcohol was considered best. However, it should not be used in a closed room, as it is toxic and might bring about blindness.

The best quality of "Completely Denatured Alcohol" may be sold as such or under a special "Trade Name."

Manufacturers of shellac are permitted to use specially denatured alcohol, Formula #1, which is nothing more than 100 gallons of pure grain alcohol to which 5 gallons of wood alcohol have been added. Specially denatured alcohol Formula #1 cannot be sold except for the production and thinning of shellac.

Varnish

General information has been previously given. (See "Varnish Finish," page 124.)

Lacquer

Lacquers have been used in the Orient for centuries. Some of the finer pieces finished with it have over 300 coats, have taken years to make, and are of such durability that they should last for centuries.

Lacquer is now made of cellulose nitrates, resins, plastics, and a fast evaporating solvent. The solvents are of a different nature than those used for paint and varnish, and cannot be mixed. Consequently, the use of lacquer over any other paint product or oil is disastrous. (For additional information, see "Lacquer Finish," page 153.)

Turpentine

The best grade of turpentine comes from the Southern Long Leaf Pine trees. It is technically called "Pure Gum Spirit of Turpentine" and is thus designated on many containers holding this grade of product. For best results none other than pure turpentine should be used in any phase of restoration work.

Professional painters now use what is commonly known as "Sub Turps" or "Painter's Thinner" for thinning paints for outside use. It is also good for cleaning paint brushes. It is a naphtha product, made from crude oil, costs about one-half as much as pure turpentine, evaporates more slowly, and is generally accepted as a paint thinner. However, it is best not to use this product in restoration work.

There is also a super-refined turpentine, costly and with little odor. It has not proved satisfactory for restoration work, as experimented with in my shop.

Linseed Oil

Only pure linseed oil should be used for refinishing. The impure, or substitute type, of which there is much on the market, is not satisfactory for good work. The pure oil is designated on the containers.

Raw linseed oil is obtained by pressing flaxseed. To produce boiled linseed oil, the raw oil is heated to about 250 degrees Fahrenheit, with lead, manganese, and driers cooked in.

Both types should always be thinned with pure turpentine, according to directions given for procedures where it is used.

A mixture of raw oil, which is thinner than the boiled, penetrates more quickly, but thinned boiled oil is better for producing a rich wood color and for preservative qualities, particularly when applied hot. (See "Coloring with Linseed Oil," page 107, and "Removing Board Warps," note 8, page 74.)

Many professional house painters, when mixing paints from prepared pastes (lead, zinc, etc.) use a large percentage of raw linseed oil in the primer coat for raw lumber, because of its penetrating qualities, and then use the boiled linseed for the succeeding coats, because of its gloss and drying qualities. To this they add a Japan drier, and turpentine or a "Sub Turps" as a thinner.

TABLE OF THINNERS OR SOLVENTS FOR FINISHING MATERIALS

FINISH	*USE*
Varnish, interior or spar type.	Pure turpentine.
Varnish, synthetic type.	See directions on container. Usually no material given.
Shellac.	Pure denatured alcohol.
Penetrating wood sealers.	Follow directions on container.
Plastic materials, all types.	Follow directions on container.
Lacquer and lacquer primer.	Special lacquer thinner.
Oil Stain.	Raw linseed oil and turpentine.
Water Stain.	Water.
Spirit Stain.	Pure denatured alcohol.
Wood Dough.	Lacquer thinner or benzol.
Enamel, standard "4 hour drying."	Pure turpentine.
Enamel, plastic type.	See directions on container. Usually no material given.
Paint, pigment and oil type.	Raw linseed oil for primer coat, boiled linseed oil for final coats, with pure turpentine or substitute (sub turps or painter's thinner).

ABRASIVE PAPERS AND EMERY CLOTH

The use of the term "sandpaper" to designate one of the various abrasive papers is a misnomer as none of them any longer use sand for the abrasive coating. Sand has round edges and corners and will not smooth a surface but only scratch it. The so-called "sandpaper" which you buy at the store is covered, instead, with a coating of crushed "flint" in various degrees of fineness. These grades of fineness are marked on the reverse side of the paper.

This "flint" sandpaper should not be used in the restoration of furniture if it is possible to obtain anything better, as it is not durable. In recent years the flint has been replaced by more effective and durable abrasive materials.

Making Abrasive Sheets Abrasive paper or cloth is produced in large sheets. These are then cut into standard or special sizes for use in hand-sanding, smoothing or polishing, or into belts, spirals, etc. for use with power sanders. They also come in sizes for attachment to discs, cones, etc., and the fineness of the grit varies according to the nature of the work to be done.

The abrasive materials are glued to a cloth or paper backing, differing in thickness and pliability as their specific use may require. The abrasive may be applied in a heavy, medium, or light coating as may be best suited for any particular job.

Types of Abrasive Papers and Cloths It is important that you understand the various kinds and types of materials used as "backing" for abrasives since only the correct type should be used in any specific step in your work. They must be of the proper grade or weight to accomplish the purpose effectively and speedily, yet without damaging the piece on which you are working.

Such understanding can best be gained by describing the various "abrasive sheets," their "backing" and the type and grades of "grit" used on them, in accordance with their distinguishing numbers. Instructions are also given in the use and proper handling of the various types and grades.

1—**Flint Paper** is coated with a species of quartz, off-white in color, which occurs as a mineral deposit in the ground. When crushed, for use as a coating for an abrasive, its cutting edges are not sharp and they crumble in use. It is by far, however, the most commonly sold of the abrasive sheets for sanding exterior paint coatings.

2—**Garnet Paper.** Garnet is also a mined stone, light reddish-brown in color and is classed as one of the semi-precious gem stones. It is crushed into grains which have hard and durable edges and corners. Garnet paper is very popular, easily obtainable, and is used largely for smoothing, finishing, and polishing wood surfaces.

3—**Silicon Carbide Papers.** This abrasive is produced in an electric furnace and ranges in color from dark gray to black. It is crystalline in form, very hard and sharp (commonly called "Carborundum"). This paper is widely used in place of garnet papers by many cabinet shops and amateur workers. It is sold under various trade names rather than by its technical name.

4—**Aluminum Oxide Papers.** This abrasive, brown in color, is also produced in an electric furnace under rigid heat control and is an almost pure cutting agent. It is dense, resists breakdown, and is the toughest and most durable of all abrasives. It, too, is sold by a trade name rather than by its technical designation.

5—**Emery Cloth.** Emery is a dull-black, mined mineral. Its cutting edges break down under pressure and is, therefore, mixed with one of the harder abrasives even though sold as "emery cloth." It is glued to a cloth backing instead of paper.

Backing

"Backing" is the material to which the various types of abrasive materials are glued. This may be paper, cloth, fiber, or a combination of them. The paper and cloth types come in standard size of 9″ x 11″ and we shall deal only with these.

Paper Backing is tough and of a special quality. It comes in various thicknesses called "weight" as follows:

1—*"A" weight* is a soft pliable grade of paper and is used where flexibility is required.

2—*"C" and "D" weight* papers are thicker and are used for the more severe hand-sanding jobs.

3—*"E" weight* is the heaviest of the backing papers and is used, primarily, for machine sanding.

Cloth Backing comes in two grades, as follows:

1—*Light Weight* material is marked "J" and is used for a backing on "emery cloth" for hand work and on some finishing and polishing cloths.

2—*Heavy Weight* material is marked "X" and is used with power tools.

Note Some manufacturers distinguish the weight of the backing by producing it in different colors.

Classifications of Abrasive Papers and Cloths

The reverse side of all abrasive papers and cloths are printed to show the grade of density or type of abrasive and often the weight or quality of the backing.

1—**"Finishing Paper"** is the name which is applied to those papers of "A" or light weight and which have a fine or extra-fine grit.

2—**"Cabinet Papers"** are the papers known as "C" or "D" (medium) weight and have grit of medium fineness.

3—**"Closed-Grain Papers."** The abrasive grains on these papers are applied thickly and these are the papers most generally used.

4—**"Open-Coat Papers."** The abrasive on these papers covers only 50% to 70% of the backing surface and there is left a certain amount of space between the grains. This increases the pliability of the paper, allows faster cutting with less pressure, and is used on the softer woods which tend to clog the surface of the paper more rapidly.

5—**"Wet and Dry Papers."** The backing of these papers is waterproofed and they are made with only the finest grades of abrasives. In restoration work, they are used for the final rub-down, with water, gasoline, or oil. They are sold under various trade names. Most of them designate whether they are for "wet" or "dry" use or are merely marked "waterproof."

Grit Numbers or Grades

On the back of all standard abrasive sheets are printed figures indicating the grit or grade. These are as follows:

	GRIT	GRADE	
	600	—	
	500	—	
	400	10/0	
	360	9/0	
Very fine	320	—	Polishing and finishing
	280	8/0	
	240	7/0	
	220	6/0	
	180	5/0	
	150	4/0	
Fine	120	3/0	Finishing
	100	2/0	
	80	0 or 1/0	
Medium	60	1/2	Cabinet
	50	1	
	40	1½	
Coarse	36	2	Rough Sanding
	30	2½	
	24	3	
Very coarse	20	3½	Coarse sanding

Note These figures (as above) are standard for both "grit" (number per square inch) and "grade." They may vary, however, in their designation as to "grit," in the naming of the classification for "cabinet" and "finishing" papers, or those with a "cloth" backing.

Markings

The form of marking on the back of the sheets may vary greatly among different manufacturers. Sometimes the grit or grade only is given and sometimes both. Also, information may or may not be furnished as to the weight of the paper or the kind of grit used but it will usually tell whether it is the "wet-or-dry" type by denoting that it is waterproof, either by using that word or a coined one.

Example of marking—"3/0—120 A," means the grade is medium fine, that it has 120 grits (per square inch) and the weight (thickness) of the paper is "A" (thinnest). You may have to guess at the kind of abrasive material used, but you should know it from the color. This paper may or may not be marked "Finishing Paper."

Buying Abrasive Sheets

Standard sheets may be purchased from paint and hardware stores and are sold more cheaply in quantity than in single sheets. Most dealers will permit you to mix grades or types when buying and if you are doing much work, it is well to have a supply on hand, since many grades are needed and they do wear out quickly.

The flint papers are by far the cheapest, but the other papers last so much longer, do the work so much better and more quickly, that they are the least expensive in the long run. The reason is because the latter stand up under service and have better "cutting edges," due to the fact that, when fed on to the paper (or cloth), the grit is "electro-controlled," which compels the particles to stand on end, with point upward, affording better cutting edges and corners.

Types and Grades to Use

Abrasive papers are used for:

1—Smoothing.

2—Finishing

3—Polishing.

No. 1 paper might be used on very soft and rough wood as the first medium in smoothing, followed by grades of "1/2" and "1/0," but it is far better to make a rule *never* to start with a coarser grade than "1/0," to be followed by those of less coarse ("2/0," "3/0," etc.), especially on hardwoods. It is always a good plan to take more time in smoothing with the finer grades of papers than to take chances of damage with the coarser ones.

For finishing, after smoothing, it is well to forget the intermediate grades beyond "3/0" and jump immediately to grade "7/0" or "8/0," for, with new paper, it is coarse enough for most woods.

For polishing, use "8/0" or finer waterproof (wet-or-dry) papers or cloths with water or proper oil as a lubricant and finish up with pumice and rottenstone (should a finish call for them).

Emery Cloth About the only use for emery cloth in restoration work (other than on tools) is, because of the strength in the "backing," for cleaning or smoothing turnings. For this work, only fine grade cloths should be used.

Cleaning and Using Old Abrasive Paper Good abrasive paper is expensive and many workers are prone to discard it long before it has become unfit for further service. Papers clog up with powdered wood but this may be removed with a small stiff hand brush. Should the material be difficult to remove, as is the case when it is gummy, and if you know the type of that material, dip the brush in the proper solvent before scrubbing. When clean, allow the paper to dry. Examples—for varnish, use turpentine; for shellac, use alcohol; for lacquer, use a lacquer thinner. By such methods, the useful life of abrasive papers may often be doubled.

Used or dulled abrasive papers are of great value and are recommended for use in many stages of work. It is well to have a special place in which to store them.

Tearing and Folding Abrasive Papers Great economy can be had from cutting or folding papers.

A paper is torn best across the short (9″) dimension to form strips about 3½″ wide. It can be torn by securing an old hack saw blade (with screws) to the side edge of a board prepared for the purpose, with the teeth of the blade slightly above the flat surface, or it may be torn over an edge of a "carpenter's steel square." The surface of the board can be marked with a scale to measure the width of the tear.

Full size sheets of thin paper may be folded in squares by first folding it in half on the 11″ dimension; folded again to ¼ size; then again to ⅛th size. The folds should be creased firmly. The edges of the folds are useful for smoothing in angles or cleaning out cracks.

Sanding Blocks

The best size for a sanding block is 3″ wide by 5″ long and 1″ to 1¼″ thick. It may be of felt, cork, or rubber. One made of hardwood (maple good) is preferred because of its weight, and the long sides may be coved or shaped so as to be easily gripped. The face of any hard material used for a block should have rubber tacked or cemented over rounded edges, so as to have no sharp corners.

A block of this size may be used best with a sheet of abrasive paper cut crosswise into 5½″ x 9″ pieces. The paper is then folded into one half that size (4½″ x 5½″) and placed over the rubber face of the block with the long dimension of the folded paper over the long way of the block. This leaves it slightly longer than the block, at both ends. The paper is turned up over the sides and gripped. When worn it may be shifted to present new edge surfaces, then turned up-side-down, thus using practically all of the abrasive paper surface. Never tack paper to a sanding block.

There are many types of hand sanding blocks which may be purchased. Some are good and some poor, but most of them require special sizes of abrasive paper and do not utilize the full surface.

A black-board eraser, such as used in schools and which may be purchased at most "10¢ stores," makes an excellent sanding block. It is padded, and of approximately the right size.

Note For the use of abrasive papers and cloth, see "Sanding and Smoothing," in Chapter 4 on "Preparing for New Finish."

POWDERED ABRASIVES

Pumice Stone Pumice stone comes in grades "F," "FF," "FFF," and "FFFF." Grade "FFF" is best for all round use in refinishing work. Pumice may usually be purchased by grade in paint stores, while that found in drug stores is much more expensive, and is usually not designated by grade.

Rottenstone Rottenstone comes in one grade only. For economy it is best purchased from paint stores.

WOOD SCREWS

Wood screws are made of steel, brass, or bronze. They come with flat, round, or oval heads and are sold by these designations and in various finishes, diameter of body (under the head), and length. (See Plate 9, page 47, "Hardware Frequently Used," for illustration of these screws and length increases.)

Steel Wood Screws are made with finishes of Bright (natural), Blue, Japan, Galvanized, Nickel, Copper, Brass, Cadmium, and Bronze plate. They come in lengths from ¼″ to 5″ (sometimes 6″) and by a "Screw Number" from "0" to "24," which designates the diameter of the screw body under the head.

Brass Wood Screws come in finishes of Brass (natural), Bronze, and Nickle Plate. They come in lengths from ¼″ to 3½″ and by "Screw Number" from "0" to "18."

Flat Head Screws are the kind used most often in furniture construction. The hole must be counter-sunk for the head to fit into and, if they are used on a visible surface, the hole for the head should be drilled into the surface with an auger bit and a wooden plug set over the head (glued in place).

Round Head Screws are for use on a surface where the head is intended to show.

Oval Head Screws are proper for use in securing hinges and other hardware to wood. The finish of the screw should match the hardware.

Phillips Screws have recently been put on the market. They have a "cross-slot" in the head, which requires a special type of screw driver. The advantages claimed are that the screw head is stronger, is more easily driven, as the screw driver stays in the slot better, and the slots do not have to be lined up for better appearance. Such screws are used in the body work on automobiles (etc.) and in modern or cheap furniture but should never be used in the repair of Antique furniture.

For Directions in the use of wood screws, see "Using Wood Screws," page 30.

TABLES OF WOOD SCREW SIZES

(See use of table below)

1—Length of Screws

SCREW LENGTH	MADE IN SCREW NOS. STEEL	BRASS
	(Nos. inclusive)	
Inches		
¼	0 to 4	0 to 4
⅜	0 to 8	0 to 6
½	1 to 10	1 to 8
⅝	2 to 12	2 to 10
¾	2 to 14	2 to 12
⅞	3 to 14	4 to 12
1	3 to 16	4 to 14
1¼	4 to 18	6 to 14
1½	4 to 20	6 to 14
1¾	6 to 20	8 to 14
2	6 to 20	8 to 18
2¼	6 to 20	10 to 18
2½	6 to 20	10 to 18
2¾	8 to 20	None
3	8 to 24	12 to 18
3½	10 to 24	12 to 18
4	12 to 24	None
4½	14 to 24	None
5	14 to 24	None

2—Sizes for Screw Numbers

SCREW NO.	DIAM. OF SHAFT	SIZE DRILL CLEARANCE HOLE	SIZE DRILL ANCHOR HOLE
		(For hardwoods)	
	Inch	Inch	Inch
0	1/16	1/16	1/32
1	5/64	3/32	1/32
2	3/32	3/32	1/32
3	7/64	1/8	1/16
4	1/8	1/8	1/16
5	1/8	1/8	1/16
6	9/64	5/32	3/32
7	5/32	5/32	3/32
8	11/64	3/16	3/32
9	3/16	3/16	3/32
10	13/64	7/32	1/8
11	13/64	7/32	1/8
12	7/32	7/32	1/8
14	1/4	1/4	1/8
16	9/32	5/16	5/32
18	5/16	5/16	3/16
20	21/64	3/8	3/16
24	3/8	3/8	7/32

NOTE—Should an Anchor hole be desired for Softwoods, use a size smaller than designated. Example —For No. 10 screw, use a 3/32″ drill in place of a 1/8″ drill.

USE OF TABLES

Table 1 gives the various lengths (first column) in which wood screws are made and the "number" of the screw in both *steel* and *brass*. (The "screw number" will be explained later under Table 2.)

Example 1—Screws ¼″ long are made of steel or brass in numbers from "0 to 4" inclusive.

Example 2—Screws 1″ long are made of steel in numbers from "3 to 16" and of brass in numbers from "4 to 14."

Example 3—Screws 4″ long are made of steel only, in numbers from "12 to 24," 3½″ being the longest brass screw made.

Table 2 gives the "screw number" (first column) followed by "diameter of the shaft" in inches, just below the head. The screw number designates the size of the screw, according to the Standard Screw Gauge. You are then given the size (diameter) of the drill to use in hardwoods for both the "clearance" (column 3) and "anchor" holes (column 4).

Example 1—No. "0" screws (column 1) are 1/16″ in diameter of shaft, so you should use a 1/16″ drill for the "clearance" hole and 1/32″ drill for the "anchor" hole.

Example 2—No. "8" screws (column 1) have a shaft 11/64″ in diameter, so you should use a 3/16″ drill for the "clearance" hole and 3/32″ drill for the "anchor" hole.

TYPES OF NAILS

The kinds of nails principally used for repairs in furniture restoration work are brads, casing nails, and finishing nails. Occasionally cut nails are used (when similar nails are found in a piece and the condition warrants), and corrugated nails are sometimes used for added strength where they will not show. For general carpentry work the most commonly used nails are common, box, or finishing nails. Use the common or box nails for crating, when shipping furniture. Only the nails mentioned above will be discussed.

The nail chart in my shop shows not only the commonly used types, but specially designed nails for 23 various industries, varying from a few to a full range in sizes. Most nails are made from round steel wire, with a few of copper. Steel nails may be zinc or cement coated, blued, barbed, or galvanized. The heads may vary in shape; their length varies from ¼″ brads to 8″ spikes and their diameter varies in size.

The size of nails and spikes is usually indicated by the word "penny" or "penny weight," which was derived from the weight per 1,000 nails. This measurement no longer holds true in modern times. The length per "penny" now stays constant, while the thickness (gauge) varies, so the weight per 1,000 would not be the same for nails of the same length but of different gauge.

The length per "penny" or "penny weight," which is always designated by the letter "D," up to 6″, is as follows:

2 D—1″	6 D—2″	10 D—3″	30 D—4½″
3 D—1¼″	7 D—2¼″	12 D—3¼″	40 D—5″
4 D—1½″	8 D—2½″	16 D—3½″	50 D—5½″
5 D—1¾″	9 D—2¾″	20 D—4″	60 D—6″

Brads are made from a thin steel wire, have a small rounded head flattened on the side, and vary in length from ¼″ to 2″. The smaller sizes are sold by length (in small pasteboard boxes) rather than by "penny" size.

Casing nails have the same shaped heads as brads, usually come in lengths from 1″ to 4″, but are made from a heavier gauge of steel wire than brads, the gauge being the same for a given length as for a common nail. The small head is usually driven below a wood surface with a nail set leaving a small hole which should be filled with wood dough or stick shellac.

Finishing nails are made of a finer gauge of steel wire than casing nails, usually come in lengths from 1″ to 4″, but differ from the casing nail, in that the top of the head is entirely flat, with conical-shaped sides sloping toward the point. This nail is driven flush with the wood surface without the use of a nail set and leaves no hole or depression around the head. For that reason it is called a "finishing" nail, as it may be covered with a colored paint material without showing its location.

Cut nails have a rectangular but nearly square shaft and large head. They are now made by specially designed power tools, usually in the same sizes as common nails. They are a copy of the first nails made, which were forged from soft steel by hand, and have great holding power as the wedge shape binds against the wood fibers instead of splitting them, as do the wire nails.

Common nails have round flat heads, great holding power, and are used for rough carpentry work, where it is not objectionable to have the head show. They are made of heavy gauge steel wire (for the length of the nail) and in lengths from 1″ to 6″ for regular carpentry work.

Box nails are of the same construction and look like common nails, except that the wire used is thinner and the head is not so thick. They may be used to better advantage in thin wood or that which is apt to split. They are not made in the long lengths and have less holding power than the common nails. They can often be purchased with a coating of resin or cement to increase their holding power and prevent corrosion.

Corrugated nails are made of flat steel wire, pressed corrugated in shape, lengthwise, are several times wider than they are deep, have a sharp edge on the bottom of the long length, and are thus driven into a wood surface directly across a joint, to the full depth of the nail, so that only a thin wavy line shows. They are often used as a reinforcement on mitered or butt joints, etc., when in a position where they will not be seen. Those used for repairs in restoration should be no longer than one inch.

PART TWO

CHAPTER
9

TOOLS FOR THE BEGINNER

It is surprising how much can be accomplished with only a few simple hand tools. However, those should be of the best quality. It is difficult and often impossible to accomplish good work with hand tools which are cheaply constructed, made of poor materials, are out of balance, or will not retain a cutting edge.

Good tools are the delight of every mechanically minded person and to use them is a fascinating hobby and often a profitable one. You realize a profit when you construct a needed article in spare time, or when repairs are completed in a satisfactory manner, which work would otherwise have had to be done by a professional.

In practically every household will be found a hammer, saw, screwdriver, pliers, rule or yardstick, and perhaps a chisel and plane. These are fine for a starter if they are quality tools which can be used for good workmanship.

In this chapter, you are given a list of those hand tools which are deemed adequate for the work you will first attempt. The balance of the tools suggested for purchase which are listed in Chapter 10, "More Hand Tools," are for those more advanced and more ambitious workers.

When purchasing tools (hand or power), it pays to buy those of a size, weight, or kind suitable to the worker or the work to be done. Do not hesitate to ask for information from a competent sales person. Buy tools of a good brand with years of reputation back of them. A friendly carpenter or cabinetmaker could be of great assistance.

In the list to follow, the tools are shown singly or in groups, according to the *type of work* for which each is to be used. This method makes it easier to select a tool for a specific purpose, by referring to the classification.

Many of the tools are shown in photographic illustrations or line drawings. Moreover, there are footnotes following the list, giving special information about some of the tools. Reference "keys" are placed before the names of those tools, as follows:

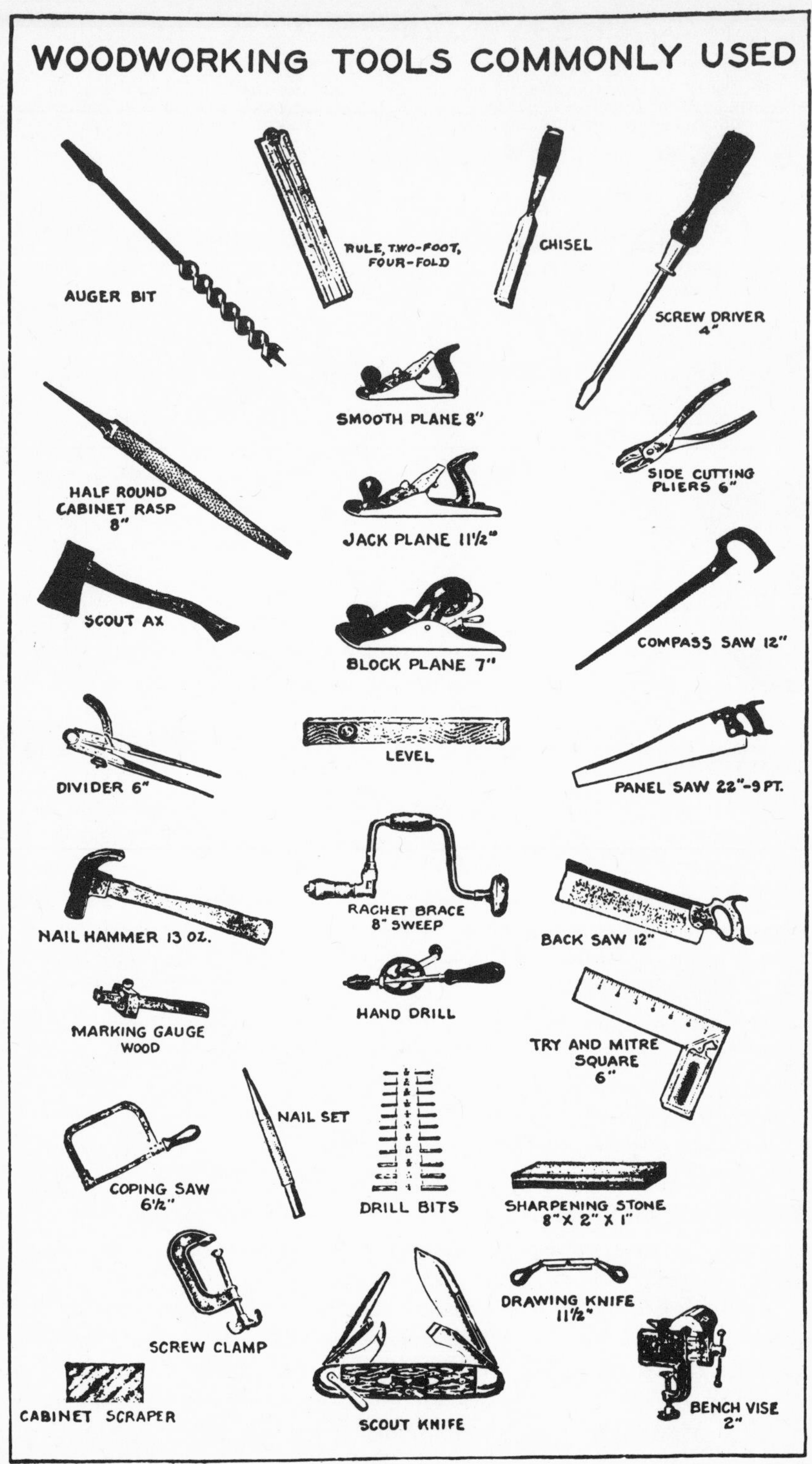

PLATE 24. Photographed from a U.S. Government book.

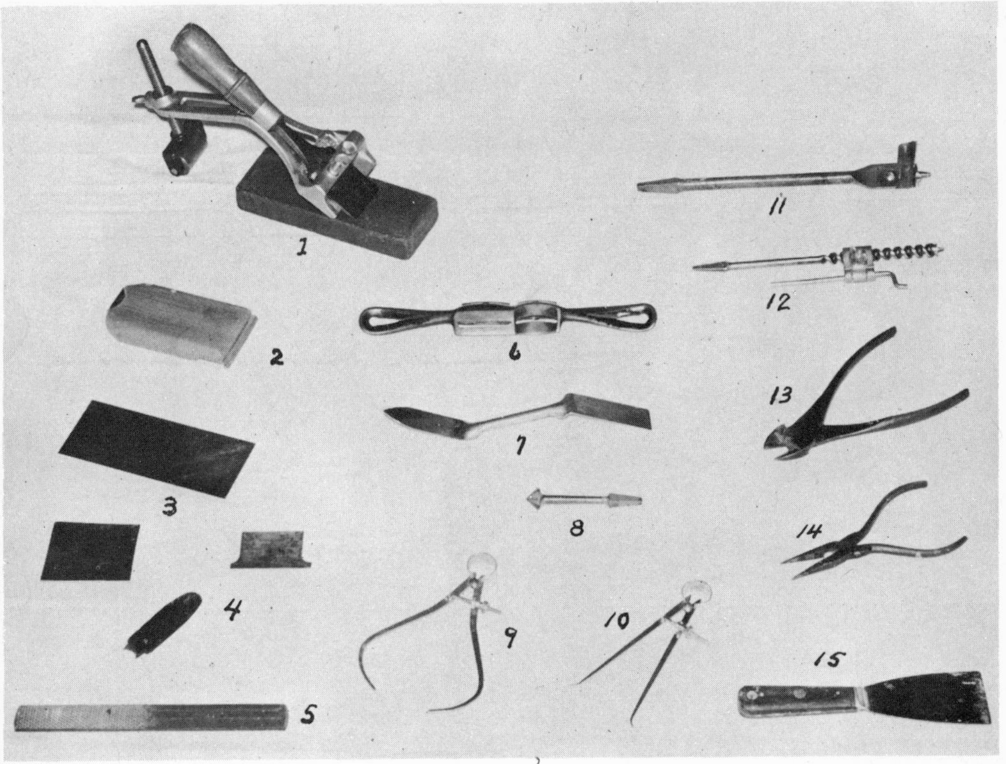

TOOLS USEFUL FOR RESTORATION

PLATE 25. 1—Stanley blade-sharpening tool and oil stone. 2—Hook cabinet scraper. 3—Rectangular hand cabinet scrapers. 4—Odd-shaped hand cabinet scrapers. 5—Shoemaker's rasp. 6—Double-bladed spokeshave. 7—Moulding and patching tool. 8—Rose countersink. 9—Outside calipers. 10—Inside calipers. 11—Expansive bit. 12—Auger bit with depth gauge. 13—Diagonal cutters (often called side cutters). 14—Long-nose pliers. 15—Putty knife.

A—Tool is shown in Plate 24, page 186.

B—Tool is shown in Plate 25, page 187.

KEY—There are numbered footnotes in some cases for a fuller explanation of the tool.

TOOLS SUGGESTED FOR PURCHASE

	KEY		
BORING	A		Bit brace, 8″ ratchet type.
	A	(1)	Auger bits, ⅜″, ½″, ¾″.
	B		Counter sink, rose head, to fit brace.
	A		Hand drill, ¼″ chuck capacity.
	A	(2)	Twist drills (drill bits), straight shank ⅛″, 3/16″, ¼″.

CLAMPING	A	(3)	Mechanic's bench vise.
	A		"C" (screw) clamps, 2 each, 3″, and 6″ or 8″. (Also see Plate 7, page 25.)
	A		Pliers, combination step-joint, 6″ or 8″.
	B		Pliers, long nose, side cutting, 5″ or 6″.
	A		Screwdrivers, 6″ and 8″ or 10″.
			Screwdriver bit, to fit brace, ⅜″ or ½″.
CUTTING	A		Pocket knife (Scout), with strong pointed blade.
			Old knife, blunt.
		(4)	Razor blade holder, with blades.
	B	(5)	Diagonal cutting pliers, 7″.
FILING	A		Half round wood rasp, 10″.
			Smooth mill file, 8″.
	B	(6)	Shoemaker's rasp.
GLUING	B	(7)	Patching tool.
HAMMERING	A	(8)	Carpenter's nail claw hammer.
			Tack hammer, claw type, light weight.
	A		Nail set, 1/16″.
		(9)	Mallet, rubber headed.
MARKING			Center punch.
			Pencil.
MEASURING			Rule, steel roll type, 6′.
			Rule, straight, wood, 6″ or 12″.
	A		Trysquare, 6″ or 8″.
PAINTING		(10)	Paint brushes, 2″.
			Paint brushes, artist's, for touch up.
REMOVING FINISHES	B	(11)	Putty knife, stiff blade, 2″.
			Tooth brushes, old.
			Meat skewers, wood.
SAWING	A	(12)	Hand saw (panel), cross cut, 26″ 8 points per inch.
SHAVING	A	(13)	Plane, "Block" 7″, or "Smooth" 8″ to 10″.
	A	(14)	Chisels, ½″ plain type (straight edges), and 1″ beveled edge.
MISCELLANEOUS			Ice pick (for marking and holding).
			Oil can (small).
			Dusting brush and pan.
			Teaspoon and tablespoon (10¢ store type).
			Cothes line (Cotton and strong).

FOOTNOTES

1—**Auger Bits** for carpentry work are made from ¼″ to 1″, increasing by 1/16″ in sizes. The size of a bit is marked on a side of the tapered square top by a figure representing the number of 1/16″ involved. Examples—¼″ size marked 4 (4/16th); ⅝″ size marked 10 (10/16th); 13/16″ size marked 13, etc. Full sets may be purchased, usually in a specially built case.

2—**Twist Drills** are made with straight shanks, to be held in chucks, for hand and power tools. "High speed" drills, for drilling hard metals, are made of tool steel; cost more but hold a cutting edge longer. "Carbon" steel drills are for drilling soft metals, so are adequate for wood. The two types look almost the same. It is best to purchase the "High Speed" for all-purpose use. Sets from 1/32″ to ¼″ or ½″ are available. The sizes are marked on the drill shank. Smaller sizes are designated by numbers or letters.

3—**Mechanic's Vise** with 3″ to 4″ wide jaw, anvil, and swivel base is preferable to a small, non-swinging type. (This vise may be used for most purposes. A Woodworker's Vise may be purchased later, if needed, listed in Chapter 10.)

4—**Razor Blade Holders,** with one blade, may be bought for a few cents in 10¢ stores, department, and hardware stores. It is a tool often used. The type for double edge blades is preferable.

5—**Diagonal Cutting Pliers,** often referred to as "Side Cutters," is one of the handiest tools in the shop, if a worker will become acquainted with its various uses. The "Crescent" brand, 7″, is a perfect tool. (See "Removing Nails," page 33.)

6—**Shoemaker's Rasp.** This is a perfect tool for shaping and semi-smoothing edges, corners, or replacement parts of wood for repairs, etc., yet it is seldom seen in a woodworking shop. The rasp is about 8″ long, one side semi-round; the other side flat. One half of each side has a coarse rasp; the other half smooth. It is surprising how rapidly and what a relatively smooth edge of wood may be obtained with the coarse teeth of the rasp when it is used with a circular motion. It can then be further smoothed with the finer teeth. The tool may usually be secured cheaply at hardware stores.

7—**Patching Tool.** Most useful when gluing or applying wood dough, because of its thin, narrow, offset blades; one pointed, the other with square end, with rounded handle in the center. Low cost. Usually found at paint stores but sometimes hard to find.

8—**Carpenter's Nail Claw Hammer.** Important to get the proper weight and balance for the individual. Weight of 16 oz. popular. The "Bell Face" type is less injurious to surfaces, if properly handled. For use in restoration, a type without too much angle to claws is best, so they can be used for prying.

9—**Mallet, Rubber Headed,** is best as it will not injure wood. Originally designed for use in automobile repair; may be bought in auto supply and hardware stores; not expensive; moderate weight best.

10—**Paint Brushes.** See "Paint Brushes," page 204.

11—**Putty Knife** with a stiff blade, somewhat dulled, and of 2″ width, is best for removing old paints and finishes. (See "Paint and Varnish Removers," page 83.)

12—**Saw.** The cross-cut saw is recommended to be purchased first as it may also be used for rip sawing.

13—**Plane.** See Footnote No. 6, in Chapter 10.

14—**Chisels.** The plain type chisel with straight edges is most commonly used. The bevel edge chisel is best for use in corners, etc., in furniture repair work.

CHAPTER
10

MORE HAND TOOLS

In this Chapter you are given a list of hand tools which, if added to those listed in Chapter 9, should be adequate for the completion of practically any woodworking job you may wish to do. The lists are thus divided, for the purpose of mentioning the more necessary tools first, and to save confusion.

If it is desired to add electric power tools, it is suggested that the first to be purchased be a grinder (also with wire brush and cloth buffers), a small hand sander, and a hand drill (¼″ capacity).

The following list of tools is divided into groups and followed by footnotes, the same as in the preceding chapter. For convenience, similar reference "keys" are used, as follows:

A—Tool is shown in Plate 24, page 186.

B—Tool is shown in Plate 25, page 187.

KEY—Footnote following for fuller explanation.

TOOLS SUGGESTED FOR PURCHASE

	KEY		
BORING	A		Auger bits, ⅝″, ⅞″, and 1″.
	B		Bit depth gauge, adjustable.
	B	(1)	Expansive bit, ⅞″ to 3″ capacity.
CLAMPING			Woodworker's bench vice, quick acting type.
			Hand screw wood-clamps, 2 each, 5″ and 12″ jaws. (See Plate 7, page 25.)
			Furniture bar-clamps, 2 each, 3′ and 5′ long. (See Plate 7, page 25.)
		(2)	Spiral ratchet screw driver.
			Monkey wrench, 12″.
			Pipe wrench, 14″.
CUTTING			Scissors, 6″ to 8″.
		(3)	Tinner's snips, combination type.
			Cold chisels, ¼″ and ⅞″.
FILING			Rat-tail file, slim and tapered.
			File brush.

HAMMERING			Mechanic's ball-peen hammer, 13 to 16 oz.
	A		Nail set, 1/8″.
MARKING	A		Wood marking gauge.
			Scratch awl.
MEASURING			Carpenter's combination square.
			Slide "T" bevel square.
			Steel square (framing), 16″ x 24″.
	A		Rule, 2′, folding.
	A		Spirit level, 18″ to 24″ long.
	B		Calipers, both inside and outside types.
	A		Dividers.
PAINTING	B		Putty knife, 2″ wide, flexible blade.
SAWING		(4)	Rip saw, 26″, 7 points per inch.
			Dove tail saw, 8″, 17 points per inch.
	A		Keyhole or compass saw.
	A		Coping saw, 6 1/2″.
		(5)	Miter box.
	A	(5)	Back saw, 12″ to 14″, 13 or 14 points per inch.
			Hack saw, type adjustable to length of blades.
SHAVING	A	(6)	Plane, "Block" 7″, or "Smooth" 8″ to 10″, whichever you do not have already.
	A		Plane, "Junior Jack" 11 1/2″, or "Jack" 14″.
			Plane, "Fore" or "Joiner," 18″.
	B		Spoke shave, 2 cutters, blades curved and straight.
	A		Drawing knife, medium size.
	AB	(7)	Cabinet scrapers.
MISCELLANEOUS			Carpenter's bar, goose-neck 18″ (commonly called a "Wrecking Bar" or "Pinch Bar")
		(8)	Electric soldering iron.
		(8)	Spatula, artist's or druggist's, with flexible 3″ or 4″ blade.
		(8)	Spirit lamp.
	B	(9)	Cutter and chisel grinder, Stanley #200.
	AB	(9)	Combination oil stone.

FOOTNOTES

1—**Expansive Bit.** Often incorrectly called an "Expansion Bit." For boring holes in wood, adjustable for size. Usually sold with a long and short blade, which must be securely tightened (with set screw) when adjusted to size for hole.

2—**Spiral Ratchet Screw Driver.** A most handy tool for saving time. When used, great care must be taken to keep the screw driver tip from jumping out of the slot and causing injury to the wood surface. Usually two sizes of screw driver points are furnished. The most useful type of this tool also supplies an assortment of wood drills which are stored in the handle.

3—**Tinner's Snips** are "Metal Shears" with offset cutting blades, which permit cutting curves, and are handier than the regular type.

4—**Hand Saws.** A good saw is a delight to use and will last for years. It does not pay to buy a poor grade of saw. The teeth will not stay sharp, causing the cut to go crooked. Saws which are "hollow ground" above the teeth are the most preferable as they are less inclined to bind in the saw cut. Those with a straight back may be used as a straight edge for marking.

5—**Miter Box and Back Saw.** A miter box assures cutting *true* angles and is used with a back saw (called so because of the reinforcing across its back to stiffen it). Most miter boxes offered for sale are both large and costly, requiring a back saw 24″ to 26″ in length. A small miter box can be made but it is apt to be untrue. There are now small, but inexpensive ones, offered for sale.

6—**Planes.** The uses for various types of planes are as follows:

"Block" planes, usually 5″ to 7″ long, are for ordinary work where frequent adjustments of plane is not required.

"Smooth" planes, 5″ to 10″ long, have a fine set for smoothing and finishing work.

"Jack" planes, usually 11″ to 15″ long, are used for trimming board edges as they come from the saw, and for preparing a surface rapidly for use of the Smooth plane. The "Junior Jack Plane" is about 11″ long and often used in training schools. (The word "Jack" comes from Jackass, as these planes are capable of doing hard and rough work.)

"Fore" and "Joiner" planes are for planing long boards and give a true surface, most important when joining boards together. The "Fore" plane is about 18″ long and the "Joiner" plane 22″ to 26″ long.

"Special" purpose planes include the Bullnose, Rabbet, Router, Dado, Circular, etc.

7—**Cabinet Scrapers.** See "Types of Cabinet Scrapers," page 103.

8—**Electric Soldering Iron, Spatula, and Spirit Lamp.** These tools are used in restoration work for filling holes, cracks, etc. with stick shellac. (See "Stick Shellac," page 36.)

9—**Cutter and Chisel Grinder and Combination Oil Stone.** It is most difficult to grind plane irons and chisels true and then finish them to a fine edge on an oil stone. The grinding tool holds a plane iron or a chisel firmly, is rolled back and forth with the cutting edge against the stone, so that, if it is properly adjusted and correctly used, the edge will be honed true. The type recommended is not expensive and, if tools used with it are to be kept sharp, it is a tool well worth owning. When buying an oil stone, inquire from a competent sales person, the type best suited to your purpose. An oil stone which has a box container is preferable, as oil must be used on the stone and the box protects it from picking up dirt. (See next chapter for methods of sharpening plane irons and chisels.)

CHAPTER 11

SHARPENING AND CARE OF TOOLS

Many workers are careless about keeping their cutting tools sharp and their other tools in shape to do good work. Quality work is largely dependent on properly sharpened, edged tools, together with the manner in which they are handled.

A worker should learn how to sharpen chisels, plane irons, and cabinet scrapers, as they need attention often, but sharpening saws is a very difficult task. A saw, made of good steel and correctly sharpened, will remain sharp a long time unless abused, and should never be sharpened by an amateur, unless he is trained to do the work properly.

In this Chapter you are given only information regarding the sharpening of a few tools. Complete information, accompanied by line drawings, is given for the sharpening of cabinet scrapers. You are also given some hints regarding the care of tools in general.

The correct handling and use of tools is an art that should be learned by every woodworker. Information on this subject is too long and complicated for the scope of this book. There are several excellent books on tools and their use, some of which include the operation of power tools and many other subjects of interest to those who wish to construct articles for use in their home, or do general home repairs. (See Chapter 16 on "Reference Books," page 229.)

SHARPENING TOOLS

Chisels and Plane Irons

1—**Grinding.** Chisel and plane irons must be ground to remove any nicks in the cutting edge, usually the result of hitting hidden nails in wood surfaces.

It is best to use a power grinder. When a hand bench grinder is used, either have someone turn the wheel (towards the tool), or make a treadle to be attached to the handle, which may be worked with the foot, as it is necessary to use both hands to hold and guide the tool evenly. The wheel should be of a fine, proper grade for the work, and its surface must be even. A grinder with an adjustable tool rest is best to assure accuracy.

Lay the bevel edge accurately on the wheel surface, and move it slightly across the wheel, to grind a new surface with no nicks appearing on the cutting edge. This edge must be straight and at a truly right angle to the side of the tool. Great care must be exercised not to burn the tool by overheating it, particularly when using a dry wheel, as this will destroy the temper in the steel. When grinding, the tool should be dipped in water from time to time to reduce the heat. Hold the tool firmly in both hands and do not exert too much pressure. Most tools are ground to a 25 to 30 degree angle.

2—**Whetting.** The tool must then be whetted to a fine and smooth cutting edge, by rubbing it on an oil stone. A small amount of oil should be applied to the stone; light motor oil is all right but "lard oil" is better.

When a tool is newly ground, the new bevel surface has a slight crosswise curvature, which follows the shape of the grinding wheel. Place the bevel of the tool flat on the stone, hold it with one hand at the upper end, and place the fingers of the other hand lightly near the base of the tool, with the tool slightly crosswise to the length of the stone.

The blade is then "whetted" by rubbing it the full length of the stone, using a circular motion, if the stone is wide enough. Test the blade on a thumb nail occasionally for sharpness. Be careful to hold the blade in a steady position and not rock it. (This work may be done better with a "Cutter and Chisel Grinder," as recommended under "Miscellaneous Tools," and told about in Note 9, in Chapter 10.)

3—**Honing.** The cutting edge is completed by honing it on the oil stone to remove the wire edge caused by "whetting." Turn the tool over with the face lying flat on the stone. A stroke or two is sufficient. A more perfect job may then be completed by rubbing the flat face of the tool over a smooth piece of leather glued on wood.

Note Chisels and plane irons, which do not need to be ground, may be resharpened by the methods given above for "whetting" and "honing."

Saws

When a hand saw fails to cut readily, it is an indication that it is dull and needs to be resharpened. When it is properly used and it will not cut in a straight line, it indicates that the saw is incorrectly "set" or the saw points are worn on one side more than the other side.

Sharpening saws is done by a carpenter or ordinarily by experts, by placing the saw blade with the teeth upward in a special long vise made for the purpose. Each tooth is sharpened with a file. The teeth are then bent, alternately, towards one side or the other, with a special adjustable tool to give them a "set." The teeth are then smoothed down, to remove the burr caused by filing, by running a smooth file or whetstone over the teeth on both sides.

As previously stated, this work should only be done by a trained expert. Hand saws are also sharpened on special automatic power machines designed for this work and which are found in shops specializing in tool sharpening.

Files

The efficiency of a file may be increased, if it is cleaned often with a special wire brush made for the purpose.

Hammers

When the face of a hammer has a tendency to slip off the head of a nail as it is being driven, this may usually be lessened or stopped by rubbing the face over a piece of medium grade emery cloth which is laid flat on a surface.

Twist Drills

The cutting edge of a twist drill is conical in shape, with a sharp cutting edge on the side of two grooves. It is hardly noticeable to the eye, but the face of the cone slants slightly back from the two cutting edges to allow clearance, for, otherwise, they would not cut. Also, the cone does not come to a true point, but is slightly wide.

Twist drills are sharpened on a grinder; an electric grinder is best for the purpose. Great care must be taken not to change the original angle of the cone, the slope from the two cutting edges, or the shape of the point. Before attempting this work, it would be well to take one or two drills to a machine shop and receive instruction.

Auger Bits

The two outside cutting edges of auger bits, which extend downward to cut a groove for the shaving blades, sometimes become dull, but generally are damaged by hidden nails or from rough handling. They may be sharpened with a small hand whetstone (called a "slip stone") to a limited degree and still be efficient. When badly damaged or dulled, it is best to buy a new one. They are not expensive.

Cabinet Scrapers

Scraper blades become dull rather quickly and have to be resharpened. Therefore, it is important that the user of such a tool know how to sharpen blades correctly so that they will operate properly. The life of the blade, in the "hook type" scrapers, may be extended by burnishing, to reset the turned edge.

In many professional shops, an electric bench grinder, with a special jig for holding scraper blades, is used to sharpen them. The instructions, given below, are for manual sharpening only.

Equipment

A "bastard mill" file with square edges (used for sharpening saws, mowing machines, knives for tools, etc. The milling slants across the file and is cut in only one direction).

A "burnisher"—a special hardened steel tool with an oval-shaped smooth blade. (The shank of a screw driver or other similar tool may be used as a burnisher.)

A high-grade "oil stone" with a truly flat surface.

A "bench vise."

Note Be very careful in your work and see that all "filing" or "whetting" on the oil stone is done in such a way that the cutting surface is flat and the angle is true. Otherwise the blade will not operate properly.

Sharpening a "Bevel" Edge Blade Scraper

The instruction given here applies to a blade that is used alone or one which has been removed from a scraper tool for sharpening. (If the blade is one of the latter, see *Note* "4" below.)

Proceed as follows:

1—Clamp the blade in the bench vise with the cutting edge of the blade away from you and about 1″ above the jaws of the vise. Test the bevel with a straight-edge (or steel ruler) to see whether it is truly straight. If not, "joint" it (make it straight by placing a mill file, flat and lengthwise, on the diagonal surface of the blade and file it back and forth. Then place the file flat against the back surface of the blade and remove any burrs left by the filing on the cutting edge. See Drawing #7).

2—Make a new bevel or work the old one over, if it is level, by placing the file, in a slanting position, on the bevel edge at an angle of about 35 degrees. (This is steeper than a 45 degree angle.) Exert a strong, even pressure on the file in the forward stroke and lift it from the work on the return. Continue filing until a wire edge has been turned over on the sharp edge. (See Drawing #8.)

3—Next, remove the blade from the vise and hone it with the bevel edge flat on the oil stone (lubricated with a half and half mixture of kerosene and light lubricating oil), by rubbing the blade back and forth on the stone, lengthwise and with a slight circular motion. (See Drawing #9.)

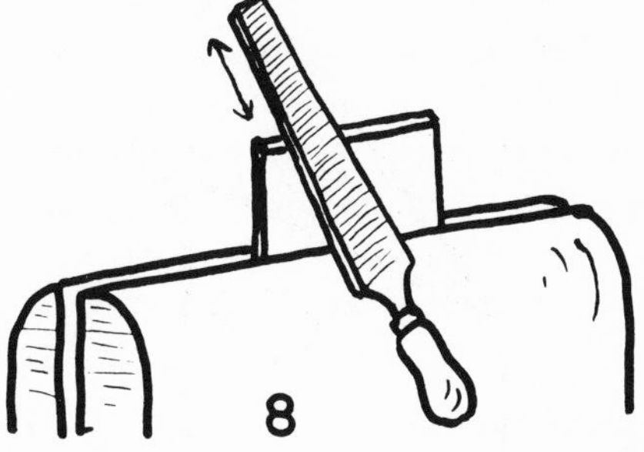

9

4—Turn the blade over and place it flat on the stone with the cutting edge next to the stone. While it is in that position, take a few strokes in order to remove any burrs from the cutting edge.

5—Remove the sharp corners by drawing them lightly over the edge of the stone.

Important

If you have followed the steps from "1" to "5" and if the work has been done correctly, you will now have a blade with a smooth true angle face (of about 35 degrees) and with a very sharp cutting edge, which is also true and straight. (If it is not, your scraper will not operate properly.) You are now ready to turn the sharp edge over (by "burnishing") to form a scraper edge, which, under a magnifying glass, will be shown to be in the shape of a hook. Continue the steps as follows:

6—Put the scraper back in the vise in the same position as it was before. (Step "1" above.) Lay the blade of the burnisher (or the shank of a long screw driver with handle) on top of the blade and at right angles to it. Hold the burnishing tool firmly with both hands, one on the handle and the other at the opposite end. (See Drawing #10.)

10

7—Adjust the burnisher blade to the true angle of the scraper and then raise the end nearest you, slightly, so that the tool touches the cutting edge of the blade only (shown by arrow at base of handle on Drawing #10).

8—Use only enough pressure to start the edge turning and push the burnisher along the blade from one end to the other. Then raise the handle slightly and make several additional strokes, raising it a little more each time. Increase the pressure on the final strokes in order to turn over a sufficient amount of the blade metal to support the scraping edge. (The edge should be turned slightly less than at right angles, say 75 degrees.) (See Drawing #11.)

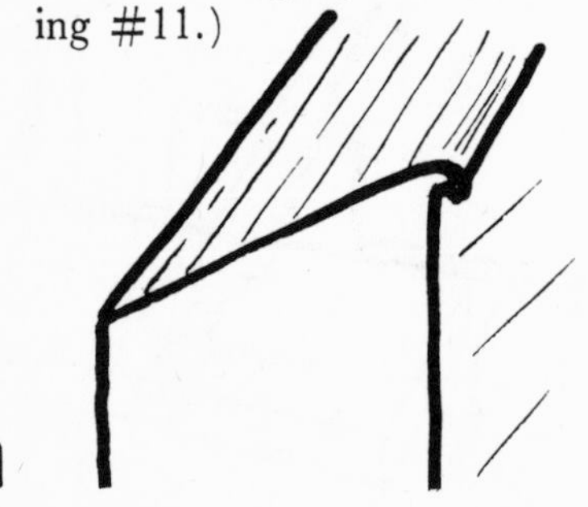

11

Note 1—By increasing the pressure slightly for each successive stroke of the burnisher, the edge is (more or less) rolled over. This gives more body (strength and support) back of the cutting edge and will increase the lasting qualities of the edge.

2—If the edge has been rolled too far, this may be remedied by running the tip of the burnisher under one end of the cutting edge and drawing it gently back to the other end.

3—The edge of a "hook" scraper, as well as the turned hooked edge of a one-piece scraper, can be resharpened many times, with a single stroke of the burnisher, applied at the proper angle.

4—The edge of the blade in a scraper plane or other such tools, should be turned over at a lesser angle, than for a blade which is to be used alone without a holder, as the plane blade is adjustable.

Sharpening a "Square" Edge Blade Scraper

All scrapers with a "square" edge are of thin flat steel, most of them with straight edges but some in odd shapes (see "Types of Scrapers," page 103). Regardless of the shape of the scraper, they are all sharpened and burnished on *both* edges of all *"square"* edges, since all edges are used.

The information for sharpening this type of scraper is for the straight edge type and for *one edge only.* The scraper is turned and treated in the same manner on all edges. If the scraper is one of the odd-shaped types (as the "swan-neck"), this must be taken into consideration in applying the directions given.

Proceed as follows:

1—It is usually necessary to remove the worn edges of a scraper blade and make new, square, and sharp edges. To accomplish this, place the blade in a bench vise with the edge slightly above and parallel to the jaws. With a mill file laid on the edge of the blade in a horizontal position and at right angles to it, take a few strokes lengthwise on the blade. Hold the file at each end and make the strokes firm, only touching the blade on the stroke *away* from you. Lift it for the return stroke. This will force "wire" edges to turn over on both edges. (See Drawing #12.)

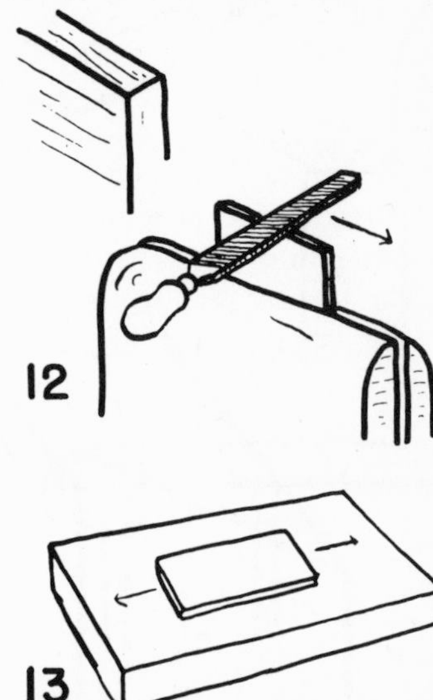

2—Remove the blade from the vice and place it with a flat side against a fine grain oil stone (with a true surface). Lubricate the stone slightly with the mixture of kerosene and light oil, as mentioned above. A few strokes on each side will remove the "wire" edges. (If the face of the stone is not true, use one of its edges.) (See Drawing #13.)

3—Next, hold the blade upright and take several strokes, lengthwise on the stone, to square the edge truly. (See Drawing #14.)

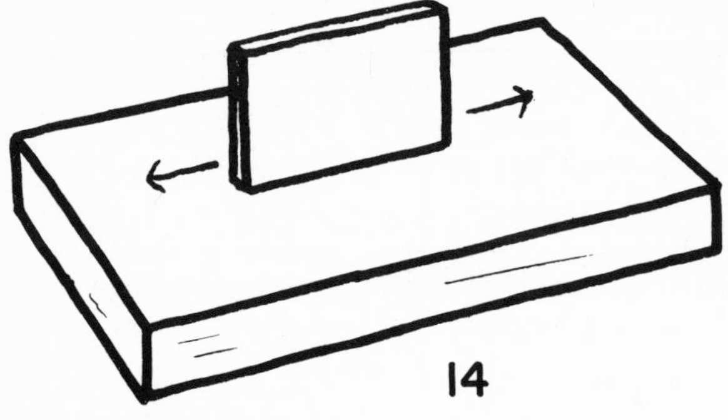

4—Wipe off the stone and repeat operations "1" and "2" if the edges of the blade are not sharp. They must be sharp or they will not burnish properly.

Important

The purpose in burnishing a square edge scraper is to form a hook-shaped cutting edge that will remove very thin shavings from a wood surface, without scratching or marring it. A durable edge must have sufficient material to support it. In order to accomplish this, the sharp edges are first forced up with the burnisher and then down over the side surface, forming a heavy hook. These steps are repeated on both edges. Continue the steps as follows:

5—Place the blade flat on the edge of a clean level surface (work bench or table) over paper. Lay the burnisher flat on the blade at a 90 degree angle. (See Drawing #15.) Take several firm strokes across the blade. Then, raise the point of the burnisher away from the surface only the slightest amount and take a single stroke. These strokes raise the cutting edge. (See Drawing #16.)

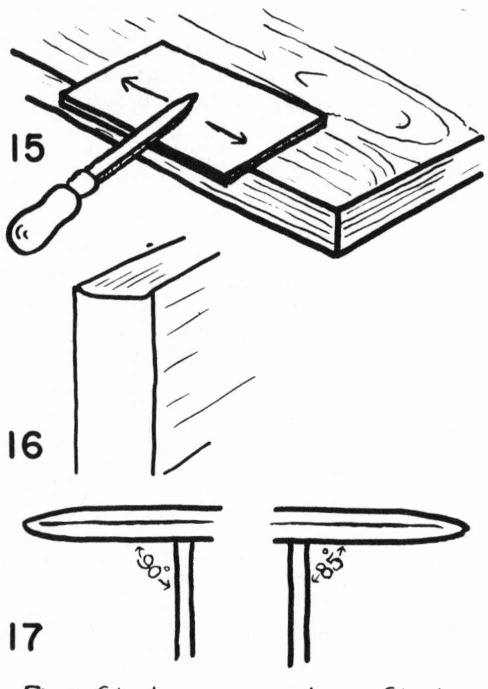

6—Put the scraper blade back in the vise with the edge about an inch above the jaws. Place the burnisher across the blade and at an angle of 90 degrees with the blade face and parallel to it. (See Drawing #17.)

Take a few firm strokes. Tip the burnisher tool down a slight degree with each successive stroke to turn a hook edge downward. (This edge should not be bent down more than 5 degrees from the flat surface.) (See Drawing #18.)

Note 1—All of the strokes with the burnisher tool should be made in one direction only.

2—For steps "5" and "6," the work should be done on both edges and on all surfaces.

3—A well-formed "hook" edge may be resharpened many times with a burnisher and without filing.

4—This method of sharpening a square edge blade is exacting work to obtain lasting and satisfactory results, but once the art is acquired it may be done rapidly.

5—If the edge has been rolled over too far, this may be remedied by running the tip of the burnisher under one end of the roll and drawing it back to the other end.

6—See "Cabinet Scrapers," page 102, "Types of Cabinet Scrapers," page 103, and "Using Cabinet Scrapers," page 104.

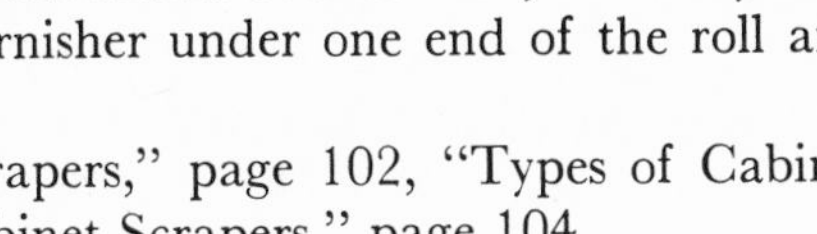

CARE OF TOOLS

The care of tools is of great importance in keeping them in proper working order. Those with cutting edges may become dulled easily by carelessly handling or storing them in the wrong manner, or they may become rusted, which may be prevented. The proper care of tools is divided into three parts, as follows:

Handling Tools More tools with cutting edges are dulled or damaged by the way in which they are handled (or stored) than through actual use. As an example, many workers lay a plane on a surface with the cutting edge down, instead of upon its side. If they had stopped to reason, they would have realized that the blade will not cut unless it extends below the bottom of the plane. When it is laid on that surface, the blade is dulled.

Also, chisels, saws, cabinet scrapers, knives, etc., in fact all tools with a cutting edge, should always be handled with the utmost care when laying them down, for fear of damage.

A good rule to follow before any work is done with a cutting tool is to examine carefully all wood for hidden pieces of metal, such as broken nails, screws, etc.

Storing Tools Saws should seldom be laid down because of dulling the offset teeth, but should rather be hung on a peg or nail, immediately after use. If they must be stored by laying them down, the cutting edge should be protected by wrapping the saw blade in a paper, or by placing a narrow "U" shaped strip of wood over the teeth and tying it in place with a string. This strip may be made on a power saw in a few minutes.

If there is a chance of damage to chisels, make a small hood for the point by folding a piece of thin cardboard, and tying it with a string, so that it may be slipped on and off easily.

Additional information for storing tools is given later with shop illustrations. (See Chapter 13 on "The Work Shop.")

Oiling Tools Tools become rusty from storing them in a damp place and from handling them. This may be prevented by cleaning and oiling them before they are stored away.

There are products especially made for this purpose. However, a mixture of 1 part of #10 grade motor oil and 1 part kerosene works perfectly. Keep some in an oil can and apply with a piece of cheesecloth. Wipe the tool with this cloth, and then lightly with a dry cloth, thus leaving a thin film of oil. Store the tool and, under normal conditions, it should not rust. No tools should ever be stored in a damp place.

Slight rust on the surface of a tool can often be completely removed by rubbing it with a pad of grade "000" steel wool dipped in kerosene. Care should be used not to injure the cutting edge. When a tool is badly rusted, it is impossible to remove all of the rust by this method, but it should be followed to remove as much as possible.

CHAPTER 12

CARE AND STORAGE OF PAINTS AND BRUSHES

Storage of Paints

There is no necessity for the great waste of paints, enamels, varnish, lacquer, or synthetic materials used for refinishing that is so commonly met with. All of these may be saved for future use with a little care.

When not properly stored, the surface of the material left in the can usually thickens into a skin, even though the lid is secured tightly, but this can be prevented. This skin cannot be dissolved merely by adding solvent or thinner and thus a part of the material is wasted.

The proper storage of these materials is a very simple matter and will save much money. Proceed as follows:

1—Clean most of the material from the groove in the top of the can but leave a small amount so that the lid will seal. If the material is heavy or dried, it must be removed until the surface is clean and even. This may be done with a screw driver, followed by a knife blade, but care should be exercised in order that none will drop into the can.

2—Clean off all dried material from underside of the lid with the same tools and wipe it clean with a cloth.

3—Pour on the surface of the material in the can a small amount of the thinner which is used with the material. Use just enough so that it will spread to a thin film; the amount to be used is dependent upon the size of the can. Use turpentine or painter's thinner for house paints, enamels, and all types of varnishes. Use a lacquer thinner for lacquers. Use the type of thinner directed on the can for synthetic and any other type of material. If no directions are given, smell the material and use a thinner that you believe will be satisfactory.

4—Place the lid on the can and set the can on the floor; step on it; move it back to the work bench; place a piece of paper over the can, and drive the lid down to a tight fit, by tapping around the edges with a hammer. (The paper over the can keeps excess material from spattering.)

5—Move the can to the storage place, using care not to rock or shake the can, so as to prevent the film of thinner from mixing with the material.

The film of thinner cannot evaporate in a tightly sealed can as there is not enough air. It is lighter than the material and will remain on top almost indefinitely, thus preventing the formation of a coating or skin. When the material is again needed, remove the lid and, after stirring, it is ready to use. It must be remembered that thinners evaporate, and it is often necessary to add more to materials before using them, but it is best not to add much thinner before storage. Materials stored in this manner may be used without being strained.

A method employed by some in storing paint materials is to cut a piece of heavy paper the size and shape of the can, and to place it on top of the remaining material in the can. This is helpful, but not as satisfactory as the film of thinner suggested above.

Materials such as linseed oils, shellac, etc., need no liquid film coating for protection. Depend upon the tightness of the container top for their proper storage.

Important

Paints which contain oils and volatile thinners are considered *inflammables*. Care must be exercised in not storing any large amount of such paints, oils, and thinners in homes. Also, great care must be taken to spread out or dispose of oily cloths, etc. (See "Inflammables," page 16.)

Reviving Old Paints

When a can of paint material has a dried skin on its top, this can best be removed by cutting around its edge with a sharp knife blade and then picking it out by taking hold of the center of the skin with two fingers. House paints and enamels should then be thinned by the addition of some raw or boiled linseed oil, turpentine, or painter's thinner with a little of Japan drier to increase its drying power. It should also be strained through cheesecloth or a sheer stocking.

Varnishes and lacquers often thicken to a point where they are worthless for further use. If thin enough to use, add pure turpentine to varnish and lacquer thinner to lacquers.

Paints, enamels, varnishes, and lacquers, made over in this manner are seldom satisfactory. It pays to use care and store these materials in a manner that will keep them without deterioration or destruction.

Paint Brushes

Paint brushes play an important part in restoration work. You are given here several thoughts with which many experienced workers in this field may not agree but which have proven practical and may save time and money. This subject is divided into subdivisions in an effort to give a clear understanding, as follows:

Selection of Brushes Cheap brushes are not worth the money paid for them. They will shed bristles and will not spread paint materials evenly. Nor is it necessary to use the best grade of brush, as does a professional painter. The best all-purpose brush is made with black China bristles which are set in rubber in the ferrule. These brushes are not cheap, but, if properly used, cleaned, and stored, they will do satisfactory work and last for years. Buy brushes from a competent sales person who will help you in their selection.

Brushes for Single Purpose Use Brushes should be used for a single purpose. That is, a separate brush should be selected for use with different kinds of painting or finishing materials, and used for that purpose only, to secure the best results.

It is seldom that any brush other than a 2″ width is used in my shop, and all are of the same grade and type. The only real occasion for the use of ½″ and 1″ brushes is for the application of stains to a small area. Turnings and carvings can often be worked over better with a 2″ brush than with a narrower one. It is also necessary to have one or two sizes of small, fine-pointed artist's brushes for touch up work, especially for stains.

It is important to have a special brush for the application of varnish and similar materials. This brush is made with a "chiseled" shape, the bristles on the side being shorter, so there is a larger surface of the split ends or "flags." These flags hold the varnish and spread it more evenly and smoothly than does a brush with the bristle ends all of one length.

Any type of an old and worn brush is satisfactory for applying "paint and varnish removers."

It is an excellent plan to mark a letter on both sides near the top of the handle of each brush, so that they indicate a single use for that brush. This letter may be made by hitting a screw driver lightly with a hammer, making straight lined letters. Having the letter near the top of the handle makes it easy to identify when the brushes are stored with paper wrapped around the bristles (see later).

The brushes in my shop are marked as follows:

"V"—"V"arnish.
"Z"—Shellac ("Z" looks like "S").
"N"—Stai"N."
"L"—"L"acquer.
"P"—"P"aint.
(No mark on brush used for paint removers as it is hung on a nail.)

There are still other single purpose brushes used in a well equipped shop.

1—A large scrub brush to be used with lye as a remover.

2—A small hand scrub brush for abrasive powders on finishes.

3—A long brush, with a horizontal handle, used for removing dust (with added wiping) before finishes are applied. A standard product in most paint stores.

4—A brush for cleaning work benches. A cheap 7″ paint brush with coarse bristles is perfect for this work.

5—A shoe brush for use for applying paste furniture wax.

Preparing Brushes A new paint brush almost always has some loose hairs which should be removed before the brush is used. This may be done by rolling a brush rapidly between the hands; then beating it lightly across spread fingers. This also removes any dust.

Many professional painters prepare their new paint brushes for use by suspending the bristles in raw linseed oil for 12 hours. The surplus oil is squeezed out with the fingers, then brushed on a clean lintless cloth, and the brush is ready for use. It is said that this preparation keeps paint from sticking too much to the bristles.

Another method of preparing a paint brush before use is to wash it in cleaning fluid, such as carbon tetrachloride, which evaporates quickly and will not catch fire.

Using Brushes Standard paint brushes are composed of three parts: the bristles, the ferrule, which binds them into shape, and the handle. This type of brush should be held by the handle and near the ferrule, very much like a pencil, for ordinary use. When applying varnish or similar products, it is better to hold the brush further down, so that the fingers and thumb rest on the upper part of the ferrule.

Most brush work should be done with a short and quick, easy motion of the wrist, and with little movement of the arm. The reason for a lower grip on the brush, when applying varnish, is to take advantage of the "V" shape of the special varnish brush. Varnish should be literally "flowed" on a surface with very little brushing, except to smooth it out and pick up sags or runs.

A brush should not be used unless it is clean, the bristles flexible, and free from dust. The bristles should never be dipped more into a material than one half their length and, before it is applied to a surface, the brush should be wiped lightly on the edge of the container. When using materials which are difficult to work with, it is well to get the brush shaped and the material flowing properly, by stroking the wet brush a few times on a dust free old newspaper.

Cleaning Brushes A brush that is thoroughly cleaned, immediately after use, by a proper method will avoid the necessity of using a solvent at a later date after the material has hardened. This weakens the bristles and is not good for them. (See Note 3 following.)

Under *no circumstances* should a brush be left or stored in a container filled with water. This makes the bristles soft and flabby, destroying their spring and resiliency, and often swells and splits the ferrule. It is a common habit in households, and is the result of carelessness, want of time, or lack of knowledge of brush cleaning. It would save time and be better to throw away the brush after use.

Cleaning a brush immediately after use is a simple matter, easy to do, takes little time, and, when completed, the brush can be stored. The brush will then be ready for future use and will be as good as ever, except for ordinary wear.

The method for cleaning a paint brush is as follows:

1—Wipe the brush on the top edge of the container to remove as much of the paint material as possible.

2—Remove more of the material from the brush by stroking it on clean newspaper.

3—The brush is then cleaned in the type of solvent, as recommended below, for the paint material used. Fill 3 containers about one-third full. For this purpose the larger sized cans (about 2 quarts) in which fruit juices are sold are ideal, when their tops have been so removed as to leave a smooth edge.

4—First hold the brush in one hand and manipulate the bristles with the fingers while the brush is submerged in the solvent in the first can.

5—Then remove the brush from the can and continue to manipulate the bristles, while holding the brush upwards at an angle of about 45 degrees, so that the solvent fluid will flow from the bristles at their juncture with the ferrule, bringing with it any paint material that has worked deeply into the bristles.

6—Repeat operations 3 and 4, using the *same* can, until the bristles and metal on the ferrule are relatively clean. Then repeat those operations in the *next* can, until the metal and bristles are thoroughly clean.

7—Finally wash the brush in the third can to remove any paint material remaining. Then shake the brush to remove surplus solvent.

The solvents to be used for the cleaning of paint brushes are as follows:

Material	**Solvent**
House paints, enamels (varnish base), and varnish (oil type).	Turpentine, painter's thinner, or kerosene.
Synthetic varnish and other similar materials, including plastic.	As directed on can for thinning or, if questionable, try turpentine or benzol.
Shellac.	Denatured alcohol.
Lacquer and lacquer sealer.	Lacquer thinner. (Sometimes benzol may be used.)
Oil stains.	Turpentine, painter's thinner, kerosene, or naphtha.
Spirit stains.	Denatured alcohol.
Water stains.	Warm water and soap.
Paste wood fillers.	Benzine and turpentine.
Paint and varnish removers.	Denatured alcohol.

Note 1—Sometimes the solvent recommended will not take the stickiness out of a brush completely. This often happens when attempting to clean a brush which has been used with a material (sometimes synthetic) which does not indicate on the label what thinner to use. (A proper thinner for a paint material will always clean a brush.) In such cases, experiment either with other solvents or try to complete the cleaning with warm water and mild soap.

2—Kerosene is a fine solvent for paint materials. It is largely used by professional house painters, particularly because it is cheap and not too volatile. It may be used over and over again, but turns a reddish-brown color. A good plan is to place the cover of a coffee can (which is slightly larger), over the fruit juice tins, and allow the washed out paint materials to settle. Then pour the kerosene into another can and the sediment can be removed with a stick. Volatile materials may be reused by the same method. However, they should only be kept in containers with tight lids.

3—Paint which has hardened on brushes may be removed by the use of products sold for the purpose.

Storing Brushes

The simplest way of storing brushes is to wrap a few thicknesses of newspaper around the bristles and ferrule, fold it back so that the bristles will not be bent, tie with a string, and lay the brush away in a clean place where there is a free circulation of air.

When a brush which has been cleaned with kerosene is stored in this manner, do so while it is somewhat wet, and allow the kerosene to soak into the paper. Before the brush is used, wash it in turpentine to remove any remaining kerosene, as kerosene is harmful to paint materials.

Paint brushes which are frequently used are often stored by suspending them in a container partly filled with either raw linseed oil, painter's thinner, or a mixture of the two. It is best that only enough of the material be used, so that only the bristles are in the liquid. The brushes should never touch the bottom of the container.

There are several ways of adapting a container for this purpose. Painter's thinner will evaporate, so that when the mixture is used, the container should be covered. A mason jar is best for this purpose as it is transparent. Cut a hole in the lid the size and shape of the brush handle. Drill a small hole through the brush handle, put the handle through the hole in the lid, insert a nail through the hole in the handle, which will hold the brush suspended in the jar, which is then filled to the proper level with the solvent. Another method is by the use of a tall tin can with a lid. Holes are drilled or punched through the sides of the can at a height where a wire can be inserted through the holes in the can and in the brush handle.

Many professionals, who wish to store a number of brushes which are frequently used, make containers from gallon paint cans. For a closed top type, a thin disk of plywood is cut to a size that will just go through the can opening. Another is cut but slightly larger. The two disks are temporarily tacked together and several holes, slightly larger than the width of brush handles, bored through the disks. The disks are then taken apart and a piece of rubber (inner tube good), cut to the size of the smaller one is placed between them, and the disks secured together with screws. Slots are then cut through the rubber at the holes. When a brush handle is inserted through the hole from the underside, the rubber holds the brush suspended in the lid.

A way of using a gallon can with an open top is to drive short nails or screws through the sides of the can near the top edge on which brushes are hung by holes in their handles. Another method is to suspend brushes from a stick, in which several oval shaped notches are cut to fit the brush handles where they are narrow. These elongated holes are cut along both sides of the stick and are shaped in such a manner that there is a narrow opening on the stick edges to permit the brush handles to pass through them.

With these open-can methods, only the raw linseed oil should be used, and the cans should be covered with a piece of cheesecloth to prevent dust from getting into them.

CHAPTER 13

THE HOME WORKSHOP—HINTS AND SHOP PRACTICE

The Home Workshop

A person who enjoys tinkering with tools is indeed fortunate if he has a home workshop. Here one may relax, gain pleasure and profit, whether it be the restoration of furniture or the construction of something which is useful. Creative hobbies may be practiced and minor repairs completed for the upkeep of the home. There is no better known cure for a tired, worried mind than working with tools.

Unfortunately, many homes do not have a space in which such a shop can be set up. That should not be a discouragement. A removable bench top may be made that can be clamped to a kitchen table, or a portable cabinet bench designed which may be stored. The floor around such a work-bench can be covered with a mass of old newspapers, over which can be spread an old piece of canvas. Many a piece of furniture has been repaired and refinished and something useful has been created under such conditions, without damage to the furnishings or the room.

When there is ample space in which to create a workshop many things must be considered. There must be a good circulation of air to get rid of the fumes from volatile materials. The place should be dry, for dampness ruins tools. Electric current must be available for any power tools, and work can best be done in a strong light as that from 100 and 150 watt lamps. The place must be of adequate size for the type of work to be done, and it must be heated for winter use.

Under certain conditions a basement is an ideal place for a shop. Attics are fine so far as space is concerned, but most of them are hot in summer and cold in winter. The side or end wall of a garage may often have sufficient space but there is the heating problem in winter in most climates. The same is true of a barn. A small service room or bedroom may often be made available for a shop and those with light and heat often make an ideal place in which to work. Under ordinary circumstances anyone who wants to work with tools can find a place where it can be done, even if it is necessary to set up a temporary platform out of doors on sawhorses.

It took six months of all available time to complete the workshop in my basement. Now it is an ideal place in which to work, particularly because of the all-year Southern California climate. The basement had no windows or floors, other than dirt, most of which was clay and had to be dug out with a pick. Concrete was poured, windows fitted, wiring installed, walls lined with plyboard, shelves and a workbench made, and all were painted. (See Plates Nos. 26-A, B, and C, on following pages.)

A shop centers around the workbench. It is needless to give directions for building one as a bench must be built to suit the available space and personal needs. A workbench for hard service must be made of sturdy material with a thick plank top. Most of the work at a bench is done while standing. A workbench with the top 36″ from the floor is ideal for a tall person. It should be made lower to a convenient height for shorter people. Hard maple is the best wood for workbench tops. Many plans are available in technical books for the construction of workbenches, but most of them are too elaborate in design for the needs of the amateur worker. (See Chapter 15 on "Reference Books.")

The following are a few practical ideas given with the thought that they might be helpful in the construction of a home workshop.

1—Measure any space available and draw plans prior to any construction. Make a list of materials, the kind and size necessary for the complete construction program. Do not deviate from the plan unless unforeseen conditions arise. Start with the workbench construction, followed by shelves and racks, unless prior work must be done on the space or room available. Construct one thing at a time and take plenty of time.

2—When laying out this plan there are a number of things to be taken into consideration. The workbench should be against a wood wall or one on which a sheet of plywood can be fastened so that loops or racks may be fastened to it, into which tools can be placed.

3—It is convenient and makes working at a bench easier if the most frequently used tools are on the wall back of the bench. Flat strips of heavy woven cloth are available at auto supply stores at low cost which are used for lacings under automobile hoods to stop rattles. These are called "Hood Lacings" or "Hood Gaskets" and are perfect for holding tools when nailed or screwed, in proper sized loops, along a wall.

To hang such tools as hammers, hatchets, mallets, putty knives, etc., on the wall, drill a $\frac{3}{16}$″ hole through the handle near the end, and use finishing nails (small headed) upon which to hang them. It is well to countersink the holes in the handle slightly on both sides with a "rose drill," which makes it easier to match the hole with the nail when hanging up the tool. If the workbench has an exposed end, it is a good plan to place nails there for hanging saws temporarily while working, rather than to lay them down and dull the teeth.

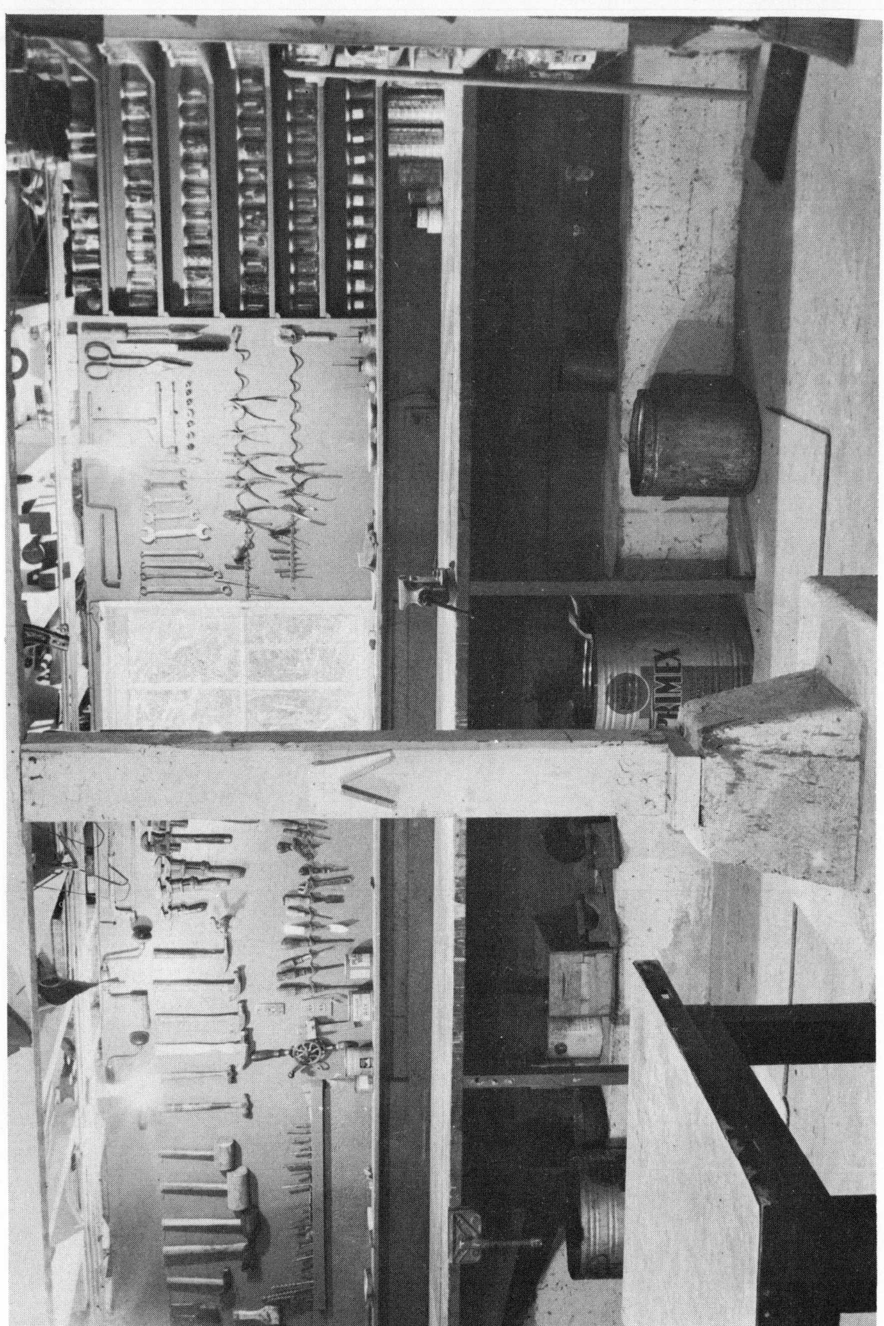

VIEW OF WORKSHOP

PLATE 26A. Center view of one end of shop, showing long homemade workbench, with handy, narrow shelf above it; method of storing tools most used (with cutting edges) on plyboard wall; trash cans (smaller one for metal and glass); celotex mat before bench; handy work table in foreground; etc.

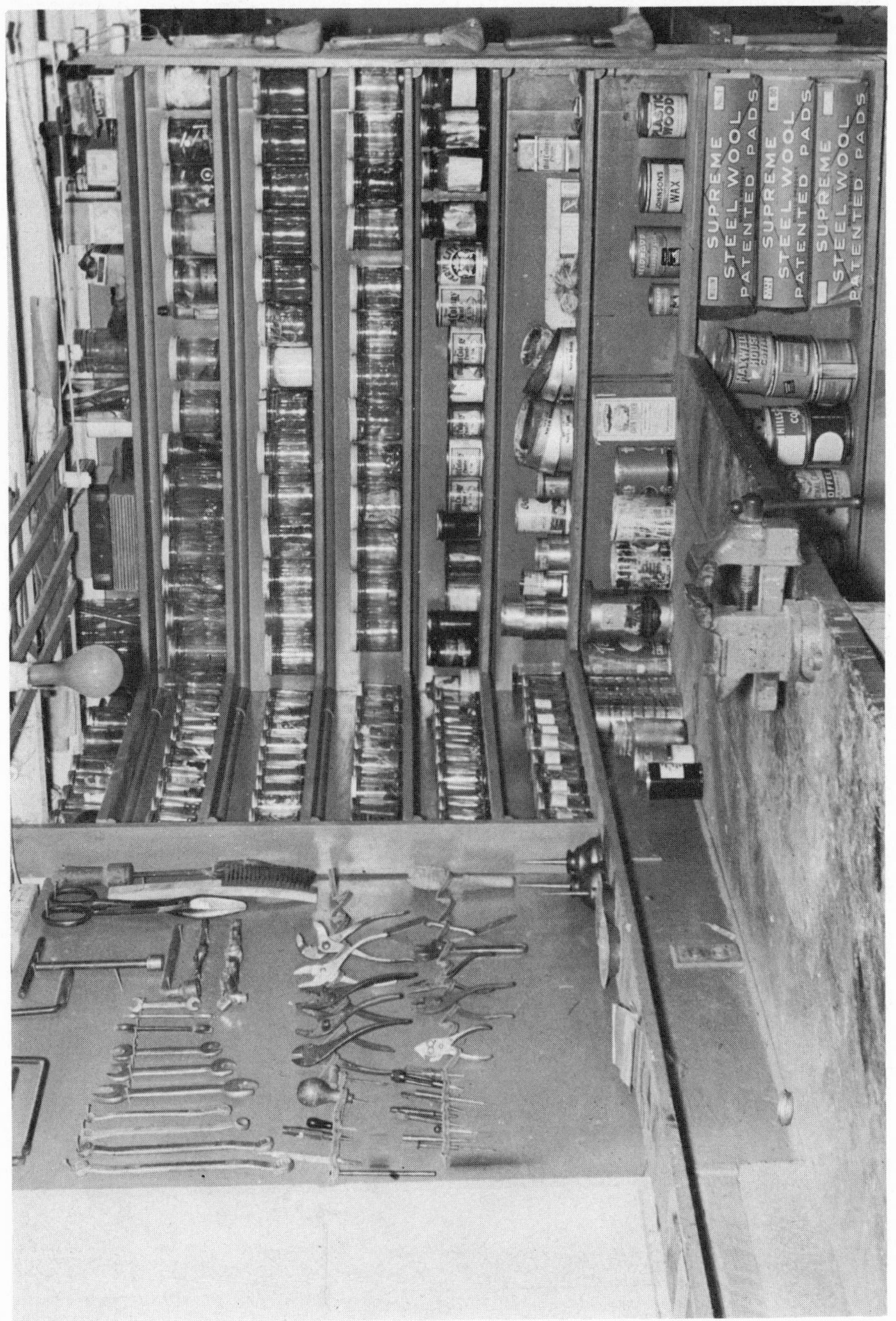

PLATE 26B. View to right, shows shelves lined with jelly glasses for small materials; peanut butter and other glass jars for larger materials; empty tin cans (handy); finishing materials; etc.

PLATE 26C. View to left, shows ceiling racks and top shelf for old wood storage; 2nd shelf for unfinished small pieces; etc.

Some workers prefer to lock up their tools and yet have them hanging on the wall back of the bench. This may be done by making two large, shallow boxes of the same size. One is secured to the wall; the other hinged to the first, so that it may be swung around as a cover and locked.

For those who wish to make their shop a bit dressy, there are enameled metal fixtures on the market which make a perfect tool rack. These come in sheets (usually white) with many small square holes in them, and with short and longer square rods, turned up at the end, or loops, that fit into the holes and may be spaced for many sizes.

4—The question of light in a shop is very important. When a workbench is short, it is best not to place it directly in front of a window as it is difficult to face the light and see the work on a bench clearly. It is better to have strong lights over the bench and near shelves for supplies. Plug outlets for power tools are handy.

5—Ample storage space on shelves is also important. Shelves 5″ wide for storage and easy display of small items and about 10″ wide for the larger are satisfactory. Vertical space will not be wasted if the height of the various sized containers is measured in advance of the laying out the shelf spacing. It is of great convenience if a shelf about 5″ wide is run along the wall about 10″ above the workbench and for its full length.

6—When there is space for a horizontal lumber rack to be placed on a side wall, it is a great convenience. When the ceiling is of rafters which are within reaching distance, as in a basement, very convenient racks may be made for the storage of dowel rods, abrasive papers, long tools, short lumber, etc., by nailing narrow cleats across the beams. Convenient triangular shaped racks for short lumber may be built in a corner. It is well to store very old lumber in a separate place.

7—There is one method of keeping track of tools which may be missing from their space on a wall or have been borrowed and not returned. This is by painting an outline of the tool on the wall where it is customarily kept.

8—It is a good plan to keep all edge cutting tools (chisels, planes, saws, etc.) in a locked cabinet or drawer, if you expect to keep them sharp, particularly if there are children in the household.

9—The storage of small items such as brads, screws, staples, corrugated nails, etc., is always a problem. Keeping them in small "jelly glasses" with a top and stored on narrow shelves, permits visibility and easy access. Likewise, nails of various sizes and types, solder, stick shellac, powdered stains, etc., which are larger in size or kept in greater quantities, may be visibly stored in "peanut butter jars" or other glass jars with tops and wide openings.

For better identification of sizes of materials thus stored, it is a good plan to make notations on small gummed paper labels and stick them on the jars. A good light should be near the shelves.

Then there is the problem of storing various types of materials which are useful for the type of work done in the shop or for repairs about the home, such as powders, light cords and sockets, hinges, locks, and door knobs, etc. Labeled coffee cans, both the 1 and 2 pound size with lids, make ideal containers.

Note Many of the ideas offered in the preceding information may be seen in the illustrations of my shop.

Good Shop Practice

Some of the thoughts or ideas given in this Chapter may be helpful to experienced workers but they are primarily intended for the beginner. Some are intentional repetitions from former Chapters, placed here as a reminder.

The workshop is considered by most workers as a sanctuary with a warning to others that "Thou shall not trespass, nor touch a thing, nor use a tool, nor clean up the place." This is not because the worker is selfish, but because he does not like work once started to be disturbed, tools taken without permission injured, not returned or lost. He likes to clean up the place himself, so that tools and materials may be put back in order where they belong and odds and ends of lumber, etc., not thrown away but put in a special place for safe keeping and future use.

All these thoughts are natural and logical, for when a person turns out work that is admired, the shop, the tools and equipment are not only held in high respect but credit is given to the material things more than to oneself.

Experienced workers get into bad habits and beginners will profit if they start out with good shop practice. A few examples are as follows:

1—Arrange the tools, which are most often used, on a wall or in a cabinet in a position from which they may be easily reached. When a tool is used, put it back where it belongs, unless it is to be used again soon.

2—Have great respect for edged cutting tools. Always lay a plane on its side and handle a chisel or saw with care. More tools are dulled or damaged by careless handling than by normal use.

3—Prevent rust on tools before it starts by wiping them with a half and half mixture of kerosene and light oil.

4—Keep the workbench neat and reasonably clean while work is in progress and brush up the entire shop as necessary.

5—Good receptacles for the disposal of sweepings from the bench and floor are 50 and 100 pound metal lard containers which usually may be purchased for very little from bake shops. They will be greasy, so must be washed. When disposing of trash, it is best to separate all metal things from the burnables. The 50 pound cans are a good size for the metal trash and for storing clean rags and burlap. (Such cans may be seen in illustrations of my workshop. See Plates 26-A and C.)

6—A shop is certain to get full of dust from use of tools and sanding. Shelves and workbench should be dusted and the floor well swept before using finishing materials.

7—Regardless of how clean a shop may be, always spread clean old newspapers under pieces that are being worked on. The paper will catch drippings from finish removers, glue, or finish materials and prevent dust;

and the work can be seen better with a lightened background.

8—Oil power tools at regular intervals. Stores that specialize in the sale of electric motors sell a type of oil that is best for motors and which will not burn if the motor should become overheated.

9—Two or more jobs may often be worked at the same time, by dovetailing the work on one piece in with another, instead of waiting for glue, finishes, etc., to become completely dry.

10—Teach children proper respect for tools.

11—Lending tools is a bad practice unless it is kept under control.

12—Take all possible precautions against fire. It is a good plan to have a fire extinguisher in the shop.

13—The best products and tools are the cheapest from every standpoint.

14—Standing on floors is hard on the legs and feet. Very often sufficiently large scrap pieces of Celotex (a coarse and rather thick wallboard) or Studio Board (thin and hard), may be bought at a most reasonable price at Builders and Supply stores. These may be placed on a floor like a rug before a workbench or work table and make standing easier.

15—It is difficult to do fine, close work at a bench while standing. A flat sturdy wooden box of the proper height makes a fine seat. It may also be used to stand on for high work (a flat box, longer than it is wide, gives 3 levels).

Shop Hints

The "Shop Hints" given herein are methods, thoughts, and ideas, some of which are old and may be known to most workers, while others may be new and of benefit. A few may be a modified repetition.

1—**"Z" Hooks** A piece of heavy wire about 12″ long, bent into a "Z," makes a fine hook for hanging up parts of furniture, chairs, and miscellaneous items and for storage or for drying, after a finish has been applied. A small staple may be driven partly into small wooden items for the wire to go through which could not otherwise be hung up.

2—**Hinge Pins** A finishing or casing nail (small headed) of proper thickness makes a perfect substitute for a missing hinge pin. Cut off an end, if too long, and it will rarely be noticed. Old pins can be knocked out of hinges with a nail set.

3—**Furniture Clamps** "C" clamps and "hand screw clamps" can be stored by clamping them on a rafter or a stick, nailed up for the purpose.

4—**Old Metal** It is well to have a box for old metal parts, etc. Do not throw them away. Many may be made over for use in repairs with a bit of ingenuity.

5—**Volatiles** Many people have an erroneous idea about explosions. Volatile liquids will burn and readily take fire, but, as they evaporate, it takes a proper mixture with the air (about 14 parts air to 1 of gasoline) to cause an explosion. That is why you are warned to apply all finishes in a well ventilated room.

6—**Crude Wooden Articles** It is surprising how some old and odd shaped wooden things may be finished and made into a piece of beauty. They are fine for experimental work. The appearance of many pieces will be improved if the corners are rounded and cracks, such as those between parts, are filled with wood dough and stained. However, do not attempt to remove all blemishes, burned marks, dents, etc. It is the finishing touches that make an admired finished piece.

7—**Ceramic and Pottery Repair** Apply pure evaporated canned milk to a break. Allow to become sticky and then bind parts together. Will not stand strain. Canned milk is much used in ceramic production for repairs.

8—**Air Pressure** In buying a spray outfit, get one with an air tank. It is advantageous to have air pressure, with hose and nozzle, for cleaning in a shop. However, for restoration, all finishes but lacquers should be applied with a brush.

9—**Hand Protection** It is difficult to do shop work wearing gloves but they must be worn for protection when using strong chemicals, such as lye. Several products (similar to cold cream) can be purchased at hardware and paint stores which, when rubbed on the hands, keep dirt and paint from entering the skin. It may not say so on the container, but it is usually considered harmful to allow the material to remain on the hands more than a few hours at a time, as it closes the pores of the skin.

10—**Hand Cleaning** Paints containing oil may be cleaned from the hands with kerosene; shellac with denatured alcohol; other finishing products with their special thinners. Also, excellent products for cleaning hands are sold.

11—**Ethyl Gasoline** Under no circumstances ever use this product in restoration work. It may be poisonous. Use the regular "White Gasoline."

12—**Killing Borers and Worms in Wood** Maple, oak, pine, tulipwood, and some others are subject to borers and worms. To kill them, apply white gasoline liberally, which evaporates quickly without harm.

13—**Sawing** For sawing a narrow strip from a board, first mark it with a pencil. Hold the pencil in a gripped hand (like holding a hammer), with the thumb pressed near the pencil end, and draw the line, using the side of the first finger as a depth guide, against the side of the wood. Make depth allowance to plane for smoothing. Always saw through from the finish side, as the lower edges of a saw cut is ragged. When starting a saw, first take an upward stroke, guiding the saw with a thumb on the edge of the wood. When continuing the strokes, stand with eyes directly over the blade, to guide it in a straight line. When the board being sawed is long enough, place it on something that is steady and low, and hold it in place with knee, opposite the hand used for sawing. When a properly handled saw will not cut a straight line, the teeth are injured or incorrectly set. (See "Saws," Chapter 11 on "Sharpening and Care of Tools.")

14—**Sawing Curves** Curves may be sawed in wood with a compass saw, or keyhole saw, but it is best done with a power band saw. A curve may also be made by sawing out "V" shaped wedges with a cross cut hand saw, a back saw, or dovetail saw. Flat areas are then sawed close to the line of the curve in straight cuts, and these may be rounded and made relatively smooth by filing with a shoemaker's rasp. The final smoothing of a curve, regardless of the tool used, is best done with an abrasive paper over a block of wood. Used in this manner, the edge may be smoothed to a true arc.

15—**Wood Dough** A dough of correct color may be made from sawdust of the wood under repair. Mix this sawdust with a small amount of powdered glue and dampen. Use at once.

16—**A Square** The edges of a cardboard box may be used as a square.

17—**Andirons, Fire Screens and Fire Tools** To refinish, if rusted, clean with coarse steel wool. Paint with "flat black" and allow to dry. Apply a mixture of 50% boiled linseed oil and 50% turpentine with a cloth. This will dry to a soft luster and will resist heat for a considerable time.

18—**Refinishing Metal Ware** Remove all loose rust with coarse steel wool. Brush on one coat of a mixture of 25% orange shellac and 75% denatured alcohol. This gives a lovely color to any rust remaining. Use on old tin candle molds, etc.

19—**Old Maps** There are special types of varnish materials prepared for renovating oil paintings, which can be used on old maps, but a light application, with a brush, of 25% white shellac and 75% denatured alcohol will usually give a soft luster.

20—**Label Paint Mixtures** Whenever a special color is made by mixing paints, it is well to label the container, giving the factory name of the colors, their numbers (if any), the names of makers of the paints, and the proportions used, especially when a portion of the mixture is stored for future use, and it is believed some of the mixture will be needed later.

21—**Alligator Finishes** These finishes are those with small check lines on a surface which resemble the hide of an alligator. They can be intentionally obtained by putting a hard finish over a primer which has not dried, or a quick drying coat over a slow drying material, before the former is dry.

22—**Outline Transfer** There are hand tools, consisting of a wooden handle, with a small wheel having many sharp points, which are used for the transfer of drawings to another surface. The drawing is first made on a smooth piece of paper that is not too thick. The paper is then placed on a flat surface which is not too hard, or, if so, it may be first covered with a bed sheet. The wheel of the tool is then run over the entire outline of the drawing and this leaves small holes in the paper.

The paper is then transferred to the surface to be marked, held in place with thumb tacks or otherwise, and the punctured outline gone over with a small bag of cheesecloth, containing a fine powder of a different color than that of the under surface. The drawing may then be copied from the visible dotted lines of the powder. Transfer by this method may be made on relatively rough surfaces. Sometimes a transfer is made with carbon paper.

23—**Steel Wool Holder** A rubber tip for crutch or fishing rod end makes a fine holder for a small amount of steel wool.

24—**Temporary Mallet** A rubber tip for cane, crutch, or fishing rod, of proper size to fit a hammer, makes a good temporary mallet.

25—**Steel Wool in Skin** Scrape the blade edge of sharp knife, over skin to remove steel wool.

26—**Tightening Loose Screws** Remove the screw, plug the hole with match sticks, and replace it. If this does not hold, fill the hole with wood dough, using a match stick as a tamper, smooth off the surface with a dampened finger, and replace the screw at once, being careful not to keep turning it beyond its full length.

27—**Wall Paper** For application on the inside of wooden cabinets, etc., use the paste which can be purchased in stores selling wall paper.

28—**Stirring Sticks** Old wooden drop-screens, the type that are made of thin strips of wood about 1/16″ thick and ¾″ wide and bound together with string, so that they can be rolled up and down, make ideal stirring sticks, when the strips are sawed in lengths of from 5″ to 7″.

29—**Cleaning Glass** Add a small amount of vinegar to water.

30—**Changing Wood Colors to Pine** Poplar and other white woods may usually be made to resemble pine by several applications of a "saturated solution of oxalic acid" and placing the piece in the sun.

31—**Chuck Keys** To avoid misplacement of keys for chucks (like the Jacobs), secure the key with adhesive tape to the electric cable for portable power tools, and tie them with a string of convenient length, to stationary power tools.

32—**Holding Lids and Covers Open** It is often desirable to apply a finishing material to lids and covers (sometimes doors), without removing them from the hinges. They may be kept open and contact with other surfaces avoided by the use of a finishing or casing nail driven lightly into a corner of a joint, so that the lid or cover will rest upon the nail head.

33—**Leather Seat for Cobbler's Bench** The old leather seat on a Cobbler's Bench usually needs replacement. A Shoe Repair Shop will gladly sell you a piece of tanned leather about ⅛″ thick suitable for the purpose. Round brass headed tacks can be purchased in small packages for 10¢ at hardware stores.

The leather seat should be hollow in the center for comfort. First cut to size, tapering the edge slightly for better appearance. Then soak the leather in warm water until soft. Lay it over the hole in the seat in correct position and with the leather flat. Secure the leather permanently in position with the tacks placed about ½″ back from the edge and about 1″ apart. Without delay start forming the hollow of the seat by rubbing the thumbs over the wet leather around the edge of the hole, gradually working toward the center. When the hollowed leather has stretched sufficiently, place the bench in direct sunlight to dry the leather and to darken it if possible.

34—**Nailing Small Brads** It is almost impossible to hold a small brad (¼″, ⅜″, ½″, and ⅝″ long) with the fingers and hit it with a hammer. If the brad is gripped in the tip of the nose of "long nose pliers" and a small headed "tack hammer" is used, you can see how to guide the brad to an exact spot, and at the angle desired.

35—**Scotch Tape for Glue Joints** A board (like a table top) may often be broken off in an irregular manner, so that the pieces are difficult to replace in their original position for gluing, and have the *finished* surface smooth and even. This may often be accomplished better if the pieces are fitted exactly together before the glue is applied, and held there by strips of Scotch Tape, applied to the top (finished) side. Then turn the fitted pieces (or the whole piece) over, open the break from the lower side, using the tape as a hinged joint, apply the glue, and clamp. Wipe off with a damp cloth and squeezed out glue, and when the glue has dried, the tape can be removed without damage to the finish.

CHAPTER
14

CARE OF FURNITURE

Furniture requires care to keep it in good condition. It requires constant attention in one way or another, to retain its smooth texture and to preserve it.

The "patina" of furniture, which develops a mellow richness of color and texture, is purely a surface condition, and a great asset in Antique furniture. Unfortunately, it is not only the surface of furniture that needs to be dusted regularly, and occasionally washed or polished, and perhaps waxed or treated with oil; it is also important that the wood should not become too dry or absorb too much moisture, thus causing it to shrink or swell.

It is not difficult to keep furniture in excellent shape, providing it is not neglected. Frequent care will help to keep wood furniture in good condition. You are given information regarding its upkeep under titled subjects, some of which have alternate methods, as follows:

Dusting

Dusting furniture in some homes is a daily routine. This is important and, when done regularly, will do much to maintain or even improve the original beauty of the finish. Keeping furniture dusted, removes the accumulation of dirt and grime, and polishes fine finishes, making their revival by more strenuous methods unnecessary or longer postponed. For dusting, use soft cheesecloth, silken rags, or chemically-treated dust mittens or cloths, which can be purchased readily.

Washing

Furniture sometimes acquires a coat of grime, which dusting will not remove, from use in a smoky city, or from greasy fumes or smoke from a fireplace or kitchen. The furniture is then best cleaned by washing or using materials prepared for cleaning. (See "Washing Soiled Furniture," in Chapter 6 on "Reviving Old Finishes.")

Polishing

It is the belief of many professional refinishers that an occasional rubbing with furniture polish is beneficial to a finish, but that excess use of oil polishes should be avoided, as they have a tendency to cause a dull and lifeless surface which collects dust more rapidly.

When using commercial furniture polishes, follow the directions on the container closely. In using most polishes, it is best to saturate a piece of cheesecloth with hot water and wring it out. When the cloth is cold, shake the polish thoroughly, apply sparingly to the cloth, and clean the furniture by brisk rubbing. Turn the cloth as it becomes dirty. When the piece is clean, rub the surface with a soft dry cloth until a fingerprint will no longer show on a surface.

A mixture of 1 part boiled linseed oil and 1 part pure turpentine makes an excellent polish for use once or twice a year on varnished and highly polished surfaces. This polish brightens the finish, removes dull, foggy appearance, and helps to stop surface checking or makes existing ones less obvious. The oil feeds the wood; the turpentine loosens dirt and helps the oil to penetrate the wood. Apply the mixture with a soft cloth, wipe off excess with a dry one, and polish with the grain of the wood until no finger print will show on the surface.

Waxing

Waxing furniture properly with a quality product has a more lasting and a softer effect than treating it with furniture polish. Once wax is correctly applied, it lasts a long time, and its polish can be revived by rubbing the surface with a soft and lintless cloth. Additional wax should be applied only when needed. This is indicated by the refusal of the surface to polish, after a firm rubbing with a dry, soft cloth. Applying wax thickly or building up too many coats, is a detriment to a good finish. It causes surfaces to become slippery and to have too high a shine, rather than the desired soft mellow appearance, and, under damp conditions, it may become sticky. The same conditions prevail when wax is used as a floor polish. (For types of wax and application, see "Waxing," page 145.)

Humidifiers

It is well to consider the humidity in a home, not only from the standpoint of health but also as to how it affects the maintenance of furniture, especially in climates with a wide range of temperature change, or those where it becomes extremely dry. A humidity from 40 to 60 percent is desirable.

Most of the modern, well-built hot air furnaces, are of the forced-air type with an electric fan, and having a built-in humidifier. During the fall, winter, and spring months, when houses in cold climates are closed in and heated, several gallons of water a day should be evaporated for good health. Pans of water on a radiator, or blocked up over a register serving a hot air furnace which has no humidifier, is very helpful in increasing the humidity.

According to U. S. Government statistics, the average moisture in seasoned lumber varies from 6 to 14 percent according to weather and other climatic conditions, and tests are based on a moisture content of 12 percent as a norm. It seems unbelievable to the layman that apparently dry wood contains so much moisture.

With this knowledge, it is apparent that wood lowers or raises its moisture content in accordance with the humidity in the place where it is stored or used. Furniture used in the desert, where the humidity is very low, often cracks or splits, or the glue gives way. Furniture used in homes or stored in warehouses which are too low in humidity are subject to the same damage. It is difficult to say which is the more detrimental to furniture—dryness or dampness.

CHAPTER
15

FORMULAS

Furniture Polish

1— 1 part Paraffin Oil
1 part Benzine

Apply with damp cloth and rub. To permit easy sprinkling from a bottle, punch a hole in a screw top or cut a slot in the side of a cork. Seal tight when storing.

2— 4 oz. Raw Linseed Oil
4 oz. Paraffin Oil
4 oz. Water
2 oz. Vinegar
½ oz. Butter of Antimony

Shake well, apply to cloth and rub.

Note Butter of Antimony, also called Antimony Chloride, Antimony Trichloride and Mineral Butter, is a white, poisonous, crystal sold in drugstores. As it spoils quickly through absorption of moisture from the air, it is often not carried in stock but may be ordered. It is also used to bronze the surface of iron and steel.

3—

(After smoothing with Pumice Stone or Rottenstone.)

½ pint Paraffin Oil
½ pint Pure Turpentine
1 oz. Oil of Cedar
1 oz. Oil of Citronella

First dampen a cloth slightly with water and wipe over the surface. Then immediately rub the surface with the mixture on a cloth pad and rub with straight strokes. Finally, put the least bit on the hands and rub the surface with a circular motion to the desired polish. Should any polish be left on the surface, put a very small amount of alcohol on a cloth, wring it out to spread the alcohol and, with this mere suggestion of alcohol, rub the surface lightly.

Furniture Wax

1 pound Yellow Beeswax
1 pint Spirits of Turpentine
1 pint Boiled Linseed Oil

Melt the wax in an old double boiler. When slightly cool, add the turpentine and oil. Use less wax if a thinner mixture is desired. Spirits of turpentine is better for use than ordinary turpentine. The linseed oil makes the wax waterproof. (This wax may be used as a substitute but it does not equal the quality of a commercial carnauba wax.)

Oil Stains

Cherry (dark)—

Italian Burnt Sienna

Cherry (light)—

2 parts Italian Raw Sienna
3 parts Italian Burnt Sienna

Mahogany (brown)—

3 parts Italian Burnt Sienna
1 part Rose Pink or Maroon Lake
1 part Vandyke Brown

Mahogany (red)—

3 parts Italian Burnt Sienna
2 parts Rose Pink

Oak (dark)—

1 part Turkey Burnt Umber
4 parts Italian Raw Sienna

Oak (light)—

Italian Raw Sienna

Walnut—

4 parts Turkey Burnt Umber
1 part Vandyke Brown

Add above colors to a mixture of—

3 parts Boiled Linseed Oil
1 part Pure Turpentine
½ part Japan Drier

Crack Filler

1 part Wheat Four
1 part Cornstarch
1 part Japan Drier
1 part Raw Linseed Oil

Mix in the order given (should be thick like putty). Will take a stain. After application, allow plenty of time to dry.

Paint and Varnish Remover

1— 1 part Tri-sodium Phosphate
1 part Sodium Metasilicate

Make saturated solution of each in water. An inexpensive remover; slow in action; may take repeated applications. Operation hastened by scrubbing with stiff brush. May raise the wood grain but this can be sanded later.

2— 4 parts Benzol
3 parts Fusel Oil
1 part Denatured Alcohol

Old English formula. Action will start in 10 minutes and paint brushes will become hard as iron but will clean in an hour or so.

Note The next two formulas contain paraffin wax and while it is objected to by some workers, others prefer it.

3— 50 parts Benzol
25 parts Denatured Alcohol
15 parts Acetone
10 parts White Gasoline
2½ parts Paraffin Wax

Dissolve shaved wax in gasoline. Add other ingredients which should precipitate the wax in flakes. Shake well before using.

4— 10 parts Benzol
9 parts Acetone
1 part Paraffin Wax

A satisfactory and less expensive remover may be made by substituting White Gasoline for ½ of the Acetone, or Denatured Ethyl Alcohol for ¾ of the Acetone.

CHAPTER
16

REFERENCE BOOKS

That a great many persons are interested in working with their hands, as a hobby, is evidenced by the fact that there are so many books on subjects dealing with such work in the Public Libraries. There you can find many books dealing with the subject of your hobby, except satisfactory books pertaining to the repair or refinishing of Antique or newer furniture. Among the books available on this subject, you will probably find none which are written in a manner that will permit their use as a manual in the workshop, with titled procedures and step-by-step methods. It was for this very purpose that this book was written.

A Public Library may, however, often have many well known books, each of which is considered an authority on various aspects of Antiques.

Listed below are a few additional books, with brief comments on them, which may be of interest to workers in the art of furniture restoration of Antique or Period furniture or for home shop work and which may not readily be found in a Public Library.

ABOUT ANTIQUES

AMERICAN ANTIQUE FURNITURE

(Book for Amateurs)

By Edgar G. Miller, Jr.

Published by—M. Barrows and Co., New York, N. Y.

Printed in two volumes; over 1,100 pages and 2,100 illustrations; includes types of period furniture, mirrors, clocks, etc. Advertised as—"The most comprehensive work on Antique Furniture ever published in America."

Published price (2 volumes)—$27.50

PRIMER OF AMERICAN ANTIQUES

By Carl W. Drepperd

Published by—Doubleday, Doran & Company, Inc., Garden City, New York.

The book has 271 pages, 1,200 drawings, and glossary of 2,200 terms, including period furniture, pewter ware, weather vanes, pottery, circus posters, lithographs, postage stamps, glassware, clocks, rugs, etc., listed in 72 divisions. The book is for the layman.

Original list price—$3.00

NOTE

Four other books written by Mr. Drepperd on specialized subjects about Antiques are also available.

ABOUT ANTIQUE FURNITURE RESTORATION

KNOWING, COLLECTING, AND RESTORING EARLY AMERICAN FURNITURE

By Henry Hammond Taylor
Published by—J. B. Lippincott Company, Philadelphia, Pa.
This book was first printed in 1930 and is well illustrated. It has much valuable information on restoration and special kinds of repair and replacement of parts for Early American pieces. Many of the methods may be adapted to other types of furniture. Most of the finishing work pertains to the use of shellac.
This book also has chapters on "Brasses and Hardware" and "Evidences of Age, Use, Wear, and Authenticity," with "Comments on Frauds and Fraudulent Methods." The book is indexed and has 156 pages.
Original list price—$3.00

HOW TO STENCIL CHAIRS

By Florence E. Wright
Associate professor, New York State College of Home Economics, Cornell University, Ithaca, New York.
A large text book of 36 pages, printed in 1949, with 68 illustrations. The first 31 illustrate the history of stenciling and show fine examples of early stenciled Hepplewhite, Sheraton, Hitchcock, Windsor, and other types of straight chairs, rockers, etc. The balance of the illustrations serve to clarify and demonstrate the complete and clearly written directions, regarding the art of redecoration, the preparation of stencils, the selection and placement of patterns, supplies, etc. It is a book worthy of attention by anyone interested in stenciled furniture, regardless of whether or not they do the actual work themselves.
The purchase price was $1.00. Sold by mail order by Miss Wright. Address above.

ABOUT HAND AND POWER TOOLS, LAYOUT OF A SHOP, ETC.

HOW TO GET THE MOST OUT OF YOUR HOME WORKSHOP WITH HAND & POWER TOOLS

Published by—Popular Science Publishing Co., New York, New York.
This book, with over 750 illustrations, gives directions for the layout of a shop, how to make a workbench, use hand and power tools, with directions for the construction of many useful articles. It is well indexed, and has 185 pages.
The purchase price was $2.75.

SUGGESTED UNIT COURSE IN THE USE OF HAND TOOLS AND PORTABLE MACHINERY

Published by—Delmar Publishers, Inc., Albany, New York.
The title of this book describes its use. No index but table of contents (192 pages).
The purchase price was $1.75

UNITS IN HAND WOODWORKING

by J. H. Douglas and R. H. Roberts
Published by—The McCormick-Mathers Publishing Co., Wichita, Kan., Atlanta, Ga., Columbus, O., New York, N. Y., and Portland, Ore.
This is a text book for a shop course in school work. It gives brief information on furniture woods and reading working drawings. It describes practically every type of woodworking hand tool and its use, many finishing materials and their application (briefly), how to do simple carpentry; and has plans for the construction of many articles, including a sawhorse, workbench, tool cabinet, rowboat, chairs, shelves, tables, bookcase, etc. It is well indexed and has 160 pages.
The purchase price was 75 cents, plus postage (ordered COD from the publishing plant at Columbus, Ohio).

ACKNOWLEDGMENTS

This book could never have been completed without the wholehearted cooperation of many people. And to the following I publicly acknowledge my debt and tender my sincerest thanks:

To Stuart M. Ketchum of Laguna Beach, California, for the tedious work of editing my manuscript and for many helpful suggestions.

To Miss Florence E. Wright, instructor in the New York State College of Home Economics, and author of the Cornell University Extension Bulletin No. 295, 'Refinishing Old Furniture.' Without her volunteered help this book would not have contained much of its refinement regarding finishes, materials used, and formulas. Miss Wright gave valuable time to criticize and make suggestions for improvement in all technical chapters. Mr. William B. Ward, head of the Department, granted permission for the use of the material for which I am duly grateful.

To Lee W. Gibbons of New Haven, Connecticut, an expert in the art of restoration, who also made suggestions for improvements in all technical chapters.

To Alvarita (Mrs. W. H.) Theobald of West Los Angeles, California, I am grateful for her timely assistance and constructive criticism when I first started to write the book.

To Mrs. Anne S. Mills of Milo, Maine, for typing and for assistance in the preparation of the final manuscript.

Several Antique Dealers were most helpful in offering technical advice. For their generous contributions, I give thanks to the following: Robert G. Hall and his Assistant, Urban McNaughton, of Dover-Foxcraft, Maine; 'The Hewett Antique Shop,' Chagrin Falls, Ohio; Lee and Dorothy Wynne of 'Wynne's Farm House' at Duarte, California, and Vernon W. Yost of 'The Pine Shop' at Pasadena, California.

Thanks is given for information about materials to Frank Butler of 'Butler's Streamline' at Santa Ana, California; Albert ('Ab') E. Billington of the 'Laguna Beach Lumber Company' and Ralph 'Jimmy' Eason, owner of the 'Laguna Paint & Glass Company' at Laguna Beach, California.

Finally, grateful thanks are given to my wife, Bertha Averill Kinney, for her cooperative support and constructive criticism during the past 24 months while I was working on the manuscript; to my daughter, Jean Kinney Laundon of Chappaqua, New York, for the pen-and-ink drawings presented herein; and to my son, Ralph P. Kinney, Jr., of Laguna Beach, California, for the most excellent photographic work which is used in the book.

INDEX